100 THINGS
PENGUINS FANS
SHOULD KNOW & DO
BEFORE THEY DIE

Rick Buker

To Nate —
On your 17th Christmas

Love
Dad

TRIUMPH
BOOKS

Triumph Books and colophon are registered trademarks of Random House, Inc.

Library of Congress Cataloging-in-Publication Data

Buker, Rick, 1957–
   100 things Penguins fans should know & do before they die / Rick Buker.
      p. cm.
   ISBN 978-1-60078-595-5
   1. Pittsburgh Penguins (Hockey team)—History. 2. Pittsburgh Penguins (Hockey team)—Anecdotes. I. Title.
   GV848.P58B84 2011
   796.962'640974886—dc23

                                    2011019463

This book is available in quantity at special discounts for your group or organization. For further information, contact:
      Triumph Books
      542 South Dearborn Street
      Suite 750
      Chicago, Illinois 60605
      (312) 939-3330
      Fax (312) 663-3557
      www.triumphbooks.com

Printed in U.S.A.
ISBN: 978-1-60078-595-5
Design by Patricia Frey
All photos courtesy of Getty Images unless otherwised noted

*This book is dedicated with loving memory to
my late parents, Susan Haley and Jim Buker;
to my sisters, Linda Buker, Karen Buker, and
Bonnie Faucheux; and to my brother, Dan Buker.*

Contents

1 Mario

The future of the Pittsburgh Penguins was forever changed on a cold, dreary night in Montreal in March of 1984. As Pens general manager Eddie Johnston looked on, a big kid wearing No. 66 dominated the opposing team like an on-ice version of Gulliver toying with the Lilliputians.

"Oh my god," Johnston muttered in astonishment.

Penguins owner Edward DeBartolo Sr. had a similar reaction after watching Mario Lemieux play. When the team's top selection in the 1984 Entry Draft put on a show during his first practice session, DeBartolo turned to Johnston and said, "Thank god you didn't trade that pick."

Perhaps no player in the history of the sport displayed more promise—or carried a heavier burden—than Lemieux. When he joined the Penguins as a fresh-faced 19-year-old rookie, he was expected to be a savior for a moribund franchise that barely had a pulse.

"Without Lemieux, they pack up the team and move to another city," said Rangers GM Glen Sather.

Standing 6'4" and weighing 210 pounds, Mario initially drew comparisons to a legendary center of similar dimensions and pedigree—Montreal's stately Jean Beliveau. Both were of French Canadian descent and each skated with a regal bearing. However, the player he was most often compared to was Edmonton's superb scoring ace Wayne Gretzky.

"I tried to gauge my career against his," Lemieux said. "It helped me to elevate my game to a level he'd reached. It was great for both of us."

The first overall pick in the 1984 Entry Draft, Mario Lemieux finished his Penguins career with 690 goals, 1,033 assists, and two Stanley Cup championships.

Mario would soon share the same rarified air as his rival. After showing steady improvement over his first three seasons, Lemieux exploded for 70 goals and 168 points in 1987–88 to emerge as hockey's most dominant player.

The following season Super Mario truly came of age. He enjoyed a magnificent season, racking up 85 goals, 114 assists, and 199 points. Opponents and teammates alike were awed by his brilliance.

"I grew up watching Bobby Orr," Pens winger Kevin Stevens said. "And Wayne Gretzky was phenomenal. But Mario is on another level."

"He just holds the puck out there on his forehand and dares to you to commit yourself," said Boston's All-Star defenseman Ray Bourque. "If you do, he slips it past you, and if you don't, he controls the blue line and has time to make the play."

With no legal means to defend against Lemieux's extraordinary talents, opponents took to fouling him and the old-guard NHL referees allowed it. The abuse he absorbed soon took its toll. On February 14, 1990, searing back pain forced Mario to remove himself from a game against the Rangers. Examinations revealed a herniated disc, an injury that would haunt him for the rest of his career.

"I saw him score in 46 straight games," marveled announcer Mike Lange. "I saw him get on the plane and he couldn't even sit down. He couldn't put his own things in the bins above the seats. But he kept at it and kept the scoring streak alive."

Displaying enormous resilience and character, Mario overcame his back problems to lead the Penguins to consecutive Stanley Cups in 1991 and 1992. Yet it was the adversity he would face the following season that elevated him to the status of a champion for the ages.

In 1992–93 Lemieux bolted from the starting gate like a thoroughbred racehorse. Piling up 101 points in his first 38 games, the big center was on pace to threaten Gretzky's single-season record of 215 points.

Once again, Mario had reached the very pinnacle of his sport. But once more, fate stepped in to deliver a crushing blow. On January 13, 1993, Lemieux was diagnosed with Hodgkin's disease.

Strange but True

The history of the Pittsburgh Penguins is filled with oddities and anomalies. First, consider a case involving three of the team's brightest stars, Michel Briere, Mario Lemieux, and Sidney Crosby. If you add the uniform numbers of Briere (21) and Lemieux (66), it equals Crosby's No. 87.

Stranger still is the eerie connection between Lemieux and Marc Boileau, the team's first French Canadian coach. Nicknamed Popeye for his fiery nature, Boileau piloted the Pens for parts of three seasons in the mid-1970s—and won 66 games.

On the evening of December 27, 2000—the night of Mario's triumphant return following a three-and-a-half-year retirement—the former Penguins skipper passed away from a heart attack.

Following surgery to remove an infected lymph node, the Penguins' captain underwent a series of radiation treatments. Displaying recuperative powers bordering on the superhuman, he returned to the lineup on March 2 and promptly went on a tear. Mario tallied 51 points over a 16-game stretch to lock up his fourth Art Ross Trophy, which is awarded each year to the league's leading point scorer, and his second Hart Trophy as the league's most valuable player.

"If he would have been healthy, he would have broken a lot of records," teammate Jaromir Jagr said. "Maybe not all of them, but I'm pretty sure a lot of them. He was the best player I've ever seen. He was the most gifted at everything—size, strength, skill, how smart he was. There is no other player like him."

Mario would make two more dramatic comebacks and win two more scoring titles before hanging up his skates for good in 2006. On April 2, 2008, he was chosen as the "Best Athlete in Pittsburgh Sports History" at the *Pittsburgh Post-Gazette* Dapper Dan awards banquet over luminaries such as Roberto Clemente and Honus Wagner.

"Pittsburgh has had some great sports heroes," Craig Patrick said, "but none of them top Mario Lemieux."

Sid

During the summer of 2003 a reporter for the *Arizona Republic* asked Coyotes owner Wayne Gretzky if he thought any player might one day break his scoring records.

"Yes, Sidney Crosby," answered the Great One without hesitation. "He's the best player I've seen since Mario [Lemieux]."

Already a celebrity in his native Canada, Crosby had been touted as the Next One since his bantam days. Following a huge 168-point season during his second year of junior hockey, there was little doubt the 17-year-old center would be the first overall pick in the 2005 Entry Draft. On July 22, 2005, the lottery balls were dropped, and the one adorned with a skating penguin logo entered the tube.

"Everybody says they know where they were when they heard President Kennedy was shot," former Oilers coach Craig MacTavish said. "Now [in hockey] we all remember where we were when Pittsburgh won the lottery."

It soon became apparent that Crosby was, indeed, worthy of the hype. Blessed with powerful legs and incredible balance, the 5'11", 200-pounder was a superb playmaker and puck handler. Displaying remarkable passion, he never took a shift off.

"He plays the game right for an elite player," former linemate Colby Armstrong said. "He can blow a game open, but he also makes other players better. He's an up-and-down player with an incredible head on his shoulders."

Crosby finished his rookie campaign with 102 points, breaking Lemieux's club record for first-year players. In 2006–07 Sid truly was a sight to behold. Displaying uncommon focus and maturity, the 19-year-old wonder rolled up a league-leading 120 points. He became the youngest scoring champion in NHL history, and the youngest ever to garner the league's three major awards—the Hart

Kudos for Crosby

From the moment he first stepped onto an NHL rink as a precocious 18-year-old, Sidney Crosby earned the highest of praise from foes and teammates alike.

"Crosby's very similar to Wayne Gretzky," noted Rangers GM Glen Sather. "Same kind of vision. Crosby sees the ice as well as anybody. And I've seen him doing amazing things. He went through us and scored a goal that was one of the best I've ever seen. He's feisty, and that's what I like about him, too."

Montreal defenseman Josh Gorges had a similar assessment of the Penguins' superstar.

"Best player in the world? Yeah," Gorges said. "Crosby and [Alexander] Ovechkin are both really good, but Crosby's better at using the players around him. Great vision. Not only can he score, but he passes the puck better than anybody. He makes plays behind his back, drop passes. You sit in the stands, and you don't even see the possibilities. You wonder how he sees them. As a defenseman you try to force him to make plays he doesn't want to make. If you allow him to make the plays he wants, he'll burn you."

Perhaps the finest testament to Sid's abilities came from Penguins owner Mario Lemieux.

"I think it's much tougher to dominate the league now, the way it's set up," Mario said. "For him to go out there and do the things he does every night, every shift, it's incredible. His toughness is unbelievable, his training, his shooting ability has gotten better the past couple years…what he's doing now is much more impressive than what I did years ago."

Trophy, the Art Ross Trophy, and the Lester B. Pearson (Ted Lindsay) Award, given to the NHL Players' Association's most outstanding player.

The Penguins' brass took note. On May 31, 2007, they officially appointed Crosby as team captain, making him the youngest player to serve as captain in league history.

Taking his new role to heart, Crosby shook off a high-ankle sprain to lead the Penguins to a Stanley Cup Finals matchup with

Detroit in 2008. Although the Pens succumbed to the powerful Red Wings in six games, Sid tied Henrik Zetterberg—winner of the Conn Smythe Trophy as MVP of the playoffs—for the post-season scoring lead with 27 points.

Following a strong 103-point season in 2008–09, Crosby once again rose to the occasion in the playoffs. He scored eight huge goals to key a come-from-behind triumph over Washington in the Eastern Conference Semifinals. During a hotly contested Finals rematch with the Red Wings, Sid helped shut down Detroit's big guns and became the youngest captain in NHL history to have his name engraved on the Stanley Cup.

Not content to rest on his laurels, Crosby worked tirelessly over the summer of 2009 to improve his game. In an effort to gain more velocity on his shot he switched to a new composite stick. The result was a career-high 51 goals and a share of the Maurice Richard Trophy. He emerged as a demon on face-offs as well, winning 56 percent of his draws.

"This is the measure of Crosby," wrote Michael Farber of *Sports Illustrated*. "He takes a flaw and burnishes it until it gleams."

In 2010–11 Crosby reaffirmed his status as the world's best player. Bolting from the starting blocks at a scorching pace, he tallied 32 goals and 66 points in just 41 games. Along the way he rolled up a 25-game point scoring streak, the longest in the NHL in nearly two decades.

However, Sid's dream season came to a thudding halt during the Winter Classic. Late in the second period he was struck down from the blind side in a brutal collision with Washington's David Steckel as he turned to follow the play. Remarkably, he dressed for a game with Tampa Bay four days later, but absorbed a second big hit from towering Victor Hedman. Afterward, the Penguins' captain was diagnosed with a concussion.

Crosby didn't resume skating until mid-March. After making it through some light-duty workouts, he increased the intensity of his

Following in the footsteps of the legendary Mario Lemieux, center Sidney Crosby led the Penguins to a Stanley Cup in 2009.

training sessions in hopes of returning for the playoffs. However, following a practice session on April 20, Sid aborted his comeback.

"I started to get some symptoms," he confessed. "I started to ramp things up a bit as far as working out and skating, and I got a little bit of symptoms. I had to take a step back."

"He looked fantastic skating, which was great news," Penguins GM Ray Shero said. "But this is an injury where when you do have something, whether it's fogginess at times or whatever, you have to step back a little bit. But the great news is, he's got all kinds of time on his side right now."

3 Birth

The Pittsburgh Penguins came into existence on a spring day in 1965 thanks to a pair of former law school classmates. While driving along the Pennsylvania Turnpike to Harrisburg, Pennsylvania senator Jack McGregor and attorney Peter Block engaged in a lively conversation about the National Hockey League's plan to expand to 12 teams.

An avid hockey fan, Block told McGregor he believed Pittsburgh was ready for an NHL team. After all, the city had a long and enduring love affair with the sport dating back to the turn of the century. Hall of Famers Lionel "Big Train" Conacher and Roy "Shrimp" Worters had plied their trade for the Pirates, an early NHL entry. Pittsburgh fans had faithfully supported the minor league Hornets for nearly 30 years. It was time to step up in class.

A strategy was soon hatched to secure an entry for the Steel City. McGregor would approach city and civic leaders arguing that

Pete and Re-Peat

Despite some early misgivings about the team's chosen nickname, the Penguins' brass quickly warmed to its new identity. They commissioned graphic artist Bob Gessner to design the now-iconic logo, which featured a skating penguin with a scarf holding a hockey stick, set upon a golden triangle background.

Late in the team's inaugural season Pens owner Jack McGregor went one better. He arranged for the Pittsburgh Aqua Zoo to loan the club a *real* penguin to serve as a mascot.

Nicknamed Pete, the flightless waterfowl made his Civic Arena debut on February 21, 1968, ironically during a game against the Philadelphia Flyers. The Penguins had CCM design a special pair of skates for Pete and arranged for the Ecuadorian penguin to receive skating lessons from a University of Pittsburgh student.

Not everyone was a fan of the team's new attraction.

"One of the least-liked ice 'skaters' was Pete the Penguin, the live Pittsburgh Penguins mascot," recalled Bob Mock, manager of the Monroeville Mall ice rink. "He may have been feathered but he was not particularly a friend to the rink workers, particularly the ones who had to carry the shovel to clean up after him as he was walked on a leash like a dog in the facility."

The Penguins planned to have Pete make regular appearances during home games. On the night of October 19, 1968, he led the team onto the ice for a contest with the Boston Bruins. Pete made six more appearances before falling gravely ill with pneumonia.

"Even Pete's battling for his life," noted *Pittsburgh Press* columnist Bill Heufelder on November 21 as the team skidded to its seventh loss in a row.

McGregor was incredulous.

"Come on, I said, penguins live outdoors in the coldest temperatures on the planet. How could he catch pneumonia?" McGregor recalled. "The vet said, 'Trust me, he has pneumonia.'"

Pete passed away two days later at the Highland Park Zoo and was promptly sent to a local taxidermist for stuffing. He was proudly on display in the lobby of the team offices until a public outcry forced the club to remove him.

Nonplussed, the Penguins arranged to have a second mascot loaned to them. Re-Peat fared a little better than his predecessor, making it through the 1971–72 season.

big-league hockey was a tool for urban renewal. Meanwhile, Block would gather information about the NHL's bidding process.

Block soon learned the NHL's expansion plan was based on geography. The league planned to add two teams from the West Coast, two from the Midwest, and two from the East. With Philadelphia already earmarked as one of the eastern clubs, McGregor and Block faced a stiff challenge.

"Our closest competition was Buffalo," McGregor recalled. "The Buffalo group went all out to pick off the sixth franchise. Two half brothers, Bruce Norris, owner of the Detroit Red Wings, and Jim Norris, owner of the Chicago Black Hawks, began leaning toward Buffalo."

Fortunately, McGregor had an ace in the hole. He enlisted the help of Pittsburgh Steelers owner Art Rooney Sr., who had connections to the Norris brothers through the horse racing business.

"I'll never forget Art calling each from his New York City hotel room, in my presence," McGregor recalled. "He said to each: 'You owe this to me. You cannot put Buffalo ahead of Pittsburgh. It would be personally embarrassing to me if you did.'"

On February 8, 1966, the NHL awarded a franchise to McGregor's 21-man syndicate, which included Rooney and some of the most prominent names in Pittsburgh business society. The other franchises were awarded to Los Angeles, Minneapolis–St. Paul, Philadelphia, St. Louis, and San Francisco–Oakland.

As fate would have it, the Penguins were the last of the new teams to receive a nickname. With suggestions pouring in, McGregor decided to sponsor a "Name the Team" contest. The fan who submitted the winning entry would receive a 25-inch color TV and two season tickets. After accepting 26,400 entries McGregor announced on February 10, 1967, the team would be called the Penguins, a name favored by his wife, Carol.

The nickname made sense in a way. After all, the team would play its home games in the Igloo, as the Civic Arena was known. But many felt the club had laid a Penguins-sized egg.

"Most fans wanted to keep the Hornets name," general manager Jack Riley admitted. "I certainly wasn't in favor of the name Penguins at the time, but it caught on."

Bob Gessner, a local freelance artist charged with designing the team's logo, certainly was no fan.

"The Penguins? No, really, what will the team be called?" Gessner asked during a meeting with the club's executives. "You can't call a hockey team 'the Penguins.' That's ridiculous."

Coach Red Sullivan hated the name, too, along with the proposed black-and-white uniform colors.

"The day after we play a bad game," he protested, "the sportswriters will say, 'They skated like a bunch of nuns.'"

After changing the color scheme to a more palatable Columbia blue, navy blue, and white, Senator McGregor signed a check for $2 million on June 6, 1967, and the Penguins became official members of the National Hockey League.

First Cup

On the morning of May 25, 1991, the Penguins found themselves on the cusp of realizing their boyhood dreams. After 24 years of unmitigated futility the Stanley Cup—the most prized trophy in all of hockey—was within their grasp.

Standing in the way was a fellow team from the expansion class of 1967, the Minnesota North Stars. Although not nearly as talented as the Penguins, Minnesota had proven to be a tough and

After 24 years of hockey futility, the Penguins brought home Pittsburgh's first Stanley Cup in 1991.

worthy adversary. After grabbing a 2–1 series lead, however, the North Stars unwittingly supplied the Pens with an extra boost of motivation. The team revealed plans to visit the White House *after* they had secured the Cup.

"Did you see that?" asked Pittsburgh coach Bob Johnson. "Did you see what they put in the paper?"

The down-but-not-out Penguins certainly noticed. Led by their all-world captain Mario Lemieux, they blitzed the overconfident North Stars in Games 4 and 5 to take command of the series.

"This team has faced a lot of adversity this year," Johnson said. "Our star players have been injured. We were down to Boston 2–0. We were down to New Jersey 3–2, without [goalie Tom] Barrasso. But this team knows how to respond."

With the series and the Cup slipping through their fingers, the aggressive North Stars decided to test Barrasso, who'd been knocked out of the latter stages of Game 5 with a groin injury. Immediately after the opening face-off, Neal Broten plowed into the Pens' netminder. However, the veteran forward drew an interference penalty, which opened the door for Pittsburgh's potent power play.

At the two-minute mark, the unlikely duo of Bryan Trottier and Peter Taglianetti set up an even more unlikely recipient—Ulf Samuelsson—for a power-play goal. The score remained 1–0 until Lemieux chased down a loose puck and beat Jon Casey on a short-handed breakaway at 12:19.

"That was a very big goal at the time," Mario recalled. "It was a four-on-three. We were shorthanded. [Larry] Murphy made a great play. He saw me going up ice and threw the puck against the boards and I picked it up at center ice."

Less than a minute later, veteran Joe Mullen scooped up a cross-ice pass from Kevin Stevens and rifled the puck past Casey.

Realizing the Penguins had Casey's number, North Stars coach Bob Gainey pulled his starter in favor of Brian Hayward to begin the second period. The move worked for a time. Hayward held the Pens off the scoreboard for 13 minutes. Despite the 3–0 deficit, Minnesota had begun to find its rhythm.

It was the calm before the storm. At 13:15 Pens mucker Bob Errey deflected a Jaromir Jagr pass behind Hayward. Moments later, Ron Francis scurried up the ice to score the back-breaker. The North Stars' discipline quickly dissolved, as Dave Gagner drew a roughing penalty. Mullen made them pay, notching his second goal of the night.

Trailing by six goals going into the final period, Minnesota was clearly demoralized. However, there would be no letup in the Penguins' onslaught. With dreams of a Stanley Cup dancing in their heads, Lemieux set up light-scoring defenseman Jim Paek at 1:19 on a two-on-one break.

The Penguins could barely contain their excitement.

"As the clock just started ticking off in the third guys started yelling, 'Sixteen minutes left, fifteen minutes left, fourteen …' all the way down," Francis said.

"It was so exhilarating to get down to where it was eight minutes left in the game, seven minutes left in the game…where you could say, 'Whew, let's just enjoy it a little bit,'" Barrasso said.

Following the traditional postgame handshake, NHL president John Zeigler presented the coveted trophy to Lemieux. With assistant captains Paul Coffey and Errey by his side, No. 66 held the Cup aloft in a moment of joyous vindication.

"You dream of this, but it's even better in real life than it is in your dreams," Lemieux said. "This is the ultimate for me. I must be dreaming. Am I?"

"To see that, to feel that, and to pick up the Cup—*pick it up*—that's the greatest feeling I've ever had," Phil Bourque added. "I can't think of anything I'd rather do in life than skate around with the Cup over my head."

5 The Goal

Over the course of his Hall of Fame career, Penguins superstar Mario Lemieux scored an astounding 690 goals—far and away the most by any player in the team's colorful and storied history. While many were of the highlight-reel variety, perhaps none was more important than his brilliant tally in Game 2 of the 1991 Stanley Cup Finals.

Although the Penguins boasted a star-studded lineup that featured no fewer than six future Hall of Famers, Lord Stanley's coveted chalice was hardly in the bag. Their Finals foe, the Minnesota North Stars, was proving to be a worthy adversary. Paced by the clutch goaltending of unheralded Jon Casey, the Campbell Conference champs had snatched a 5–4 victory at the Civic Arena in the series opener. The Pens desperately needed a victory to keep pace.

Determined to even the series, the home-standing Penguins responded with a strong effort in Game 2. Buoyed by the return of All-Star defenseman Paul Coffey, they carried the play to the North Stars through the early going. Speedy Bob Errey struck for a short-handed goal, and big Kevin Stevens victimized Casey in the waning moments of the opening period to stake the team to a 2–0 lead.

Meanwhile, Mario, who had scored a shorthanded goal in Game 1, noticed how aggressively Casey played the puck. Number 66 filed the nugget away for future reference.

Entering the second period with a two-goal edge, the Penguins appeared to be in good shape. But 55 seconds into the frame, North Stars prodigy Mike Modano scored a power-play goal that threatened to turn the tide.

Frankie's Rush

When Penguins general manager Craig Patrick plucked towering defenseman Francois Leroux from the Ottawa Senators in the 1994 Waiver Draft, he wasn't expecting Bobby Orr numbers. Indeed, the former first-round pick of the Oilers had registered just four assists in 32 career NHL games.

While Leroux quickly became a fan favorite in the Steel City for his bone-crushing hits and willingness to drop the gloves, the lumbering 6'6", 247-pounder rarely ventured past his own blue line. Yet during the 1995 playoffs Frankie authored one of the signature plays in franchise history.

Down 3–1 in their opening-round series against Washington, the Penguins were fighting for their playoff lives. Although Pittsburgh rallied to send Game 5 into overtime, the underdog Capitals were dominating the action. The Pens needed a big play. Remarkably, Leroux provided the heroics.

As the game clock ticked past the four-minute mark, the big defender astonished everyone—including his own teammates—by lugging the puck deep into the attacking zone.

"He looked like Dagwood running to catch a bus," noted an observer.

With the bewildered Caps frozen in place Leroux dished a backhand pass to Luc Robitaille, who directed the puck past goalie Jim Carey. As the Capitals skated dejectedly off the ice, the Penguins joyously mobbed Leroux and Robitaille.

"For a minute there, the way he beat the guy to the corner, I thought he was Mario," Robitaille quipped.

"It was funny on the bench," Jaromir Jagr added. "The players screamed at him, 'Stay back. Don't go there. Just dump it.' All of a sudden he beats this guy, passes, [Robitaille] scores the goal, and he's a big hero."

The stage was set for one of the most spectacular goals in Stanley Cup history, one that would simply and eloquently become known as the Goal. The play began innocently enough as Lemieux gathered in a short pass from Phil Bourque deep in the Penguins' end. Gaining speed with each stride, Mario flashed through the neutral zone and caught the young defensive tandem of Shawn Chambers and Neil Wilkinson by surprise.

Still accelerating as he crossed the blue line, Lemieux sliced past Wilkinson and slipped the puck between Chambers' legs, turning the young defenseman into spaghetti. Skating at warp speed, he bore down on Casey. Staying true to form, the little goalie aggressively moved out to the top of his crease to cut down the angle. Mario was practically on top of Casey when he swerved sharply to his left and swept the puck into the net.

"What a burst of speed by Mario Lemieux," gushed Pens play-by-play announcer Mike Lange. "He left [Casey] on the parkway going to the airport. Brilliant goal."

"Lemieux just said, 'Give me that thing, I'm going coast to coast,'" added color man Paul Steigerwald. "He was flying through center ice and he had the defensemen backing in. He put it right between [Chambers'] legs, cut in on Casey, and [made] a tremendous final play to turn it over to the backhand as he was falling down. Oh, what a goal."

Mario's awesome effort took the starch out of Minnesota. Moments later Stevens banged home his second tally of the night to clinch a resounding 4–1 victory.

The Goal immediately found its rightful place in Penguins lore. It also proved to be the turning point of the series. Mario had provided his teammates with an enormous lift, not to mention a blueprint for beating Casey. With the plucky North Stars goalie under siege, the Penguins won three of the next four games to capture their first Stanley Cup.

6 Jags

When Jaromir Jagr was 13 years old, he traveled to Prague to watch Wayne Gretzky and Mario Lemieux compete in the World Cup Championships. Inspired by the two superstars, the youngster made up his mind he that he, too, would one day skate in the National Hockey League.

Following an impressive showing at the 1990 World Junior Championships, the kid from Kladno achieved his dream. On June 16, 1990, the Penguins selected the rangy right wing with the fifth overall pick in the Entry Draft.

Although he possessed a world of talent, Jagr's transition to the NHL was hardly a smooth one. Speaking little English, the 18-year-old grew terribly despondent and homesick. To remedy the situation, Pens general manager Craig Patrick acquired fellow Czech Republic native Jiri Hrdina from Calgary.

"Jags was really down low when I got there," Hrdina said. "He wasn't going to go home or anything, but he felt alone. I could talk to him about his problems. He's a very smart guy for his age. Very unusual to have the goals he does. He wants to be the best player in the game."

The move worked like a charm. With Hrdina serving as his companion and mentor, Jagr's extraordinary gifts soon bubbled to the surface. During Game 2 of the Pens' opening-round playoff series with New Jersey, he scored a spectacular overtime goal to lift his team to victory.

More than one observer likened him to a young Mario Lemieux. Certainly there were striking similarities. Both were strong, powerful skaters with a flair for the dramatic.

The Jagr Saga

After enjoying unprecedented popularity in Pittsburgh during the early stages of his career, Jaromir Jagr wore out his welcome in the early 2000s. Weary of the superstar's declining attitude, Penguins general manager Craig Patrick peddled the five-time NHL scoring champ to Washington in 2001. For the remainder of his career, Jagr became the man Penguins fans loved to hate.

The Jagr saga appeared to come full circle, however, during the summer of 2011. Following three seasons in the Kontinental Hockey League, the 39-year-old icon expressed a desire to return to his original team.

"My heart is in Pittsburgh," Jagr said.

On June 27, Pens GM Ray Shero extended the expatriate winger an olive branch by offering him a one-year deal for $2 million.

"We feel he's a guy who could help us this year and retire as a Penguin," Shero said.

The situation quickly unraveled. When a mystified TV reporter asked Paul Steigerwald if he thought No. 68 would sign with the black and gold, the play-by-play announcer flashed a wry smile and shook his head.

"I wouldn't bet on it," he said.

Steigerwald proved to be prophetic. Like a scene from the movie *Runaway Bride*, the legendary Czech left the Penguins standing at the altar while he entertained proposals from other suitors. Refusing to enter a bidding war, Shero withdrew his offer on July 1. Jagr promptly signed with the archrival Philadelphia Flyers.

"If I hurt somebody, I apologize," he said afterward. "I didn't mean it, but this is my life and I want to make the choice. I didn't think I was going to go [to Philadelphia], but after the conversation with the coaches and [Flyers defenseman] Chris Pronger, I started to like it."

"You all know that if you jumble 'Jaromir' you come up with 'Mario Jr.,'" sports personality Stan Savran noted.

Others felt Jagr more closely resembled one of hockey's most iconic stars.

"He reminds me of Maurice Richard," said Pens coach Scotty Bowman. "They both played the off wing, and both had so many moves. I don't think either of them knew which moves they were going to make until they did them. Totally unpredictable."

Jagr was electrifying during the Pens' march to their second Stanley Cup in 1992. With Mario out of action the 20-year-old star stepped forward in style, notching the winning goal in three straight games. All told, the brilliant young winger tallied 11 goals and 24 points in 21 postseason contests.

The fans loved his exuberance, the way he would remove a glove and shake his fist after scoring an important goal. Signs reading "Zivio Jagr" ("Cheers Jagr") hung from the balconies at the Civic Arena like championship banners. Charismatic and rock-star handsome, he became the darling of the Steel City faithful, especially the fairer sex.

"Me and Jags were in a bar one night playing a pinball machine," teammate Rick Tocchet recalled. "There were, like, a thousand girls and Jaromir. When he needed change, they started throwing quarters at him."

When Mario was forced to sit out the 1994–95 season, Jagr truly emerged as a world-class player. Skating on a line with crafty setup man Ron Francis, he came into his own and captured his first Art Ross Trophy. The following season he exploded for 62 goals and 149 points, an NHL record for right wings.

After Lemieux retired in 1997, Jagr became far and away the most dominant player in the game. Beginning in 1997–98, he won four straight scoring titles, a feat topped only by Gretzky. For good measure, he garnered the Hart Trophy in 1999 and the Lester B. Pearson Award two years' running. Even opponents were quick to sing his praises.

"With no disrespect to the other guys," said rugged New Jersey defenseman Ken Daneyko, "you've got [Eric] Lindros, [Paul] Kariya, [Teemu] Selanne, and [Peter] Forsberg here, and Jagr is head and shoulders above them, up there."

By the late 1990s, however, things started to sour for Jagr in Pittsburgh. Although quick with a smile or a joke, beneath the

The fifth overall pick in the 1990 Entry Draft, Jaromir Jagr scored 439 goals as a Pittsburgh Penguin.

surface he was a deeply sensitive young man given to periods of brooding and introspection. He often gave the impression of being selfish or overly critical of his teammates and coaches.

"He's a very emotional kid," noted announcer Mike Lange. "I don't think people realize how emotional he is, day to day."

The turbulence came to a head during the 2000–01 season. On three separate occasions Jagr asked to be traded. Bound by financial constraints and weary of No. 68's declining attitude, Craig Patrick called his bluff. On July 11, 2001, he dealt arguably the finest hockey player in the world to Washington for three raw prospects who never panned out.

For the remainder of his NHL career Jagr was greeted by boos and catcalls every time he visited the Mellon Arena. It was a sad requiem for arguably the second-greatest player in franchise history.

7 The Trade

After years of unfulfilled promise and frustrating failures, the Penguins appeared to be ready to turn the corner in 1990–91. Although superstar Mario Lemieux would miss nearly four months of the season due to complications from back surgery, the team performed surprisingly well during his absence. One of the big reasons was the inspired play of John Cullen, a former minor league scoring champion who had blossomed into one of the NHL's best playmakers.

Following a solid first half, however, the Pens hit the skids in February. During a western swing they were trounced by Los Angeles, Vancouver, and Calgary by a combined score of 18–7.

"We were in Calgary [on March 1]," Paul Steigerwald recalled. "There was a replay of a play around the net. The camera was from above and every Calgary Flames player was around our goal cage. We had no presence in front of our net whatsoever."

The Hartford Whalers were struggling as well. Although they'd made the playoffs five years in a row, the Whalers clearly were a troubled team. At the eye of the storm was the team's franchise player, Ron Francis. Long considered a model citizen, Francis had been stripped of the captaincy after running afoul of owner Richard Gordon and coach Rick Ley.

As the trade deadline approached, Whalers general manager Eddie Johnston was under intense pressure from Gordon to move Francis or else.

"I was told if certain players were still here after the [trade] deadline, I'd be the next one to leave town," he said.

Johnston and Penguins GM Craig Patrick had hooked up for a trade earlier in the season, with Scott Young joining the Pens while scoring ace Rob Brown went to Hartford. Instinctively, they dialed each other up.

On March 4, 1991, the headline in the *Pittsburgh Post-Gazette* sports section blared, "Penguins pay a big price for a big payoff." Less than 24 hours before the trade deadline, Patrick and Johnston had swung a blockbuster of epic proportions. The Pens had parted with two of their best young players, Cullen and puck-moving defenseman Zarley Zalapski, along with minor league forward Jeff Parker. In exchange they received Francis and backline thumpers Ulf Samuelsson and Grant Jennings.

"It started out as a one-for-one deal," Patrick recalled, "but neither of us was comfortable. We kept adding players until we felt comfortable."

Although in hindsight it's hard to imagine, the Trade, as it would come to be known in Penguins lore, did not receive universal acclaim. Cullen's best friend, Kevin Stevens, stopped just short of calling the swap a mistake. *The Hockey News* analyzed the deal and declared it a win for Hartford.

"We knew the trade was giving us certain parts that we needed to be even more successful than we were," Patrick said. "It was hard to give up what we did, especially Johnny Cullen. Zarley Zalapski had a lot of promise at that point in his career, too. But we were really concerned about our chemistry because John was a big part of our chemistry on the team at that point. So it was a major concern."

It soon became apparent that Patrick had filled in the missing pieces to the Penguins' jigsaw puzzle with one bold stroke.

"Ronnie was a No. 1 center in Hartford, but he was a No. 2 center here and he was the perfect second-line center because he could give you offense, but he could check and win draws,"

Steigerwald said. "Ulfie was a mean man in front of the net. So you had the combination of a guy [Francis] who really created a defensive structure for the team all by himself and then you had another guy [Samuelsson] who could zero in on the best scorer on the other side and ruin his night with the way he played. It was great."

Ignited by the Trade, the Penguins tore through the homestretch at a 9–3–2 clip to capture the Patrick Division crown, the first division title in the club's 24-year history. On the night of May 25, 1991, they hoisted the Stanley Cup.

8 Crazy Eights

During his first four seasons in the National Hockey League, Penguins superstar Mario Lemieux enjoyed many big games. On December 31, 1985, he recorded his first career hat trick, notching four goals to pace an 8–4 rout of St. Louis. By the end of the 1987–88 campaign Mario had a dozen hat tricks to his credit, already the highest total of any Pens player.

In 1988–89 the big fellow really heated up. Far and away the most dominant player in the game, the 23-year-old phenom rolled up an astonishing 85 goals, 114 assists, and 199 points to capture his second straight Art Ross Trophy. Along the way he accomplished a feat that no other player has achieved before or since.

On the evening of October 15, 1988, Mario became only the 12th player in NHL history to tally eight points in a single game, registering two goals and six assists during a 9–2 demolition of the Blues. It was a harbinger of bigger things to come.

Barely two months later, Lemieux enjoyed a game for the ages. Skating against New Jersey before a sellout crowd at the

Civic Arena on New Year's Eve, Mario tied a league record with his second eight-point game. Even more remarkably, he became the first player in NHL history to score five goals in five different ways. The rangy center struck at even strength, shorthanded, on the power play, and on a penalty shot. For good measure, he capped off his astounding evening with an empty netter.

"I think we all just saw Mario's gift, a little late for Christmas, to me and the fans," coach Gene Ubriaco said. "I'm not going to say 'awesome,' I've said that too many times."

"Some of the things he did out there were amazing," added linemate Rob Brown. "They're going to have videotapes of tonight's game for kids to buy and watch, because it was just amazing."

Mario wasn't finished writing his name in the record books. During the 1989 Patrick Division Finals he turned in perhaps the single greatest performance in Stanley Cup history.

The Penguins were locked in a titanic struggle with the battle-hardened Flyers. By his lofty standards, Lemieux had been comparatively quiet. After collecting a goal in each of the first three games of the series, he was held off the score sheet in Game 4. Worse yet, he'd collided with teammate Randy Cunneyworth late in the contest. The Penguins' captain retired to the locker room after suffering what trainer Skip Thayer described as "a whiplash-type injury."

Heading into Game 5, there was tremendous concern over Mario's condition. With the series tied at two games apiece, the Pens could ill afford to have their superstar on the sideline. The Civic Arena faithful exploded with a loud roar when No. 66 took to the ice for the pregame warmups.

Shaking off the lingering effects of his injury, Lemieux appeared to be in his usual top form.

"The first shift, he had extra jump in him and you knew he was going to have a good game," Brown said.

Philadelphia goalie Ron Hextall stopped Lemieux's first shot. It would be the high point of the evening for the All-Star netminder. On the next rush Mario streaked up ice and beat Hextall on a breakaway. The wail from the goal siren had barely faded when Le Magnifique scored again at 3:45. Three minutes later Mario banged the puck past the flustered goalie to record a natural hat trick. He'd potted three goals on three shots, all within a span of four minutes and forty seconds.

"With a great player like Mario, it's only a matter of time," Paul Coffey said.

Incredibly, Lemieux wasn't finished. At 17:09 he struck for his fourth goal of the opening period, a power-play tally that gave the Pens a 5–1 lead.

Mario was content to play the role of setup man in the second period, dishing out three assists. When the Flyers closed the gap with a furious third-period rally, he sealed the Pens' victory with an empty-net goal.

Thanks to his amazing exploits, Lemieux tied Patrik Sundstrom's mark for most points in a playoff game. He also became the only player in NHL history to register three eight-point games.

9 The Save

During his NHL career goaltender Frank Pietrangelo earned a reputation as a fierce competitor who hated to lose, even at a game of cards. Although he served mainly in a backup role for the Penguins over four-plus seasons, the former University of Minnesota star played to win each and every night.

Pietrangelo's competitive nature was put to the ultimate test during the opening round of the 1991 Stanley Cup playoffs. The New Jersey Devils were proving to be more than the Penguins bargained for. While they were far and away the more talented team, the Pens trailed the nettlesome Devils 3–2. The series was shifting to the hostile surroundings of the Brendan Byrne Arena, where the Steel City sextet had enjoyed little success.

To make matters worse, starting goaltender Tom Barrasso suffered a shoulder injury and would be unavailable for the pivotal Game 6. Pietrangelo, who'd started only three games during the second half of the season, would start in goal. Indeed, the only question was not whether New Jersey would win but by how much.

As they had done throughout the series, the Devils took command early thanks to a fluke goal by John MacLean. However, power forward Kevin Stevens struck twice to stake the Penguins to a precarious one-goal lead.

It was then that Pietrangelo stepped forward to literally save the day. Fifteen minutes into the first period Peter Stastny found himself all alone in front of the Pittsburgh net with the puck cradled on his blade. A deadly accurate shooter, the New Jersey sniper rarely missed a scoring opportunity from point-blank range.

"When I saw Stastny moving into the puck I turned the other way because I know that's a goal," Pens winger Bob Errey said.

Stastny confidently whipped the puck toward the wide-open net and waited for the red light to signal the game-tying goal. From out of nowhere Pietrangelo's gloved left hand flashed like a phantom. Straining every fiber and sinew in his body to its limit, No. 40 reached across the goal crease at the last possible moment to snatch the puck out of midair.

The Devils were stunned. They could not believe the puck hadn't gone in. Yet there was Pietrangelo, casually flipping the vulcanized rubber to a linesman.

"I don't believe that save," gushed play-by-play announcer Mike Lange, "and neither does Stastny. [Pietrangelo] should get five to ten for that."

Deflated by the Save, the Devils' attack lost its steam. Thanks to Pietrangelo's stellar relief work, the Pens clipped New Jersey 4–3 to force a deciding Game 7 in Pittsburgh. What figured to be a barn burner turned out to be anticlimactic as Frankie stuffed the Devils again.

"He is a hot goaltender, red hot," color man Paul Steigerwald said. "They're just not gonna beat him."

Backed by Pietrangelo's sparkling 27-save performance, the inspired Penguins ran roughshod over their rivals en route to a 4–0 win. Using the series victory over New Jersey as a springboard, the Pens rolled past Washington, Boston, and Minnesota to capture their first Stanley Cup.

Team captain Mario Lemieux credited Pietrangelo for helping turn the playoffs around.

"Frankie came on in a tough situation in Jersey," Mario recalled in the highlight video *One From the Heart*. "We had to win the game facing elimination and he made a key save on Peter Stastny. That was probably the turning point of the playoffs for us."

Following the season Pietrangelo reflected on the Save in an interview with Tom McMillan. "I just reached back and [Stastny] kind of put it in my glove for me," he said modestly. "It's just one of those things where you've got to be lucky to be good."

10 Geno

Evgeni Vladimirovich Malkin burst on to the international hockey scene in the spring of 2004 when he led his native Russia to a gold medal at the World Under 18 Junior Championships. During one memorable play, the lanky 6'3", 192-pounder vaulted Kazakhstan's sprawling goalie to score a big goal.

Impressed with the youngster's boundless potential, Penguins general manager Craig Patrick selected Malkin with the second overall pick in the 2004 Entry Draft. However, bringing the gifted center to Pittsburgh proved to be infinitely more difficult. Malkin's team, Magnitogorsk Metallurg, was owned by Viktor Rashnikov, one of the richest and most powerful men in Russia. He was in no hurry to release his most prized player.

Much to the Penguins' surprise, Rashnikov announced on August 7, 2006, that he had signed Malkin to a new one-year deal. The prodigy contacted his North American agent, J.P. Barry, with the news.

"He was distraught when he called me the next day," said Barry. "He asked for help."

With Barry's assistance, Malkin defected when the team traveled to Helsinki on August 12. Upon his arrival in the United States, he made it clear that he had been pressured into signing with Magnitogorsk.

Malkin finally made his much-anticipated debut on October 18 against New Jersey. He gave a tantalizing preview of what was in store. Bursting into the slot, he faked future Hall of Famer Martin Brodeur out of position and whipped a backhander past the stunned goalie.

The 20-year-old promptly exploded, scoring at least one goal in each of his first six games, a pace unmatched by a rookie in 90 years. Displaying the mercurial brilliance of a Rachmaninoff concerto, Geno piled up 85 points to earn the Calder Trophy as the league's top rookie.

Malkin came of age during the 2007–08 campaign. When fellow supernova Sidney Crosby went down with a high-ankle sprain on January 18, the responsibility for pacing the attack fell on the quiet Russian's shoulders. Proving he was up to the task, No. 71 tallied a team-high 47 goals and 106 points to place second in the NHL scoring race behind countryman Alexander Ovechkin.

Russian superstar Evgeni Malkin joined the Penguins in 2006 and, along with Sidney Crosby, formed the foundation of Pittsburgh's Stanley Cup winners in 2009.

"That's when he elevated his game," teammate Sergei Gonchar said. "That was a real turning point for him."

Unfortunately, the magic dust wore off during the postseason. Following a strong performance through the first three rounds of the playoffs, Malkin faded during the Pens' loss to Detroit in the Stanley Cup Finals.

"You know, Sid got hurt and missed 29 games, and Geno had to carry the team on his shoulders basically," Max Talbot said. "He just couldn't do it anymore."

Although it was revealed that Malkin was suffering from the flu, questions surfaced about his ability to produce at crunch time. The criticism only strengthened the big center's resolve. Entering his third season, he was a more confident, mature player. Skating as if he had something to prove, Geno captured the Art Ross Trophy on the strength of a 113-point season.

Determined to lead his team to a Stanley Cup, Malkin shifted into top gear in the 2009 playoffs. He paced all postseason scorers with 36 points, including a team-high eight points during the Pens' scintillating victory over Detroit in the Finals. At age 22, he became the youngest forward ever to win the Conn Smythe Trophy.

"It's a big day in my life," he said. "My friends, my parents are happy; I'm happy."

Malkin had emerged as perhaps the most dominant player in the game. However, the injury bug bit hard just as he was reaching top form. Hampered by shoulder and foot problems, his production dipped to 77 points in 2009–10.

Primed for a big comeback in 2010–11, Malkin suffered through another injury-plagued season. Shaking off the effects of a troublesome left knee, he tallied 37 points in 43 games. However, on February 4, 2011, he collided with Buffalo's Tyler Myers and tore the anterior cruciate and medial collateral ligaments in his right knee. Six days later he underwent season-ending surgery.

Dynamic Duo

When Evgeni Malkin arrived at his first Penguins training camp in 2006, the team already boasted one of the game's brightest young stars in Sidney Crosby. It wasn't long before the dynamic duo began to engage in a little friendly one-upmanship, constantly pushing themselves to outdo the other.

"The competition is great," Malkin said with a smile. "Competing against Sid is great."

"They bring out the best in each other," Pens defenseman Brooks Orpik said. "They're team-first guys, but they don't want to let the other guy get too far ahead."

A debate soon arose over who was the better player. Crosby held the early edge, outpointing Malkin 120 to 85 during the 2006–07 campaign to win the Art Ross and Hart Trophies. However, after Sid was sidelined with a high-ankle sprain in 2007–08, Geno stepped forward. He piled up 219 points over a two-year span to earn an Art Ross Trophy of his own.

"Malkin makes everyone around him better," NHL defenseman Brian Pothier said. "Not to say Crosby doesn't. But [Malkin's] more potent. He scares guys a little more, and they give him a little more space."

Others backed Sid the Kid.

"Watch their body language on the bench," noted a scout. "It's Crosby doing the talking and Malkin doing the listening. No question, Crosby makes that team go."

Perhaps teammate Craig Adams summed things up best. After watching the precocious pair shred the Carolina Hurricanes during the 2009 Eastern Conference Finals, he said, "They're unbelievable. To me, they're 1 and 1A, and I don't know which one is which. Just so competitive, so talented. They just want to play in these big games and score the goals, and they're doing it."

Fortunately, Geno's MCL wasn't damaged as severely as the ACL and didn't need to be surgically repaired. Following two months of rehab the big center laced up his skates and took his first strides on the CONSOL Energy Center ice, fueling hopes for a complete recovery.

"I'm glad to start skating," Malkin said. "We just work hard every day and see what happens tomorrow. I feel pretty good. I want to play."

11 The Architect

It's safe to say that no one aside from Mario Lemieux had a greater hand in turning the Penguins into a winning organization than Craig Patrick. Prior to his arrival, the Pens perpetually had a minor league feel about them, accompanied by minor league results.

"It is easy to forget that when Patrick walked into the building in December 1989, the Penguins were worse than a joke," wrote Gene Collier of the *Pittsburgh Post-Gazette*. "They were an old, bad joke."

Patrick immediately breathed new life into the franchise while instilling a much-needed air of professionalism. Perhaps no general manager in the history of the sport did better work than Patrick during his first full season at the Pens' helm. In the summer of 1990 he hired well-respected hockey men Bob Johnson and Scotty Bowman to assist him. Noting that his talented young team lacked leadership, Patrick imported seasoned veterans and Stanley Cup winners Joe Mullen and Bryan Trottier. At the Entry Draft he selected a gangly, mullet-topped kid from the Czech Republic named Jaromir Jagr. Belying his no-trade reputation, he acquired future Hall of Famers Ron Francis and Larry Murphy, as well as established pros Gordie Roberts, Ulf Samuelsson, and Peter Taglianetti. In little more than 18 months he transformed the team from perennial also-rans into Stanley Cup champions.

The following season Patrick faced even bigger challenges. In the wake of Johnson's tragic and untimely death, he convinced Bowman to take over the coaching reins. With the club sagging at the two-thirds pole, he displayed the brass of a riverboat gambler by trading popular stars Paul Coffey and Mark Recchi for Kjell Samuelsson, Rick Tocchet, and Ken Wregget. Infused with sorely needed grit and fire, the Penguins heated up and rolled to a second straight Stanley Cup.

"Quite simply, Craig Patrick is the finest general manager in the National Hockey League," said appreciative Penguins owner Howard Baldwin.

Royalty

As a descendant of hockey's royal family, Craig Patrick was destined to make his mark in the sport. His grandfather Lester Patrick—the legendary Silver Fox—helped form the Pacific Coast Hockey Association and later gained fame as the first coach and general manager of the New York Rangers. Craig's father, Lynn Patrick, was a Hall of Fame left wing who starred for the Rangers' 1940 Stanley Cup champions. Uncle Murray "Muzz" Patrick, a rough-and-tumble defenseman, likewise won a Cup with New York. For good measure his great-uncle, Frank, also was inducted into the Hall of Fame.

It was only natural for young Craig to pursue a career in hockey. A right wing of some promise, he considered entering the Canadian junior ranks until his family intervened.

"My uncle Muzz…he demanded I go to Denver University," Patrick recalled. "When the man is the heavyweight boxing champ of Canada, I thought I'd better listen."

Craig would soon carve out an enduring legacy of his own. After leading Denver to national titles in 1968 and 1969, he enjoyed a solid NHL career that spanned 401 games. In 1980 he served as the assistant coach and assistant general manager for Team USA's gold-medal winning Miracle on Ice squad. A year later he became the youngest GM in New York Rangers history.

On December 5, 1989, the DeBartolo family hired Patrick to turn the fortunes of the sagging Pittsburgh Penguins. It was a move that would change the course of a franchise.

During the next nine years, Patrick kept the team on the short list of Cup contenders. He continued to display a Midas touch, acquiring an endless succession of stars such as Alexei Kovalev, Petr Nedved, Luc Robitaille, Tomas Sandstrom, and Sergei Zubov. When the team was rocked by bankruptcy in the late 1990s, he did some of his finest work. Showing a sharp eye for undervalued talent, he added solid performers Robert Lang, Jiri Slegr, and Martin Straka.

In recognition of his outstanding achievements, Patrick was inducted into the Hockey Hall of Fame in November of 2001. New owner Mario Lemieux flew the entire team to Toronto to take part in the ceremony. Clearly humbled, the soft-spoken GM misted up several times during his speech.

"What an experience," he said. "Simply overwhelming."

Following his induction, some of the luster began to fade from Patrick's sterling reputation. A string of poor drafts, combined with the club's ever-tightening finances, caused the Pens to falter. In the summer of 2001 he dealt Jagr to Washington for three prospects who never panned out. The trade effectively ended the team's glorious run of 11 consecutive playoff seasons.

Undaunted, the veteran general manager stockpiled an incredible collection of young talent in the early 2000s. Under his watch promising first-round picks Evgeni Malkin, Marc-Andre Fleury, and Ryan Whitney joined the fold. Plums such as Ryan Malone, Alex Goligoski, and Kris Letang were picked in later rounds. Patrick struck gold at the 2005 Entry Draft when he selected phenom Sidney Crosby with the first overall pick. Teeming with good young players, the Penguins were poised for a comeback, one that would ultimately lead to a third Stanley Cup.

Patrick hoped to preside over the team's resurgence. Sadly, it was not to be. After 17 years of service he was relieved of his duties on April 20, 2006, by club president Ken Sawyer.

Penguins GM Craig Patrick was the driving force behind two Stanley Cup champions during his 17 years with the franchise.

"This was a difficult decision that we did not take lightly," Sawyer said. "It involved all the members of our board [of directors] and after much discussion, we all came to the same conclusion: that it was time to make a change."

Stung by the dismissal, Patrick avoided hockey-related functions for a time. But on April 2, 2008, he accepted an invitation to join Lemieux in the owner's box. He watched with pride as the team he helped build defeated the Flyers to clinch the Atlantic Division crown.

12 Heart of a Champion

Entering their 1992 Stanley Cup Finals matchup with the Penguins, the Chicago Blackhawks were brimming with confidence. A tough, veteran team, the Blackhawks had rolled to an NHL-record 11 straight postseason victories. Paced by 50-goal man Jeremy Roenick and superb young goalie Ed Belfour, the high-flying Hawks were poised to bring the Stanley Cup back to the Windy City.

The Penguins, however, were a team of enormous fiber and character. During the season they'd unflinchingly weathered the tragic death of coach Bob Johnson; the trading of Paul Coffey and Mark Recchi; and postseason injuries to stars Mario Lemieux and Joe Mullen.

"We stay on an even keel and do what it takes to win," said forward Kevin Stevens.

The tone was set in the series opener. Led by their All-Star defensive tandem of Chris Chelios and Steve Smith, the Blackhawks snatched a 4–1 lead and banged Lemieux and the other Penguins stars around without mercy. But the Pens weathered the storm and rallied to beat the Hawks on Mario's scintillating last-minute goal.

Nonplussed, Chicago continued to employ its trademark body-bending style in Games 2 and 3. However, the Penguins adjusted and matched their physical foe check for check.

"We're not the most aggressive team in the world," Rick Tocchet said, "but we do play aggressively when we have to. We're just as big and strong as they are, and it's not the worst thing in the world to take a hit."

Beating the Blackhawks at their own game, the Steel City sextet prevailed in a pair of tight, defensive struggles.

"I look at some of the great teams of the past, the Islanders and the Oilers, and one of the strengths they had was adaptability," defenseman Gordie Roberts said. "This team's the same. We can change gears. We can play any style. We do what we have to do to win hockey games."

With his team in dire straits, Chicago coach Mike Keenan threw caution to the wind in Game 4. Playing before a frenzied throng at Chicago Stadium, Blackhawks captain Dirk Graham responded with a first-period hat trick. However, the Penguins countered with three goals of their own, including one each by big guns Jaromir Jagr, Stevens, and Lemieux.

The second period featured furious end-to-end action. The rugged Tocchet staked the Pens to a 4–3 lead with his sixth goal of the playoffs. Lemieux and Stevens sprung loose for numerous breakaway opportunities. They were repeatedly denied by unheralded Dominik Hasek, who had replaced Belfour between the pipes. Thanks to Hasek's brilliant play, the Hawks knotted the score late in the period on a tally by Roenick.

However, the folly of engaging the talent-laden Penguins in a shootout soon took its toll. Five minutes into the final frame, Mario separated Chelios from the puck with a crisp check. Tocchet pounced on the rubber and fed it to Larry Murphy, who fired a beautiful shot into the upper-right corner of the net. Moments later, Ron Francis steamed into the Chicago zone. Using linemate Shawn McEachern as a decoy, he blew the puck past a fading Hasek.

The goal clearly took the starch out of Chicago. In one memorable sequence Lemieux and Jagr played keep-away with the puck, reducing the bewildered Hawks to an on-ice version of the Keystone Kops chasing after Buster Keaton and Harold Lloyd.

Although Roenick scored his second goal of the game with nine minutes remaining, the outcome was never in doubt. Settling into their one-four delay, the Pens set up a protective cocoon around Tom Barrasso. The veteran goalie stopped a final shot by Chelios in the closing seconds and thrust his hands into the air. The Penguins had won their second straight Stanley Cup.

"When you win once, people wonder," Stevens said. "When you win twice, it's no fluke."

13 Lucky 13

As a general rule, sports teams and athletes avoid the number 13 like the plague. This is especially true in hockey, whose players tend to be famously superstitious.

Penguins head equipment manager Dana Heinze vividly remembers the reaction of Ivo Jan, a European who was assigned the number as a member of the Johnstown Jets back in 1997–98.

"He was beside himself," Heinze said. "I was like, 'Oh, okay, okay, I'm sorry.' That happened a couple of times, so we just took [13] out of the rotation."

Superstitious Sid

Penguins superstar Sidney Crosby is widely regarded as the finest hockey player in the world. He may well be the most superstitious, too.

Sid was outed a few years ago by teammate Ryan Malone during an interview with Karen Price of the *Pittsburgh Tribune-Review*.

"Usually if I'm scoring, I try to do the same thing over and over. Or if the team's winning, I try to do the same stuff," Malone explained. "But I'm not too crazy. You probably want to talk to Sidney. *He's* crazy. If we go somewhere on the road, if we win, like when we went to New York and we beat the Rangers there, we all had to go to the same spot to eat and order all the same food. He's a different bird."

Former Penguin Hal Gill agreed.

"Sidney is pretty superstitious," the hulking defenseman said. "But it's more stupid things, like going over the train tracks [on the team bus] he touches a screw and lifts his feet...I don't know, stupid things like that."

Crosby was quick to defend himself.

"I don't do anything too crazy," he said. "I just do the same thing."

"The same *everything*?" Price asked.

"Yeah, pretty much, if we're winning," Sid responded. "If we're not winning, I pretty much keep it the same, but I might change something. It's just a mind-set. But for me, it's still pretty much the same as anyone else. Come to practice, after practice grab a bite to eat, have a nap, and then come to the rink."

The one thing the Pens' captain never alters is his pregame ritual. He always starts from the right side when he puts on his equipment. No one is allowed to touch his stick after it's been taped. Sid also likes to have his teammates go down the runway and onto the ice in the same order.

"If you have the mentality that you've done everything the right way or the same way to prepare for a game, you know that you've done everything right and you just have to go out and do it on the ice," he said. "That's the most important part."

Far from being a bad-luck number, 13 has come to symbolize accomplishment and success for the Penguins. Over the course of the team's 44-year-history, 13 players have worn the captain's "C" on a full-time basis. The list includes luminaries such as Sidney Crosby and Jaromir Jagr, as well as Hockey Hall of Famers Ron Francis and Mario Lemieux. Others who served as captain include All-Stars Mike Bullard, Randy Carlyle, Rick Kehoe, and Jean Pronovost, along with Dan Frawley, Earl Ingarfield, Ab McDonald, Terry Ruskowski, and Ron Schock.

In recent seasons the Penguins have virtually annexed the Art Ross Trophy. Beginning in 1987–88, Pens superstars such as Lemieux, Jagr, Crosby, and Evgeni Malkin captured the award an astounding 13 times in 23 seasons—including a remarkable run of seven straight years from 1995 through 2001. It is an achievement unparalleled by any other team in NHL history.

The first Penguins player to don No. 13 was Jim Hamilton. A swift-skating left wing out of Barrie, Ontario, Hamilton was the club's second-round pick in the 1977 Amateur Draft. He served most of his eight-year pro career as a fringe player, splitting time between the Penguins and their top minor league affiliate.

However, during the 1979 Stanley Cup playoffs the blond-haired winger enjoyed a shining moment in the sun. Recalled from Binghamton of the American Hockey League for a winner-take-all Game 3, Hamilton magically scored two huge goals to lift the Penguins to a 4–3 victory over Buffalo.

Fast-forward to the 2008–09 season. After reaching the Stanley Cup Finals the previous spring, the Penguins were struggling to keep pace in the chase for a playoff berth. With the season hanging in the balance, general manager Ray Shero acquired Bill Guerin from the Islanders for a conditional draft pick.

The 39-year-old veteran, who'd worn No. 13 since the 2000–01 season, immediately helped tip the scales for the Penguins. With Guerin providing badly needed leadership and clutch goal scoring, the team went on a 12–2–3 tear to lock up second place in the Atlantic Division. Guerin was a solid performer and a stabilizing influence during the playoffs, notching seven goals—including two game winners—to help the Pens capture their third Stanley Cup.

"All our kids want to wear [No. 13]," Guerin said. "They all wear it on their teams now. They all try to get it."

Two other players wore No. 13 while skating for the Penguins. Big Charlie Simmer, a two-time 50-goal scorer and All-Star, eschewed conventional wisdom by donning the number for the 1987–88 campaign. Promising young defenseman Alex Goligoski briefly sported No. 13 during his first go-around with the team.

"My first year of pro, I kind of got stuck with it," Goligoski said. "I had three numbers to choose from, and I didn't like the other two, so I went with 13, and I just grew to like it, I guess. I'm the least superstitious guy you know, and I'm sure a lot of people who wear that number say that."

14 Third Time's a Charm

The 2008–09 season would prove to be one of the most challenging—and rewarding—in Penguins franchise history. After bowing to Detroit in the 2008 Stanley Cup Finals, the Pens suffered a string of devastating defections. Several key players, including Ryan Malone, Gary Roberts, and Jarkko Ruutu, signed with other teams. The biggest free agent of them all, Marian Hossa, spurned a lucrative long-term offer to sign a one-year deal with the Red Wings.

Hossa's defection set the tone for the season. The Penguins got off to a quick start but struggled mightily through January and February. The extended cold snap cost coach Michel Therrien his job. General manager Ray Shero named Dan Bylsma, a bright but relatively unproven coach, as Therrien's successor.

Playing Bylsma's up-tempo style, the Penguins responded with a dazzling stretch run to nail down a playoff berth. They continued their hot streak through the first three rounds of the playoffs, ousting the Flyers, Capitals, and Hurricanes to earn a return match with the Red Wings in the Finals.

The defending Cup champions once again proved to be a difficult foe. When the Red Wings won Games 1 and 2 by identical 3–1 scores, they appeared to be set for a repeat.

This time, however, the Penguins refused to fold. Displaying remarkable resilience, they took three of the next four games to set up a winner-take-all Game 7 in Detroit.

"We've given ourselves a chance to go up there," Max Talbot said. "One hundred and eleven games down for the season, and it comes down to one."

"Now, it's anyone's game," captain Sidney Crosby added. "We have to battle and find a way to pull it off."

The Penguins were faced with a daunting task. No visiting team had won Game 7 of a Stanley Cup Finals series since Montreal turned the trick against Chicago in 1971. To make matters worse, the black and gold had lost five of their previous six playoff contests at Joe Louis Arena, including an embarrassing 5–0 shellacking in Game 5.

Despite the Pens' dubious track record in Detroit, owner Mario Lemieux had faith in his team. The morning of the series finale he sent a special text message to each player.

"This is a chance of a lifetime to realize your childhood dream to win a Stanley Cup," Mario wrote. "Play without fear and you will be successful! See you at center ice."

Mario's message galvanized the team. Following an early Red Wings salvo, the inspired Penguins settled into their speed game

After losing to Detroit in the 2008 Stanley Cup Finals, the Penguins got their revenge by beating the Red Wings in their rematch one year later.

and seized control. Early in the second period Evgeni Malkin harassed Detroit blue-liner Brad Stuart into a turnover. The puck squirted loose to Talbot, who snapped a low wrist shot between Chris Osgood's pads.

Less than 10 minutes later the ubiquitous Talbot struck again. Gathering in a pass from Chris Kunitz, he sped into the Detroit zone and ripped the puck over Osgood's shoulder. Thanks to the supreme efforts of Mad Max, the Penguins were up by two.

Unfortunately, the Pens soon swallowed a heaping spoonful of adversity. While chasing down a loose puck in the neutral zone, Crosby was smashed into the sideboards by hulking Johan Franzen. Sid came away from the collision hobbling on a banged-up left knee. He would skate only one shift during the crucial third period.

"We tried to make it so I couldn't feel it anymore," Sid said, "but it just didn't work."

Sensing an opportunity, the Red Wings pounced. They dominated play in the final 20 minutes, outshooting the Pens by a margin of 7–1.

Thrust into the spotlight in the biggest game of his career, Penguins goalie Marc-Andre Fleury responded with a magnificent performance. His positioning flawless, his rebound control superb, the Flower held Detroit off the scoreboard until a Jonathan Ericsson rocket found the mark at 13:53.

Fleury's confidence never wavered. He made a pair of brilliant saves in the closing seconds, including a spectacular lunging stop on sharpshooting Wings captain Nicklas Lidstrom.

"I saw the shot coming in, and I just tried to do everything I could to get over there," Fleury said.

As the puck skipped harmlessly to the corner, his teammates poured into the crease and mobbed the victorious goalie. After a 17-year hiatus, Lord Stanley's coveted Cup was returning to the Steel City.

15 Badger Bob

Perhaps no individual left as an indelible imprint on Penguins hockey as the late Bob Johnson. His tenure was brief, tragically cut short by the brain tumor that would prematurely end his life. But during his stay he had a profound influence on everyone around him.

An excellent teacher and communicator, Johnson first gained national attention when he was hired to coach the University of Wisconsin in 1966. Under his steady hand, the Badgers became a powerhouse, capturing three national titles during his 15-year reign. It was there that he was given the enduring nickname Badger Bob.

In 1982 Johnson made his grand entrance into the NHL when he took over as coach of the talented but underachieving Calgary Flames. With a lineup seasoned with American-born stars he led the Flames to the Stanley Cup Finals in 1986.

Although he possessed an outstanding technical knowledge of the game, it was Johnson's effervescent personality that earned him lasting fame.

"I remember the night in Calgary when we were beaten 9–0 by Hartford—it was our 10th consecutive loss," former Flames GM Cliff Fletcher recalled. "If someone had parachuted me into the coach's office after that game and I didn't know the score, I would've sworn we'd won the game. He found something positive in everything."

In 1987 Johnson left Calgary to become the executive director of USA Hockey. A wonderful administrator, the position seemed to suit him well. But when Pittsburgh general manager Craig Patrick approached him in 1990 with an offer to coach the Penguins, Badger Bob couldn't resist returning to his first love.

Badger Bob Johnson led the Penguins to their first Stanley Cup victory in 1991. His life was tragically cut short by brain cancer that same year.

Guiding the Penguins would be no easy task. An exceptionally talented team, they were a prickly bunch that had a history of overthrowing coaches. Never one to back down from a challenge, Johnson dove into his new assignment with his typical unbridled enthusiasm.

"He created an atmosphere where you wanted to play for him and you wanted to win for him," Phil Bourque recalled. "And he taught us to play defense, something I never thought any coach could do."

By the sheer force of his personality, Johnson began to transform the Penguins from a group of talented individuals into champions. He became a surrogate father to many of the players, who found his positive, upbeat personality irrepressible.

"He approached every day with an enthusiasm that I've never seen in anyone except little children," Tom Barrasso noted. "He was able to translate his enthusiasm for life and hockey to the people around him."

The Pens had their tough times under the veteran coach, including a disastrous road trip in early March that left the club in peril of slipping out of playoff contention. Through it all the buoyant Johnson remained the same—optimistic and wholly confident in his team's abilities.

The rest, as they say, is history. In rapid succession, the underdog Penguins gunned down the Devils, Capitals, Bruins, and North Stars—each in comeback fashion—to capture their first Stanley Cup. Badger Bob became only the second American-born coach in modern NHL history to win a Cup.

"I've coached at every level of the game, but I never thought I'd put on a Stanley Cup ring," he said following the team's Game 6 triumph over Minnesota. "This is an unbelievable night."

Sadly, tragedy would follow on the heels of his greatest triumph. While preparing Team USA for the Canada Cup Tournament that summer, he began to experience slurred speech. During a six-game road trip in August his condition worsened dramatically and he was hospitalized.

Tests revealed two brain tumors. Doctors performed emergency surgery to remove one of the tumors, but the second had to be treated with radiation. Following a courageous battle, Johnson

The Option Line

Despite the prolonged absence of Mario Lemieux due to complications from back surgery, the 1990–91 Penguins stayed in the thick of the playoff chase thanks to the big-time scoring of John Cullen, Mark Recchi, and Kevin Stevens.

The trio was dubbed the Option Line because each member of the unit was in the option year of his contract. In keeping with his optimistic nature, Pens coach Bob Johnson had an entirely different take on the line's nickname.

"He thought we were called the Option Line because we had so many options available to us on the ice," Recchi recalled.

passed away at his home in Colorado Springs on November 26, 1991.

Although his time in the Steel City was brief, Badger Bob left an enduring legacy that will never be forgotten.

"He's the man most responsible for turning the whole thing around," play-by-play announcer Mike Lange said. "He established an attitude here that we'll never lose. Finally, it meant something to be a Penguin."

16 Conn Smythe Would Be Proud

After missing 75 games due to back miseries the previous two seasons, the 1991–92 campaign was comparatively kind to Penguins superstar Mario Lemieux. The big center appeared in 64 games and piled up 131 points to reclaim the Art Ross Trophy.

Shaking off the effects of an injured shoulder, No. 66 sparkled during the Pens' opening-round playoff series. Super Mario rang up seven goals and 17 points as Pittsburgh rallied to down Washington in a thrilling seven-game set.

Lemieux's fortunes took a decided turn for the worse during the Patrick Division Finals. After he set up a pair of goals to pace a 4–2 win in the series opener, frustrated Rangers coach Roger Neilson urged his team to "take Lemieux out of the game."

Late in the first period of Game 2, Adam Graves complied. With the Penguins working on a power play, Ron Francis won a face-off and drew the puck back to Mario at the left point. As the Pens' captain gathered in the pass, Graves skated toward him with bad intentions.

"When I saw Adam coming," Lemieux recalled, "I knew he wasn't kidding around."

Wielding his stick like a baseball bat, the Rangers' penalty killer swung for the fences and caught Lemieux with a wicked two-handed slash across the left wrist. Mario crumpled to the ice.

Afterward, the Penguins' worst fears were realized. Lemieux had a broken bone in his left hand. Amid speculation that Neilson had placed a bounty on Mario, Pens coach Scotty Bowman urged his players to forget about revenge and concentrate on winning the series.

Remarkably, they did just that. With their captain watching from the press box, the Penguins shocked the Rangers by winning three straight games to advance to the next round. Following a hard-fought 4–3 victory over Boston in Game 1 of the Wales Conference Finals, Lemieux was ready to make his triumphant return.

Initially, Bowman planned to use him exclusively on the power play. However, after a couple of shifts it was obvious the big fellow was fit for regular duty. Showing few ill effects from his injury, he notched two goals and an assist to key a 5–2 Pittsburgh triumph.

Following a Herculean three-assist effort in Game 3, Lemieux stepped forward to deliver the knockout blow early in Game 4. After picking off a wayward pass, Mario set sail for the Bruins' end. At the red line he encountered Ray Bourque, who was back-pedaling furiously in an attempt to gain position. With stunning precision No. 66 threaded the puck between the future Hall of Famer's legs and raced toward the Bruins' goal, where he beat Andy Moog with ease.

"There wasn't a guy on the bench who wasn't picked up two feet when he scored that goal," Francis said.

It would not be the last of Lemieux's heroics. In Game 1 of the Stanley Cup Finals the Penguins trailed the physical, determined

Chicago Blackhawks 4–2. Once again Mario provided a boost when his team needed it most.

Late in the second period he wove his way into Chicago ice on a two-man foray with Kevin Stevens. While Stevens ran interference, Mario veered off to the right side of the Blackhawks' zone. Stationed along the goal line, he appeared to be out of options. However, in an amazing display of skill, he faked a look to Stevens in the slot and banked the puck off of goalie Ed Belfour's right leg and into the net.

The goal proved to be the turning point. Revitalized, the Penguins rallied to tie the score in the third period. The stage once again was set for Le Magnifique.

In the final minute of play he drew a hooking penalty to Hawks defenseman Steve Smith. Seventeen seconds remained on the clock, enough time to mount one last attack.

He decided to gamble. Mario knew if Francis won the face-off he would try to move the puck to Larry Murphy at the right point. As soon as the puck was dropped he bolted toward the net. Play-by-play announcer Mike Lange picked up the call:

"They'll drop the puck…it's free…out right side to Murphy…shooting…save made…rebound to Lemieux… *he shoots and scores*! Mario Lemieux has given the Penguins the lead!"

Six days later the Pens hoisted the Stanley Cup.

It was only fitting that Mario was awarded the Conn Smythe Trophy. Displaying an abundance of courage and character he overcame a broken hand to lead all playoff scorers with 16 goals and 34 points, including a record-tying five game-winning goals.

17 Doctor in the House

Prior to Paul Coffey's arrival in the Steel City in 1987, the Penguins were (not so) loveable losers—a mediocre bunch that was perpetually consigned to the infernal regions of the NHL standings. Following his arrival, the team embarked on a glorious run that included 11 consecutive playoff berths and two Stanley Cup championships.

Coffey was a superb offensive defenseman the likes of which hadn't been seen since Bobby Orr. In many ways he was a throwback to the early days of the sport when teams played with seven players a side. The extra man—called a "rover"—played a hybrid position of forward and defense. This described Coffey's style to a T.

Like Orr, the cornerstone of Coffey's game was skating. Wedging his feet into skates that were two sizes too small, he could accelerate to warp speed in a matter of strides. Then he simply glided through the neutral zone past would-be checkers.

Teaming with Wayne Gretzky, Coffey helped turn the Edmonton Oilers into a dynasty. Serving as the quarterback for Edmonton's lethal power play, he paced the Oilers to three Stanley Cups in four seasons. Along the way he captured two Norris Trophies as the league's top defenseman and broke Orr's record for most goals in a season by a blue-liner (48). During the 1985 playoffs he piled up 37 points—an incredible total for a forward let alone a defenseman.

In 1987 Coffey became embroiled in a contract dispute with Oilers general manager Glen Sather. While he sat out the first two months of the season, Penguins GM Eddie Johnston—desperate to find a superstar to team with Mario Lemieux—approached the

Bobby Orr's Knuckle Sandwich

Perhaps no player in the annals of hockey history had a more profound influence on the game than former Boston Bruins great Bobby Orr. Prior to Orr's arrival, defensemen rarely ventured into the attacking zone. Thanks to his incredible speed and supreme offensive skills, Orr made daring end-to-end rushes seem routine.

"He's the perfect hockey player," marveled his coach/GM Harry Sinden. "[Gordie] Howe could do everything, but not at top speed. [Bobby] Hull went at top speed but couldn't do everything. The physical aspect is absent from [Wayne] Gretzky's game. Orr would do everything, and do it at top speed."

Orr was surprisingly tough for a superstar. Late in his rookie season, the 18-year-old phenom raised eyebrows when he beat up Montreal's rugged Ted Harris, regarded as one of the top fighters in the league.

When the Penguins visited Beantown on February 10, 1973, the three-time Hart Trophy winner was at the very peak of his abilities. Most teams were intimidated before they ever set foot on the Boston Gardens ice, but the Penguins were a spirited bunch. Determined to give a good showing, they did not go down quietly. After Lowell MacDonald and Boston's Phil Esposito opened the second period with a pair of rapid-fire goals, the action heated up.

On the next rush Esposito began pushing and shoving with Pens blue-liner Duane Rupp. They shed their sticks and gloves and engaged in a brief skirmish, with Rupp dropping the Bruins' scoring ace to his knees with a right.

As players from both sides grabbed a man, Orr paired off with Darryl Edestrand. Known more for his goal scoring than his physical play, the Pens' defenseman didn't have an especially fearsome reputation. Orr decided to test the second-year defender, popping him on the chin with a half-hearted jab.

In an instant Edestrand lashed out, catching Orr flush with a bolt of a right hand. Stunned, the Boston superstar could do little more than cover up as Edestrand fired off a volley of crisp rights. Realizing his teammate was in big trouble, Don Awrey tackled Edestrand to set off a donnybrook at center ice.

Predictably, the Bruins beat the Penguins 6–3 that afternoon. But the blue-and-white-clad visitors had shown their moxie by battling an infinitely stronger and tougher foe. For Orr, it was the first blemish on his previously spotless fight card. Edestrand, meanwhile, had made an impression. Eight months later the Bruins acquired him from Pittsburgh for Nick Beverley. He occasionally shared the ice with the man he had recently bested in the punch-up.

Oilers about a trade. On November 24, 1987, a deal was finally struck and Coffey headed east to Pittsburgh.

Sports Illustrated hailed it as the biggest trade in hockey since the 1967 expansion.

"There are three impact players in this league, and now Pittsburgh has two of them," noted Washington general manager David Poile. "It'll solidify the franchise in Pittsburgh."

The trade marked an audible shift in the Penguins' fortunes. In his first game wearing the black and gold, Coffey tallied three power-play assists to ignite a comeback victory over Quebec.

"You couldn't have scripted it any better," an elated Johnston said. "Our fans were on their feet every time Coffey touched the puck. He brings a dimension to our team like Orr did to the Bruins. He skates so well that it opens up ice for everyone else."

Nicknamed the Doctor by Penguins play-by-play announcer Mike Lange for the way he surgically exploited the tiniest of openings, Coffey instilled qualities that were in short supply in the locker room, including leadership and a winning attitude.

"Hockey's a funny game," he said. "You have to prove yourself every shift, every game. It's not up to anybody else. You have to take pride in yourself."

During the next three seasons Coffey flashed his Norris Trophy form. In 1988–89, the defenseman struck for 30 goals and 113 points to help lead the Pens to their first playoff berth in seven years. The following year he rolled up 103 points and filled the leadership void when Mario was struck down with back miseries.

In 1990–91 Coffey and the Penguins hit pay dirt. Once again putting up big-time numbers (24 goals and 69 assists), the 29-year-old defenseman helped the team capture its first division title. Although injuries limited him to a dozen games in the postseason, he returned in the Finals to reinvigorate the power-play and lead the Pens to their first Stanley Cup.

If there was a chink in Coffey's armor, it was his less-than-stellar defensive play. It was a flaw that didn't escape the critical eye of the Penguins' new coach, Scotty Bowman. Although Coffey was named to the Wales Conference All-Star Team for the fifth straight year, it did little to sway Bowman's opinion. On February 19, 1992, the speedy blue-liner was dealt to the Kings in a big three-team trade that netted the Penguins Kjell Samuelsson, Rick Tocchet, and Ken Wregget.

Upon learning of the trade Coffey headed to the empty Civic Arena. He laced up his too-small skates and glided around the ice until 2:00 AM, thinking about "the good times" he had in the Steel City.

Coffey would play eight-plus seasons after leaving Pittsburgh. He retired as the NHL's all-time leading scorer among defensemen (since surpassed by Raymond Bourque) and a surefire Hall of Famer.

18 Ronnie Franchise

It's only fitting that Ron Francis was inducted into the Hockey Hall of Fame in 2007. His numbers alone are staggering—1,731 games, 549 goals, 1,249 assists (second all time), and 1,798 points (fourth all time). But statistics tell only part of the story. They say nothing of the leadership, heart, and desire he displayed over the course of an exemplary 23-year career that enabled him to coax every ounce of ability from his 6'2", 200-pound frame.

Francis' character was formed to a large degree by his parents, Ron and Lorita.

"I was brought up that if I spoke too much 'me' and 'I' stuff, I got a real tongue-lashing," he said. "I was taught to be team-oriented, to be family-oriented. I was told to do whatever I was doing as well as I could do it, but to share the credit."

The lessons served him well. By the age of 18, Francis was starring for the Hartford Whalers. When the Penguins acquired him along with Ulf Samuelsson and Grant Jennings in a blockbuster trade on March 4, 1991, Ronnie Franchise already was the Whalers' all-time leading point getter.

"He was in Hartford for 10 years scoring 80, 90, 100 points a year," Lemieux said. "He was one of the best two-way center men in the league, and he still is."

Ignited by the trade, the Penguins responded with a 9–3–2 stretch run to nail down the Patrick Division crown. Teaming with burly Kevin Stevens and old pro Joe Mullen on a solid second line, Francis provided superb all-around play and helped propel the Penguins to their first Stanley Cup.

"Ronnie just had an uncanny way of settling things down whenever we got a little bit scrambled," Phil Bourque said. "He wasn't a guy of a lot of words, but those few words were right on the money every single time. He had so many different dimensions to his game, too. He could be a checking center; he was obviously unbelievable on face-offs and won some great draws for us; plus, he scored some big goals for us. He just complemented our team so perfectly."

Perhaps no player in the history of the sport read the game as well as Francis. Although by no means a great skater, he possessed an uncanny knack for arriving at the right place at the right time. Unselfish with the puck, he was an outstanding playmaker. Combined with his superb defensive play, tireless work ethic, and sterling leadership, he was one of the most complete players the sport has ever seen.

His value was never more evident than during the 1992 Patrick Division Finals. With Lemieux sidelined with a broken hand, Francis brought the Penguins back from the brink, scoring two huge goals in Game 4 to turn the tide of the series. In Game 4 of the Finals he notched the game winner to clinch the Penguins' second straight Stanley Cup.

Firmly entrenched as one of the most beloved and popular players on the team, Francis remained at the very core of the Penguins' success for six more seasons. In 1994–95 he stepped up to assume the captaincy when Lemieux sat out a year due to the lingering effects of radiation treatments. The hardworking center was rewarded for his unselfish play with the Lady Byng and Selke Trophies, awarded to the league's best sportsman and defensive forward, respectively.

He enjoyed a career year in 1995–96, piling up 119 points and a league-leading 92 assists to help lead the Penguins to the Eastern Conference Finals. When Mario entered his first retirement in 1997, Francis once again was awarded the "C."

"He's the ultimate professional," Tom Barrasso said. "He doesn't make the big headlines, doesn't get the big contract. He's just a very special player who's quietly become one of the all-time greats."

Sadly, Francis and the Penguins parted ways during the summer of 1998. It was not due to a lack of respect—general manager Craig Patrick simply couldn't afford to sign him to a new deal. Although he was now 35 years old, Francis enjoyed a wonderful second career with the Carolina Hurricanes (nee Whalers).

Displaying his trademark consistency, he averaged nearly 22 goals and 65 points during five full seasons in Carolina. In 2001–02 he led the Hurricanes to the Stanley Cup Finals.

Prony

As a young boy growing up in Shawinigan Falls, Quebec, Jean Pronovost idolized his big brother, Marcel. The older Pronovost had carved out a career as a Hall of Fame defenseman that spanned nearly 20 years. Jean hoped to follow in his brother's footsteps.

The youngster soon gained the attention of the Boston Bruins. Skating for the Bruins' junior A team, the Niagara Falls Flyers, Pronovost developed into a solid all-around player who paid equal attention to his offensive and defensive chores. Following his junior career Jean enjoyed two strong seasons with Boston's top farm team, the Oklahoma City Blazers. However, the Bruins were loaded at right wing, boasting stars such as Ken Hodge, John McKenzie, and Tommy Williams. There was no room for a rookie, even one as promising as Pronovost.

The Pittsburgh Penguins, on the other hand, were in desperate need of young talent. Immediately following the 1967–68 season, general manager Jack Riley acquired the raw-boned winger for a first-round draft pick.

The Steel City was not an easy place to begin a career.

"It took me some time to adapt to the city of Pittsburgh," Pronovost recalled in Jim O'Brien's book, *Penguin Profiles*. "I reported to the team's training camp in Brantford, Ontario. Then I remember coming to Pittsburgh, being surprised by the

Acquired from the Boston Bruins in 1968, Jean Pronovost would retire as the Penguins' all-time leader in goals and points scored.

cobblestone streets I saw everywhere. I remember checking in at the old William Penn Hotel. I had such a small room, a dimly lit affair. I was a little disappointed."

Despite his misgivings, Prony proved to be one of the few bright spots of an otherwise dismal season. Displaying good speed and a nose for the net, he scored 16 goals to win the Pens' Rookie of the Year award. In 1969–70 he reached the 20-goal plateau while skating on the Jet Line with Michel Briere.

Pronovost's career took off the following January when the Penguins acquired silky smooth setup man Syl Apps from the Rangers.

"It was funny how we clicked so quickly, right from the first game," Pronovost said. "I didn't even know who Syl Apps was—I mean, I knew him as a player for the New York Rangers, and that was it—when we were put together on the same line. We just played well together. We read each other well."

The duo quickly emerged as one of the most prolific combinations in team history. In 1971–72 Pronovost established a new team high with 30 goals, while Apps set club records for assists and points.

After being separated for a season, they were reunited during the 1973–74 campaign along with a new left winger, Lowell MacDonald. Nicknamed the Century Line, the trio became one of the most lethal combinations in the league.

Serving as the unit's triggerman, Pronovost blossomed into a bona fide sniper. Over the next three seasons he tallied a whopping 135 goals. On March 24, 1976, the hardworking winger beat Boston goalie Gilles Gilbert to become the first player in Penguins history to score 50 goals in a season.

Despite his lofty production, Pronovost never strayed from his two-way foundation. A complete player, the 6'0", 185-pounder worked the corners and back checked with authority, qualities that endeared him to the Steel City faithful. "Let's Go Pronovost," was a popular chant at the Civic Arena throughout the 1970s.

When Ron Schock was traded in the fall of 1977, Prony assumed the captain's "C." Although the All-Star winger enjoyed another 40-goal season, the Penguins fell on hard times. Weary of the team's nearly endless rebuilding cycle, Pronovost approached general manager Baz Bastien and requested a trade.

"Baz said, 'No, we want to keep you,'" Pronovost recalled. "Baz finally granted my wish, and sent me to Atlanta. I look back now and think I made a mistake."

The future Penguins Hall of Famer departed as the club's all-time leader in goals (316) and points (603). Teammate Rick Kehoe eventually topped his point total. His goal-scoring mark stood for over a decade until it was broken by another French Canadian—a big center who wore No. 66.

20 Learn How to Skate

I grew up a basketball fan. My father, Jim Buker, played hoops at Oliver High School in Pittsburgh and, later, at Muskingum College. He passed his love for the sport on to his eldest son.

On weekends, Dad and I would watch the NBA Game of the Week. Afterward, we would go out to our driveway and play our own game, lofting jump shots at the not-quite-regulation-height hoop and plywood backboard Dad had toggled into the front wall of our red-brick suburban home.

It wasn't until I entered my teens that I became a hockey fan. One day, while I was laid up in the hospital recovering from surgery to remove a ruptured appendix, I happened to catch a Penguins-Bruins game on TV. In an instant, I was hooked.

Not long after being released from the hospital, I decided to give ice skating a try. My new Penguins heroes made it look so easy. While I'd never been on skates before, I was fairly athletic. How hard could it be?

Emboldened by the thought of becoming the next Syl Apps, I went to the old South Park skating rink one night with some friends. I laced on a pair of flimsy white rental skates and eagerly took my first steps onto the ice. Seconds later I was on my fanny. Stung by my lack of success, I quickly clambered to my skates, only to take another pratfall. Thoroughly embarrassed, I crawled to the wooden sideboards and hauled myself up, gaining a death grip on the round metal railing that ran atop the boards.

Determined to circle the rink at least once, I displayed all the grace of a drunken sailor. I'd let go of the railing, take two or three strides, and tumble to the ice in a heap. This process was repeated countless times until I mercifully made my way to the exit ramp. It must've taken a half hour to complete one lap.

Nursing my wounded pride—not to mention countless bumps and bruises—I resolved to give it another shot the following weekend. Unfortunately, the results were the same. Tucking my tail between my legs, I turned in my skates and spent the rest of the evening huddled among the mass of wannabe gliders.

It would be a dozen years before I gave skating another try. I was discussing the Penguins with a co-worker at Consolidated Gas—Tony Bartczak—when the subject of skating came up. I confided in him about my past failures. Tony assured me that it would be a different story if I had a pair of hockey skates, which provided a lot more ankle support. I recalled the way my ankles had wobbled in the old rental skates, as if there'd been a mini hurricane roiling six inches above the ice surface. Maybe he was right.

Thanksgiving Day

Entering the fall of 1987 the Penguins had missed the playoffs five years running and were hardly a cinch to end their seemingly endless streak of futility. While the Pens had assembled a talented young core in Mario Lemieux, Craig Simpson, and Doug Bodger, the team's long-suffering fans wanted a playoff team and they wanted one now.

Perhaps the most glaring need was a superstar to team with Lemieux. GM Eddie Johnston had few options. He tried mightily to pry sniper John Ogrodnick away from Quebec, but Rangers GM Phil Esposito beat him to the punch.

"Ogrodnick beside Lemieux in Pittsburgh would have 55 or 60 goals," Esposito said. "So forget it."

Instead, Johnston settled for aging former stars Charlie Simmer and Wilf Paiement. Each was in the twilight of a distinguished career and failed miserably as Mario's new linemates.

Suddenly a window of opportunity burst open. Edmonton defenseman Paul Coffey, a two-time Norris Trophy winner, was holding out for a new contract. Oilers owner Peter Pocklington was desperate to hold the line on his burgeoning payroll, leaving general manager Glen Sather no room to renegotiate. Coffey expressed a desire to play with Lemieux, and Pittsburgh was one of the few teams that possessed the young talent Sather sought in return.

For weeks a trade was rumored to be in the works but nothing came of it, further frustrating the Penguins faithful. But on November 24, 1987, Johnston proudly announced that he had acquired Coffey in a huge seven-player swap. The Pens parted with a considerable chunk of talent, including Simpson, promising rookie Chris Joseph, and veterans Moe Mantha and Dave Hannan, but the return was well worth the price.

"A player of Paul Coffey's caliber comes along probably every 15, 20 years," Johnston said. "We're looking at a world-class player. They put him in the category of Bobby Orr. There's not too many guys like that who come around."

Although it would be several seasons before the Pens sipped champagne from the Stanley Cup, Coffey's arrival marked an immediate upturn in the team's fortunes. Coffey's blazing speed and skilled puck handling forced opposing checkers to back off at every turn. Soon he was springing No. 66 loose with his patented home run passes. Even without an accomplished set of wingers Mario caught fire and nailed down his first scoring title.

Sadly, the Penguins once again fell short in their quest for a playoff berth—a failure that cost Eddie Johnston his job. Yet his signature trade put an end to the darkest era in franchise history and paved the way for future glory.

Tony just happened to have a pair of hockey skates he was willing to sell. I bit. The next weekend, I decided to try them out during a public skating session at the Mt. Lebanon rink. Gingerly, I took my first tentative strides onto the ice in over a decade. Much to my amazement, I stayed upright.

My tenuous confidence restored, I began to chug around the rink. I was aware of the little kids whizzing past at twice my speed, but I didn't care.

Twentysomething and full of vinegar, I decided to push the envelope. Strange as it seems, I'd always wondered how it felt to crash into the boards like an NHL player. Slowly gathering steam, I skated straight toward the sideboards. When I was about five feet away, I lost my balance and nearly tumbled headlong into the wall.

Okay, bad idea. I'd just be content to circle the rink. After all, Rome wasn't built in a day. As I made my way to center ice, however, my skates flew out from beneath me and I slammed to the ice on my back. The wind was completely knocked out of me. I'd never felt so much pain. As I dragged myself off the ice, I gained a new level of appreciation for the toughness of hockey players.

Call me chicken, but I've never gone skating since.

21 Shooting Star

Years before Mario Lemieux hoisted the Penguins onto his broad shoulders and carried them to Stanley Cup glory, another center of French Canadian descent wowed the Steel City faithful with his slick moves and clever, determined play.

Like No. 66, Michel Edouard Briere was a junior hockey scoring champion. Unlike Mario, he was not expected to be a franchise player. Although he piled up a whopping 320 points during two seasons with the Shawinigan Bruins, he was overlooked by the other NHL teams in the 1969 Amateur Draft. Even the Penguins passed on the will-o'-the-wisp center.

"We took Rick Kessell on the second round and Michel Briere on the third round," general manager Jack Riley recalled. "He was the 26th player picked in the draft. We made a mistake there."

Scout Dick Coss, who pleaded with Riley to select the La Belle Province scoring sensation, knew Briere was something special.

"This kid spent his life playing against and beating boys who towered over him," Coss said. "Michel knew what the other pro scouts were saying about him as a junior, that he was too small. But every summer, he'd go down into the mine or to the sawmill and build himself up."

Briere clearly believed in himself, too. When Riley offered him a $4,000 signing bonus, the rookie demanded an additional $1,000.

"It's really not that much extra money," Briere said, "because I'll be playing for the Penguins for the next 20 years."

The youngster proved to be a quick study.

"At the start of the season, Penguins coach Red Kelly tried to protect Briere, keeping him out of matchups with stronger, more experienced centers," wrote former *Pittsburgh Press* sports editor Roy McHugh. "On face-offs it seemed that Montreal's Jean Beliveau beat him to the draw every time—at the start of the season. By the end of the season, Briere was beating Beliveau, getting his stick on the puck before it hit the ice."

In an era when few players made the jump from junior hockey to the NHL, Briere flourished. Slotted between Val Fonteyne and Jean Pronovost on the speedy Jet Line, he led the club in assists and finished third in scoring.

"He looked like a kid, he looked like a little boy, and he was out there doing great things," Pronovost said.

Kelly marveled at Briere's elusiveness. One night in Philadelphia two Flyers lined him up in their crosshairs. At the last second Michel squirted through an opening and the unfortunate foes cracked heads, knocking each other unconscious.

"If they looked at the puck, he'd be gone," Kelly said. "He was slippery, he could shift and make movements, but all the time he was doing this he was still skating. A lot of guys, when they shift, aren't going anywhere. Michel kept on skating at the same rate of speed."

Considered the Pens' brightest star, Briere soon was targeted for abuse. During the 1970 Stanley Cup Semifinals, St. Louis coach Scotty Bowman assigned the rugged tandem of Noel Picard and Bob Plager the task of stopping the precocious rookie by any means necessary.

Using his quickness and wits to fullest advantage, Briere made the brawny defenders look foolish. With Picard and Plager lumbering in his vapor trail, he enjoyed an extraordinary series, racking up a team-high four goals.

It appeared that Briere would make good on his promise to play in Pittsburgh for 20 years. However, on the evening of May 15, 1970, fate intervened to deliver a crushing blow. While traveling with friends near his hometown of Malartic, Quebec, Briere's car skidded off the road. As a result of injuries sustained in the accident, the 20-year-old lapsed into a coma.

The Penguins rallied around their fallen teammate. In a touching display of support, they took his jersey on road trips during the 1970–71 season. During trips to Montreal the team visited Briere in the hospital.

"You'd walk in and sit down, you'd take hold of his hand," Kelly recalled. "He'd turn his head toward you and his eyes would open, staring. He couldn't talk. I was always optimistic, but the last time I saw him…"

Michel tragically passed away on April 13, 1971. To honor his legacy, the Penguins retired his No. 21. Over the team's 44-year history, only Mario Lemieux was afforded the same tribute.

22 The Streak

When the Penguins visited Philadelphia during the 1970s and '80s, talk invariably turned to the Streak. As incredible as it seemed, the Pens had not won a game in the Spectrum since January 20, 1974, when they beat the Flyers 5–3. Since that fateful day, the Penguins had gone *42 games* without a win in the "City of Brotherly Shove."

Marc Boileau was the coach of the Penguins when the Streak began on February 7, 1974. Over the next 15 years it took on a life of its own. No fewer than seven Steel City coaches—Boileau, Ken Schinkel, Johnny Wilson, Eddie Johnston, Lou Angotti, Bob Berry, and Pierre Creamer—failed to win in Philly. Worse yet, the team rarely came close. The 42-game skein included only *three* ties. The rest were Philadelphia wins.

"I graduated from high school, graduated from college, got a job, got married, got divorced, moved to San Diego, moved back to Pittsburgh, and the Penguins still hadn't beaten the Flyers in Philadelphia," Penguins vice president Tom McMillan said.

The Streak reflected the disparity between the clubs. Winners of consecutive Stanley Cups in the mid-1970s, the Flyers were a perennial powerhouse who played a bruising, take-no-prisoners style. By contrast, the passive Penguins were mediocre at best.

"We weren't the only team that got clubbed by the Flyers," Phil Bourque recalled. "But when we went to the Spectrum, as much as you wanted to believe you were going to win, you just knew something bad was going to happen. You had the feeling you were going to get beat up, and not just on the scoreboard. They never took their foot off the gas pedal. They kept hammering us. It wasn't enough to rub our noses in it, they grabbed us by the hair on the back of our heads and shoved our faces into the pile."

By 1988–89, however, the roles were beginning to reverse. With superstars Mario Lemieux and Paul Coffey leading the way, the resurgent Pens would soon equal Philly's feat of back-to-back Stanley Cups. Meanwhile, the Flyers were on the verge of a Penguinsesque streak of missing the postseason five years in a row.

Still, the Streak was very much alive when the Pens rolled into the Spectrum to challenge the Flyers on February 2, 1989. In an effort to disrupt the bad karma, Penguins coach Gene Ubriaco gave goalie Wendell Young—a former Flyer—the starting nod. Determined to help the team break the hex, local radio personalities Jim Krenn and Scott Paulsen arrived at the Spectrum that night dressed as witch doctors.

Midway through the opening frame, rookie center John Cullen staked the Pens to an early lead. Bourque padded the advantage at 18:19, but Ron Sutter struck for the Flyers in the final minute of the period.

The Penguins proceeded to shake off any lingering bad juju. Bob Errey and Rob Brown scored in the second period. Dan Quinn supplied the frosting on the cake in the final frame. The Flyers mounted a mild rally, but Young stood tall, kicking out 39 shots. The final score was 5–3, which was the same score as the last Penguins victory in Philly all those years ago. The Streak was finally over.

"We're not the fire hydrant anymore," Bourque said. "We're the bigger dog."

"It's a great thing for the organization," added teammate Troy Loney. "Especially the guys who have been around here four or five years and put up with this."

That included play-by-play announcer Mike Lange, whose broadcasting career with the Penguins stretched back to the origins of the Streak. The Hall of Fame announcer recalled that his Philadelphia counterpart, the late Gene Hart, carried around a special stat sheet documenting the disparity between the two clubs.

"When it finally ended, I didn't have to say a word," Lange said. "I carried that stat sheet around with me for a long, long time, too. The Flyers, on the whole, have been so successful it's scary. It wasn't because they were lucky. They were better than us all those years."

23 Mario Returns

By the fall of 2000, Mario Lemieux was firmly established in his new role as Penguins owner. The team's front office staff had grown accustomed to seeing the big fellow in the office, sporting a suit and tie. He seemed perfectly content in retirement.

Mario Lemieux made his improbable return to the ice on December 27, 2000, after retiring for the first time in 1997.

There was, however, a loose thread. His young son, Austin, had never seen him play.

"He's only four years old," Lemieux said. "Of course we watch tapes here from the Stanley Cup years, but I don't think he realized how many years I played."

Inspired by the thought of playing for his son, Mario contacted former teammate Jay Caufield in November of 2000 and asked the fitness guru to whip him into shape. Working in secret, they began a series of grueling training sessions. Soon Lemieux had honed his 6'4" frame to a rock-solid 238 pounds.

On December 11, Mario officially announced that he was making a comeback. It was a great relief to Penguins insiders, who found it nearly impossible to keep hockey's most closely guarded secret.

But first he broke the news to Austin.

"Daddy is coming back to play with [Jaromir] Jagr," Mario told him.

Needless to say, his teammates were thrilled.

"We were struggling," explained Jagr, "and [general manager] Craig Patrick told me 'Mario wants to talk to you.' I had nobody to play with. I told Mario, 'We need a center man.' He told me, 'I might have one for you.' I said, 'Who is it?' And he said, 'He's pretty good.'"

Two days after Christmas, Lemieux made his triumphant return versus the Toronto Maple Leafs. When he stepped onto the Mellon Arena ice for the pregame warmups, he was showered with one of the longest and loudest ovations of his storied career.

It took Mario all of 33 seconds to make an impact. On his first shift in a competitive game in three and a half years, he set up a goal by Jagr with a nifty pass from behind the net. The roar from the crowd was so loud it nearly blew the retractable dome off the Mellon Arena.

(Un)Lucky Luc

Following an early playoff exit in 1994, Penguins general manager Craig Patrick sought to revitalize his sagging team. On July 29 he struck gold, acquiring left wing Luc Robitaille from the Kings in a deal for popular but injury-prone Rick Tocchet.

One of the premier snipers in all of hockey, Robitaille had averaged 49 goals a year during his eight seasons in Los Angeles. In 1992–93 he potted a career-best 63 while skating alongside Wayne Gretzky.

Steel City fans were thrilled by the possibility of Lucky Luc teaming with Mario Lemieux. So was Robitaille.

"I'd love to play with Mario," said the future Hall of Famer. "He's one of the greatest players ever to play, the greatest now."

Unfortunately, things didn't quite work out. Plagued by back problems and anemia resulting from Hodgkin's disease treatments, Lemieux sat out the 1994–95 campaign. Nonplussed, Robitaille flashed his All-Star form. He notched 23 goals during the lockout-shortened season—a 40-goal pace over a full schedule.

When Mario announced he would return from his one-year hiatus in 1995–96, it appeared Luc would once more serve as the triggerman for an all-time great. Once again, however, the stars failed to align. On August 31, 1995, Patrick shipped Robitaille to the Rangers in a huge four-player trade.

The 35-year-old marvel was just getting started. Midway through the second period he gathered in a pass from Jagr in the left face-off circle and snapped the puck past Toronto goalie Curtis Joseph for career goal number 614. At 14:23 he scooped up a loose puck and fed a blind backhand pass to Jan Hrdina, who beat Joseph from the left circle.

"What was disappointing was that after two periods, he had three times as many points as me, and he's been out for three and a half years," defenseman Ian Moran joked.

Remarkably, Mario didn't earn the game's No. 1 star. That honor went to Austin's favorite player, Jagr, who collected two goals and two assists in a 5–0 Pens victory. But by all accounts Lemieux's return was a rousing success.

"I'm not sure I can describe what we just watched," offered an elated Craig Patrick.

"I didn't know what was going to happen," Jagr said. "But I didn't expect anything like that."

"That was unbelievable to come back and play like that," Martin Straka added. "He could have had seven or eight points, easy. That was an awesome show."

While acknowledging that he was a bit rusty, Mario was no less pleased with the results.

"I think that with a lot of hard work and dedication, I feel like I could still be the best in the world," he said. "I'm still only 35 years old...I have a fresh start physically and mentally, and I feel that I can achieve my goal to be the best again."

24 Captain Clutch

By the end of his fourth season in the National Hockey League, Sidney Crosby was firmly established as one of the game's brightest young stars. At the callow age of 21, he'd already captured the Hart Trophy, the Art Ross Trophy, and the Lester B. Pearson (Ted Lindsay) Award. Handsome, humble, and well spoken, the Penguins' captain was the poster child for the new post-lockout NHL.

However, one prize—the one that mattered the most of all—eluded him. In the spring of 2008 Crosby had led a talented young Penguins squad into the Stanley Cup Finals against the seasoned

Detroit Red Wings. Despite Sid's best efforts the Pens fell to the powerful Red Wings in six games.

In the hush of the losing locker room the players understandably were heartbroken, none more so than Crosby.

"This feeling, it's not a good feeling at all," Sid said, his voice cracking with emotion. "It's not something I want to experience [again]."

Crosby and the Penguins fell flat through the early stages of the 2008–09 campaign. A series of free-agent defections over the summer, including the departure of gifted winger Marian Hossa, had robbed the team of scoring punch and depth.

Worse yet, Sid's heretofore sterling reputation was taking a hit. When asked to comment on Crosby during an interview with *Sovetsky Sport*, Washington's Alexander Semin offered some unflattering observations.

"What's so special about Crosby?" Semin asked. "I don't see anything special there. Yes, he does skate well, has a good head, good pass. But there's nothing else. Even if you compare him to Patrick Kane from Chicago…Kane is a much more interesting player."

Crosby shrugged off the criticism and piled up 31 points during the final 21 games to lead the resurgent Penguins to a second-place finish in the Atlantic Division. Setting his eyes on hockey's most coveted prize, Sid elevated his game to another level in the postseason. In Game 6 of a hotly contested opening-round series with Philadelphia, he scored two huge goals to vanquish the Flyers.

Next on the Pens' dance card was a marquee matchup with his archrival, Alexander Ovechkin, and the high-flying Washington Capitals. After spotting the Capitals a 2–0 lead, the Penguins roared back to win the series in a pulsating seven-game set. Once again Crosby rose to the occasion, scoring a pair of goals during the winner-take-all Game 7. His riveting performance against Washington (eight goals and five assists) earned the respect of friends and foes alike.

"The way Crosby played in this series, they should build a monument to him," a chagrined Semin said.

"He's the best all-around player in the NHL," added former critic Don Cherry. "I like Ovechkin. He's exciting. The wild bull of the Pampas. And he was everybody's darling. But I said before this series that Crosby wins draws now, he hits, he blocks shots, he plays down low, he's dropped the gloves twice. He's a complete player."

Sid's extraordinary play continued through the Eastern Conference Finals. Teaming with fellow superstar Evgeni Malkin to form a two-headed monster, he tallied seven points to pace the Pens to a four-game sweep of Carolina.

The impressive showing against the Hurricanes earned the Penguins a return match with Detroit in the Finals and a chance for redemption. In a virtual replay of the previous year's matchup, the Red Wings grabbed a quick 2–0 series lead. However, Crosby and his teammates would not be denied. Thanks in part to Sid's game winner in the pivotal Game 4, they clawed their way back to defeat the Red Wings in seven games.

Although he was edged out in the voting for the Conn Smythe Trophy by Malkin, nothing could dim the luster of Crosby's remarkable achievements. He topped all playoff scorers with 15 goals while providing a shining example for his teammates. Best of all, he'd won the Stanley Cup—the youngest captain in NHL history to do so.

"It's everything you dream of," Sid said. "It's an amazing feeling."

25 Artie

The town of Brockton, Massachusetts, lays claim to two of boxing's all-time greats, Rocky Marciano and "Marvelous" Marvin Hagler. It's also the birthplace of one of the Penguins' greatest goal scorers—Kevin Stevens.

Like his pugilistic cousins, Stevens packed a wallop. Over a four-year span in the early 1990s, the burly left wing piled up 190 goals while establishing himself as the premier power forward in hockey.

Nicknamed "Artie" after his father, Stevens was acquired from Los Angeles by general manager Eddie Johnston on September 9, 1983, for journeyman winger Anders Hakansson. Although the trade eventually gained fame as one of the best in Penguins history, it received little fanfare at the time.

"I was a late bloomer," Stevens told Jim O'Brien in an interview for *Penguin Profiles*. "In high school, I was one of the top three or four players on our hockey team. Baseball was my love, until I got to the level where someone could throw 20 curve balls in a row and put them all over the plate. It was the bender that took me out of baseball."

Baseball's loss was hockey's gain. Following a strong career at Boston College, Stevens earned regular duty with the Penguins during the 1988–89 stretch run. In his first full season he struck for 29 goals and 70 points.

The 6'3", 215-pounder burst into prominence in 1990–91. Skating on a line with fellow up-and-comers John Cullen and Mark Recchi, he netted a team-high 40 goals. At his best in big games, Stevens tallied three straight game-winning goals against

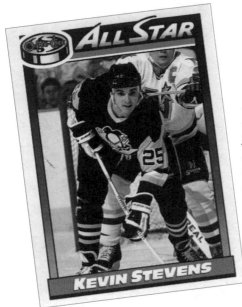

Powerful winger Kevin Stevens became the first player in NHL history to top 50 goals and 200 penalty minutes in the same season in 1991–92.

Washington during the Patrick Division Finals. When the Pens fell behind the Bruins 2–0 in the Wales Conference Finals, he guaranteed a victory in Game 3 and backed up his pledge by scoring the all-important first goal. Arguably the Penguins' most valuable player, he went on to lead all playoff scorers with 17 goals.

In 1991–92 Stevens was virtually unstoppable. A veritable freight train on skates, he set a slew of records, becoming the first player in NHL history to reach 50 goals and 200 penalty minutes in a season. With 123 points, he set a new high for American-born skaters and placed second in the scoring race between Lemieux and Wayne Gretzky.

"Imagine that," he said. "Mario, Gretzky…and me."

The following season Stevens was even better, banging home a career-best 55 goals to earn NHL Second Team All-Star honors.

"Kevin's probably the purest power forward in the league," marveled linemate Rick Tocchet. "He reminds me of a big running back in the NFL who just wears you down."

Sadly, a tragic incident during Game 7 of the 1993 Patrick Division Finals derailed the popular winger's career just as he was reaching his peak. Playing with his typical gusto, Stevens collided with Islanders defenseman Rich Pilon while chasing down a loose puck. Pilon's protective shield caught Artie full force and knocked

Owch

With all due respect to Darius Kasparaitis and current Penguin Brooks Orpik, arguably the hardest hitter in franchise history was a Dryden, Ontario, native who wore No. 25 and patrolled the Pens' blue line in the mid-1970s. Blessed with a powerful 5'11", 190-pound frame and a rock-solid base, Dennis Owchar delivered hits that seemed to register on the Richter Scale.

The husky defender's specialty was the shoulder check. Like a snake in the grass, Owchar would lie in wait for an opposing puck carrier to venture across the middle of the ice with his head down. In most cases the would-be goal scorer was separated from the puck— and his senses—with brutal efficiency.

Appropriately nicknamed Owch, the youngster first made an impact during the 1974–75 season. Called up from Hershey in November to replace Jean-Guy Lagace, Owchar responded with a slew of thundering hits. Possessing a cannon of a shot and a flair for offense, he showed genuine promise.

Following an injury-plagued 1975–76 campaign Owchar, quite literally, hit his stride in 1976–77. In a little over half a season he knocked three opponents out of action with booming body checks. His prowess as a hitter soon gained the attention of *The Hockey News*.

"The source of the youngster's destructiveness isn't a lead pipe," chimed the publication, "but a shoulder buried into the chest of an unsuspecting puck carrier."

Ironically, Dennis became a casualty of his own aggressive play. In January of 1977 he suffered torn knee ligaments during a collision with Boston's Mike Milbury. Struggling to regain his form, he was traded to Colorado the following season.

him unconscious. He landed on the ice face-first with a sickening thud. Kevin's nose and forehead were shattered the way a pane of glass would if struck by a hammer.

"Losing him hurt us quite a bit," Larry Murphy said. "We had a lot of scoring chances and he has a tremendous touch. He's a key guy for us."

During four and a half hours of emergency surgery, doctors made an ear-to-ear incision along the hairline and peeled Kevin's skin back in order to reconstruct his forehead with metal plates.

Remarkably, Stevens recovered from his injuries to score 41 goals in 1993–94, but he was never quite the same. In 1995–96 he was traded twice, first to Boston and then to Los Angeles. As his career continued to spiral downhill, he was arrested on January 23, 2000, for using crack cocaine.

Teammates and friends were quick to support the affable winger.

"Kevin would give the shirt off his back to anybody who needed anything," Gretzky said. "A ride. Somebody to talk to. Kevin was always there. He was comfortable hanging with the captain or the young guys on a team. He was one of those guys nobody disliked."

After entering the NHL's Substance Abuse Program, Artie enjoyed one more season in the sun. In January of 2001, Craig Patrick acquired him from Philadelphia and placed him on a line with Mario Lemieux, who had recently come out of retirement. The old magic returned as Stevens began to score once more. He helped to lead the Pens to the Eastern Conference Finals.

26 Sly Syl

When Syl Apps first skated out onto the Civic Arena ice on January 27, 1971, it was hardly to a hero's welcome. The day before, Penguins general manager Red Kelly had sent Glen "Slats" Sather to the New York Rangers for Apps and young defenseman Sheldon Kannegiesser.

A player of modest ability but enormous spunk and charisma, Sather had been wildly popular in Pittsburgh. The huge banner that hung directly across from the Penguins' bench said it all—WHY SLATS?

Apps quickly provided the answer. Gathering in a lead pass from Jean Pronovost, he broke free in the Toronto zone, deked Hall of Fame goalie Jacques Plante to the ice, and ripped the puck into the net. Not a bad way to make an entrance.

"You never forget certain games," Apps told Jim O'Brien in an interview for *Penguin Profiles*. "I remember my first game in Pittsburgh. I scored a goal and assisted on another."

Although Apps had tallied just three points prior to his Steel City debut, there was no questioning his ability. An early scouting report summed up his play in glowing terms: "Apps Jr. is a splendid skater, a good puck handler and playmaker, just like his father."

The father happened to be Syl Apps Sr., a Hall of Fame center who established himself as one of the game's greatest players while starring for Toronto in the 1930s and '40s.

Slotted between fellow rising stars Pronovost and Greg Polis on a promising young line, Apps finished the 1970–71 campaign with nine goals and 16 assists in 31 games. The next season he led the Penguins in scoring while setting new club records for assists (44) and points (59).

"He just didn't get enough ice time in New York," said Syl Sr. "I was pleased when he was traded to Pittsburgh because Red Kelly, in my estimation, is one of the outstanding NHL coaches and Syl is playing a lot of hockey."

Kelly took a bit of a gamble during the Pens' 1972 training camp. Hoping to come up with two strong scoring lines, he broke up the PAP Line and assigned a new set of wingers to Apps—Lowell MacDonald and Al McDonough. Both were unknown quantities; MacDonald was a former 20-goal scorer who was trying to bounce back from knee surgery; McDonough was talented but green.

The trio meshed beautifully. McDonough struck for a club-record 35 goals while MacDonald culminated an amazing comeback by scoring 34 goals. The silky-smooth Apps enjoyed one of his finest seasons, collecting 29 goals, 56 assists, and 85 points.

McDonough was traded to Atlanta midway through the 1973–74 season. Pronovost rejoined the line, which quickly emerged as one of the most lethal combinations in the league. With Syl setting the table and his opportunistic wingers finding the net with stunning frequency, the Century Line struck for a whopping 107 goals.

Realizing he had a bona fide superstar on his hands, Penguins owner Tad Potter signed Apps to a record contract for $125,000 per year. The darkly handsome center proved to be worth every penny. Over the next two seasons he rolled up 178 points, including a career-high 99 in 1975–76 to place 10th in the league in scoring.

Apps enjoyed a moment in the sun when he was selected to play in the 1975 NHL All-Star Game. It was a proud moment for his family; young Syl was the first son of an All-Star Game participant to play in the game. With his parents in attendance, he scored two goals and earned MVP honors while leading the Wales Conference to a resounding 7–1 victory.

Vic

During the summer of 1974 Penguins general manager Jack Button took advantage of a fire sale by the Rangers and landed All-Star Vic Hadfield in exchange for journeyman defender Nick Beverley. One of the first big-name players ever to skate for the Pens, the rugged left wing brought the team instant credibility.

"He was a great leader, a great guy all the way around," Syl Apps said. "He was having trouble with his knees. It was unfortunate. If he had been healthy, he could have taught everyone a lot."

Hadfield began his career as a brawler, but gradually emerged as a player who could fight and score. Skating on the famous GAG [Goal-A-Game] Line alongside superstars Rod Gilbert and Jean Ratelle, he became the first Ranger ever to tally 50 goals in a season.

Following his arrival in the Steel City, Hadfield enjoyed similar success. In 1974–75 he scored 31 goals—the fourth-highest total on the team—and 73 points. The next season the 35-year-old veteran was nearly as potent, lighting the lamp 30 times.

His leadership was never more evident than during the team's playoff series with Toronto in 1976. When the Pens lost Game 1 to the less skilled but infinitely tougher Leafs, Hadfield took it upon himself to show the way. Moments after the opening face-off in Game 2, he dropped the gloves with Toronto's aggressive young center, Darryl Sittler. Inspired by their old warrior, the Penguins carried the physical play to Toronto for the rest of the evening.

"We had to show Toronto right off the bat we weren't going to lie down for them," Hadfield said.

Vic knew how to have fun, too. One of the team's most popular players, he earned a reputation for being an avid prankster.

"He was always playing tricks on the maintenance crew at the Civic Arena," recalled Rick Kehoe.

Sadly, Hadfield's aching knees gave out in 1976–77. After skating in just nine games, the old pro retired. A scratch golfer, he opened up the Vic Hadfield Golf and Learning Center.

"It was kind of fun," he said. "The only time I usually got to play in front of my family was when we played in Toronto. That made it even more special."

The 28-year-old center was just entering his prime. However, during the 1976 playoffs he suffered a knee injury. As was often the case in the days before arthroscopic surgery, he was never quite the same.

In November of 1977 the Penguins traded Apps to Los Angeles, where he finished his career. Syl departed as the team's all-time assist leader, a distinction he would hold until Mario Lemieux surpassed him.

27 Wayne Who?

In many ways, the dramatic Canada Cup tournament during the summer of 1987 marked a coming of age for Mario Lemieux. Thrust into hockey's center stage, the 22-year-old center shone like a diamond. He paced all scorers with 11 goals in nine games, including a dramatic overtime tally in Game 3 of the Finals to win the tournament for his native Canada.

It also represented a changing of the guard. Prior to the tournament, Lemieux had played second fiddle to Edmonton supernova Wayne Gretzky. During Mario's first three NHL seasons, the Great One had outdistanced his young rival by the whopping margin of 606 points to 348. That was about to change.

Mario clearly benefited from the time he spent with Gretzky and the other NHL stars. Perhaps there were some lingering doubts in the back of his mind about whether he truly belonged. After the tournament, he was ready to take his rightful place among the game's elite.

"Playing with Gretzky and all those great players, it made a difference," Mario admitted. "It taught me how to win."

His confidence growing by leaps and bounds, Lemieux enjoyed a breakout year in 1987–88. Although he often shared the ice with a grab-bag collection of wingers that included career minor leaguer Jock Callander and fading former stars Wilf Paiement and Charlie Simmer, Mario piled up an astonishing 70 goals, 98 assists, and 168 points to capture his first scoring title. In recognition of his sterling play, he was awarded the Hart Trophy and the Lester B. Pearson (Ted Lindsay) Award.

To veteran observers, No. 66 was on the cusp of greatness.

"He's unbelievably good now, and we don't know how good he will be," said the legendary Gordie Howe.

"I'm not sure if *dominant* is a strong enough word to describe what Mario will be this year," Washington GM David Poile added.

Poile proved to be prophetic. Skating on a line with speedy Bob Errey and fellow scoring sensation Rob Brown, Mario exploded for a monster season in 1988–89, racking up 85 goals, 114 assists, and 199 points. Although Gretzky had posted slightly higher totals, it's doubtful that anyone ever enjoyed a better year.

So accomplished was Lemieux that he was a threat to score every time his skates touched the ice. Opponents routinely took to fouling him but nothing worked. During a game against Washington, Larry Murphy hog-tied Mario at the blue line in a desperate attempt to slow him down. Like a bull shrugging off a flea, Lemieux dragged the exasperated defenseman to the net and scored.

"Once he gets behind you, he cannot be legally stopped," said coach Gene Ubriaco.

Former linemate Randy Cunneyworth vividly recalled watching Lemieux weave through the Vancouver Canucks one night.

Le Magnifique

Throughout his career, Mario Lemieux received the highest of praise from his fellow players, who marveled at his abilities.

Former NHL defender and hockey analyst Brian Engblom gave perhaps the most eloquent description of what it was like to compete against big No. 66.

"The toughest one-on-one player I ever faced was Mario Lemieux," Engblom said. "He was pure magic. At 6'4" and around 215 pounds, he could do things to you with his stick-handling ability like no one else before or since...not even Gretzky. Mario needed no help, either. Just the two of you straight up. Try and stop him. Deceptive speed, fluid motion, magic hands, and perfect depth perception, he could put moves on you that left you feeling violated!

"He was too big and strong to be intimidated physically, too fast for you to get a half step on him, too smart to allow himself to be boxed into a small space, and way too good at stick handling to allow you to risk trying to steal the puck from him. To this day, I have no answer as to how to stop Mario when he's on his game."

"They were literally falling at his feet, one after another," Cunneyworth said. "I froze that picture: three guys behind Mario on the ice, in a heap. I'll never forget that. He ended up behind the net and just reached around and stuffed the puck in."

Remarkably, Mario finished second to Gretzky in the voting for the Hart Trophy, despite eclipsing No. 99 by 31 points. However, nothing could detract from the plain and simple truth—Lemieux had emerged as the finest player in the game.

"If you asked me three or four years ago who is the best player, there's no question I would have said Gretzky," said Detroit coach Jacques Demers. "But right now, the best player in the world is Mario Lemieux. He's taken over. He's the most talented. No one can dominate a team the way he can."

28 Scotty

Scotty Bowman was a rare breed. In terms of relations with his players, he was decidedly old school. He felt a team performed at its best when it was on edge. To that end, he constantly challenged his players in an effort to keep them motivated.

In terms of strategy, however, he was an innovator. There may never have been a finer "in game" coach than Bowman. Rarely caught off guard by an opponent's tactics, he always seemed to be 10 steps ahead. Long before "Captain Video" Roger Neilson earned notoriety for studying film, Bowman was using game tapes as an instruction tool.

In his book, *The Game*, Hall of Fame goalie Ken Dryden gave an honest description of his former coach. "Abrupt, straight-forward, without flair or charm, he seems cold and abrasive, sometimes obnoxious, controversial but never colorful," Dryden wrote. "He is not Vince Lombardi, tough and gruff with a heart of gold. His players don't sit around telling hateful-affectionate stories about him…. He is complex, confusing, misunderstood, unclear in every way but one. He is a brilliant coach, the best of his time."

No one could argue with the results. Starting in 1968, Bowman-led teams appeared in the Stanley Cup Finals eight times during a 12-year span. His Montreal teams of the 1970s—among the greatest of all time—posted an extraordinary winning percentage of .734 over seven seasons and won five Cups.

In 1979–80, Bowman took over the helm of the Buffalo Sabres, serving as both coach and general manager. It was the one and only time during his storied career that success eluded him. By the end of his seven-year term the Sabres had dissolved into a losing team.

As incredible as it seemed, it would be several seasons before Bowman was given another opportunity to coach. He served as an analyst on CBC's *Hockey Night in Canada* until Penguins general manager Craig Patrick brought him to Pittsburgh in 1990. The hiring took on added significance the following summer when coach Bob Johnson was stricken with a brain tumor. In the wake of the tragedy, Patrick asked Bowman to step behind the Pens' bench.

"It wasn't like Craig said, 'Come in and coach for the year,'" Bowman recalled in an interview with E.M. Swift of *Sports Illustrated*. "It was, 'Keep the job until Bob comes back.' We hung on to the hope that a miracle would happen. But a month into the season, we knew he wasn't coming back."

Grasping the delicate nature of the situation, the veteran coach went easy on the players through the early going.

"I was aware that if I coached the way I did in the past, it wouldn't have brought the same results," Bowman said. "I knew I had to be different. If you're critical of a player today, especially openly, it's perceived as being negative. Bob Johnson was so positive. You have to stroke them more."

However, as the Pens began to stumble in January, Bowman turned up the heat. He was especially critical of All-Star defenseman Paul Coffey, one of the team's most established and popular players.

The Penguins had a long history of rebelling against coaches. Their frustration boiled over during a western road trip in March of 1992. With Bowman spending an extra night at home in Buffalo, Patrick held a meeting with the players. Many complained bitterly of Bowman's tough-love approach.

"We were frustrated with him," Bryan Trottier said.

"He was such a hard-line coach in the past," Tom Barrasso added, "and we were such a relaxed team that there was a period of adjustment."

The tension seemed to ease following the meeting. In the postseason, Bowman masterfully guided the Penguins to comeback victories over the Capitals and Rangers. With the coach and team in perfect sync, the Pens proceeded to sweep Boston and Chicago to win their second Stanley Cup.

"As great as our teams were in Montreal, we never won 11 [games] straight," Bowman said proudly. "We got on a roll and never looked back."

29 Flower

When Penguins general manager Craig Patrick traded up on draft day in 2003 to select Marc-Andre Fleury with the first overall pick, he clearly expected great things from the youngster.

"We were looking to build a championship team from goal on out," said Pens goaltending coach Gilles Meloche. "Not too many goalies like Marc-Andre come along."

The willowy Fleury made quite a first impression. On October 10, 2003, the 18-year-old netminder turned in a dazzling 46-save performance during a 3–0 loss to the Kings. In his next start, the precocious youngster earned his first victory, shutting down the powerhouse Red Wings.

However, things soon began to sour. Playing behind a woeful defensive corps, he tried to win games single-handedly.

"Sometimes he'd get there too quick and sort of slide by the shot," teammate Brooks Orpik said. "He used to make the first save and be out of position."

Undaunted, the unflappable goalie with the ready smile worked long hours with Meloche to improve his fundamentals while learning to rely less on his extraordinary reflexes. The hard work paid off handsomely in 2006–07. His positioning and rebound control dramatically improved, Fleury helped lead the surprising Penguins to a stunning 47-point improvement and a postseason berth.

The following season would prove to be the most challenging of his young career. After an uneven start, Fleury suffered a high-ankle sprain on December 8, 2007. During his three-month absence veteran Ty Conklin turned in a superb performance, prompting coach Michel Therrien to assert that Fleury would have to earn the starting job upon his return.

The youngster proved that he was up to the task. Displaying an intensity that belied his easygoing nature, Fleury outshone Conklin to snatch the goaltending reins.

"It's almost like two different goalies the way he's playing now," Sergei Gonchar noted. "He's much more comfortable."

In the playoffs he came of age. Posting a sparkling 1.97 goals-against average and three shutouts, he led the Penguins to within two wins of the Stanley Cup. His efforts were rewarded with a brand-new, $35 million seven-year contract.

He proved to be worth every penny. With Flower in top form, the Penguins tore through the competition to set up a Finals rematch with Detroit. In the closing seconds of Game 7 he made a spectacular save on Nicklas Lidstrom to seal the Pens' Stanley Cup triumph.

"It's only fitting that he made that save with a second left to clinch it for us," Mark Eaton said. "You can't say enough about the way he's played, and what he did for us."

Fleury once again carried the load for the Penguins in 2009–10. He appeared in 67 games—tying his own club record—and registered 37 wins, the third-highest single-season total in team history. Fleury's strong play earned him a spot on the Canadian Olympic team.

The first overall pick in the 2003 Entry Draft, Marc-Andre Fleury sparkled in goal during the Penguins' run to the Stanley Cup in 2009.

An Eye for Color

During the early stages of his career, flamboyant Penguins goalie Marc-Andre Fleury earned notoriety for his Gumby-like flexibility, lightning-fast reflexes, and his bright-yellow pads.

In November of 2007, Pens general manager Ray Shero received a surprising letter from Janet Leduc, an Ottawa optometrist, regarding Flower's color of choice. She explained that yellow is the most noticeable color to the human eye and suggested that Fleury change to white pads to better blend in with his on-ice surroundings.

"If there were a sniper walking around, I wouldn't be dressing in yellow," she explained to Michael Farber of *Sports Illustrated*. "It's too visible. That's why the Golden Arches are yellow, why school buses are yellow."

Taking the advice to heart, Fleury made the switch. Perhaps not by coincidence, his numbers improved dramatically. By season's end he'd recorded a 2.33 goals-against average and a career-high .921 save percentage.

However, during the 2010 playoffs an old bugaboo—inconsistency—seeped back into his game. In a winner-take-all Game 7 versus Montreal in the Eastern Conference Semifinals, he yielded a backbreaking tally just 32 seconds into the contest. After leaking for four goals in 25 minutes he was unceremoniously pulled in favor of backup Brent Johnson.

The disturbing trend continued early in the 2010–11 campaign. He allowed four goals on only 14 shots during an early-season loss to Toronto, a shabby performance that drew criticism from Pens coach Dan Bylsma.

"There's a time when Fleury has got to come up with the save," Bylsma said.

Determined to regain his form, the slender netminder responded like a champion. In a sudden and dramatic turnaround, he became one of the hottest goalies in the league. When injuries to superstars Sidney Crosby and Evgeni Malkin threatened to derail the Pens' playoff hopes, Flower placed the team on his shoulders and carried it to a postseason berth. He enjoyed an extraordinary season, posting a career-best 2.32 goals-against average, along with 36 wins and a .918 save percentage.

"He's our MVP," Bylsma noted, "and I think he deserves to be mentioned as the league MVP with his play this year."

30 Visit the CONSOL Energy Center

Tuesday, July 27, 2010, was a banner day in Penguins history. While staff members and construction workers looked on, owner Mario Lemieux and the team's reigning superstar, Sidney Crosby, took the very first skate on the CONSOL Energy Center ice to officially christen the sparkling new arena.

"It felt great to be able to skate for the first time with Sid," Lemieux said. "I think it was pretty special for all of us. It was a long time coming. We worked hard to get this accomplished. I'm glad we were able to do this today."

Indeed, the CONSOL Energy Center represented a triumph of perseverance and patience stretching back over a decade.

Upon gaining control of the Penguins in the fall of 1999, Lemieux and his partners immediately began to petition Pittsburgh mayor Tom Murphy and other local leaders for public funding for a new arena to replace the aging Mellon Arena. However, the city coffers were strained following the construction of Heinz Field and PNC Park.

Undeterred, the Penguins purchased a tract of land on November 30, 2000, for $8 million. Located directly across Center Avenue from Mellon Arena, the site would be used for the construction of a new arena.

It would take the Lemieux Group another seven years to come up with the necessary funding. After an innovative deal with casino developer Isle of Capri fell through, the Penguins finally reached an agreement with Pennsylvania governor Ed Rendell and state and local officials on March 12, 2007.

The Penguins formally signed a 30-year lease agreement on September 20, 2007. With the team's future in Pittsburgh secured until 2040, planning for the new arena took center stage. Populous (formerly HOK Sport), the design firm that conceptualized Heinz Field and PNC Park, presented drawings to the Pittsburgh City Planning Commission on April 8, 2008. The initial design was rejected as being "too cold and uninviting."

"If I put a Home Depot sign on that," local architect Rob Pfaffman said, "it looks like a Home Depot."

One month later Populous presented a second set of plans that featured a spectacular atrium facing downtown Pittsburgh. The design was unanimously approved.

"The atrium in the front allows everyone to see the energy and electricity inside the building during events," former Penguins CEO Ken Sawyer said. "When you're inside, you get to see the most beautiful city skyscape in the country."

On August 14, 2008, Lemieux met with club officials and a group of local dignitaries at the future location of center ice for the ground-breaking ceremony. Using shovels crafted with the shafts from Sidney Crosby's old hockey sticks, the first clump of dirt was turned. The new arena was christened CONSOL Energy Center on December 15, 2008, when the Penguins signed a 21-year naming rights agreement with Pittsburgh-based energy giant CONSOL Energy.

Slowly but surely the magnificent new building took shape. The structural steel was erected by August of 2009. Construction was completed on schedule in the summer of 2010.

The Puck Drops Here

The Penguins officially opened the CONSOL Energy Center on October 7, 2010, with a regular season matchup against their bitter cross-state rivals, the Philadelphia Flyers. During a stirring pregame ceremony, team owner Mario Lemieux christened the new arena by pouring a bottle of water from the melted Civic Arena ice onto the virgin ice surface.

"Winning exhibition games is nice and took some polish off the seats, but the real thing will be something different," coach Dan Bylsma said. "It's opening night, and it's Philly. There are a lot of things that make this game special."

Tyler Kennedy struck for the first Penguins goal 44 seconds into the third period. Try as they might, the Pens were unable to deliver a win for the overflow crowd of 18,289, dropping a 3–2 decision to the Flyers.

Remarkably, it would take the Pens four tries to finally gain a victory at their new home. After losing to Montreal and Toronto, they nipped the Islanders 3–2 on October 15, thanks to Alex Goligoski's game winner in overtime.

"It's good to get the first one, for sure," Goligoski said. "Especially for the fans. Just to get it over with."

In honor of Sidney Crosby's number 87, CONSOL Energy Center seats 18,087 for hockey. This includes 2,000 box seats and 66 suites—an homage to Mario Lemieux. To ensure the new facility offers the latest innovations, the Penguins partnered with the Pittsburgh Technology Council, a consortium of more than 1,400 local businesses. The luxury suites feature on-demand replays from touchscreens. "Yinz Cam"—a system developed by Carnegie Mellon students—provides instant replays from any angle to fans on their cell phones. A Penguins All-Time Team zone features touchscreen displays, videos, photos, and bios about the team's greatest stars, executives, staff members, and personalities.

"This is going to be, technologically, one of the most advanced buildings in the country," said Penguins CEO and president David Morehouse.

The Penguins moved into their new digs on August 1, 2010. Three days later they announced that the CONSOL Energy Center had attained Leadership in Energy and Environmental Design (LEED) gold certification, making it the first NHL arena to achieve that lofty standard. Understandably proud of their beautiful new facility, the Pens held a series of open houses later in the month for season ticket holders and the general public.

The sparkling new arena quickly earned rave reviews. In December of 2010 it was voted the best NHL arena by the readers of the *Sports Business Journal*.

31 Murph

When Jim O'Brien interviewed Larry Murphy for his book, *Penguin Profiles*, he asked the veteran defenseman to describe his style of play. Murphy gave a typically thoughtful answer.

"I don't have blazing speed, so you have to compensate somehow," he said. "Using my head, playing the game smart has always been my strong suit. I rely on anticipation and concentration. I rely on being in the right place at the right time."

Indeed, Murphy's game was a triumph of substance over flash. He didn't fly around the ice at warp speed like a Bobby Orr or a Paul Coffey. Yet he controlled the flow of a game like no other with a subtle shift in speed or an artful pass. He didn't throw booming checks or pound opponents into submission in the manner of a Scott Stevens. Instead, he relied on superb positioning and the brilliant use of his stick. In short, Murphy was the ultimate thinking man's defenseman, relying on intelligence, creativity, and superb positioning.

Entering the NHL with Los Angeles in 1980–81, Murphy enjoyed one of the finest seasons ever by a rookie rearguard. At the callow age of 19 he piled up 16 goals and 76 points—a record for first-year defensemen. Remarkably, the Scarborough, Ontario, native finished second to Quebec center Peter Stastny—his senior by five years—in the voting for the Calder Trophy.

Shaking off the snub, the 6'2", 210-pounder continued to perform at a high level. Following a trade to Washington in 1983, he emerged as one of the best two-way defensemen in the league. In 1986–87 he tallied 23 goals and 58 assists to earn Second Team NHL All-Star honors.

Curiously, Murphy's play took a dip the next season. Struggling to find the net, he scored only eight goals. Disenchanted with their erstwhile All-Star, the Cap Centre boobirds were quick to pounce. They made a strange whooping sound every time he touched the puck, described by *Sports Illustrated* as a "faux turkey mating call." By the spring of 1989 the situation became untenable, forcing general manager David Poile to peddle Murphy to the Minnesota North Stars.

It was a second trade—to the Penguins in December of 1990—that restored Murphy's sagging reputation and revived his career. Given a badly needed boost of confidence by coach Bob Johnson, Murphy flourished in the Steel City. Teaming with the physical Ulf Samuelsson to form an exquisitely balanced tandem, he scored 23 points in the postseason to help pace the Pens to a Stanley Cup victory over his former club, the North Stars.

During the next several seasons Murphy was at the top of his game. While he would never win a fastest skater competition, he possessed outstanding agility and lateral mobility. On the power play, he was a master at gobbling up wayward clearing attempts and

Acquired from the North Stars in 1990, defenseman Larry Murphy would later pass Bobby Orr on the NHL's all-time assists list.

turning them into scoring opportunities. Defensively, he was cool and poised under fire. He always seemed to make the right read and the proper play.

"Murph was a smart and studious player," said his admiring coach, Scotty Bowman. "It was his understanding of what he could do that made him special."

One of his patented moves was "the Murphy Dump." At opportune times, Murphy would adroitly loft the puck out of the Penguins' zone and into the other team's end of the rink. Thanks to his marvelous touch, he executed the maneuver time and again without icing the puck. Often the rubber would land behind an unsuspecting defenseman and onto a teammate's waiting stick.

"He's a very, very smart hockey player," said Eddie Johnston, echoing Bowman's sentiments. "He does the little things that help you win hockey games."

Following a banner year in 1992–93 (22 goals, 85 points, and a plus-45) Murphy reached a significant milestone on November 27, 1993, when he passed Orr on the all-time assists list.

"Bobby Orr is probably the greatest defenseman to play the game," he said. "By no means do I measure myself equally with him. But still, when you're able to have your name mentioned in the same sentence as Bobby Orr, that's something I take as a true compliment."

Eleven years later Murphy once again would have his name mentioned in the same breath as Orr's when he was inducted into the Hockey Hall of Fame.

32 The Ice Bowl

The Penguins made history on New Year's Day 2008 when they participated in the NHL's first Winter Classic. It was the second NHL regular season game ever to be contested outdoors. In 2003 more than 57,000 fans had flocked to Commonwealth Stadium in Edmonton to watch the Oilers take on the Canadiens in the Heritage Classic.

Two days before Christmas, work crews began the arduous task of constructing an NHL rink at Buffalo's Ralph Wilson Stadium.

"We tarped the field and removed the goalposts and spent the next few hours just doing a site survey, getting our points that we start to level the field with since there's a nine-inch crown in that football field," said Don Renzulli, the NHL's Senior Vice President of Events and Entertainment. "We started with that and slowly started leveling that field off with about 3,000 sheets of plywood and Styrofoam. Then, we started the rink and the ice process."

The Pens' creative department was hard at work, too. The club planned to unveil a new third jersey for the event, featuring the logo and powder blue color scheme worn by the team in the late 1960s.

By game time, more than 71,000 fans had packed Ralph Wilson Stadium to watch the Penguins and Sabres do battle. They were greeted by 30-degree temperatures and a healthy dose of wind, sleet, and snow. Millions of additional viewers tuned in on NBC, making "the Ice Bowl" the highest rated regular season hockey game in more than a decade.

The Penguins wasted little time in lighting the lamp. On the opening shift, Colby Armstrong gathered in a Sidney Crosby rebound and whipped the puck past Ryan Miller.

"It just popped right to me," Armstrong said.

That goal stood up until 1:25 of the second period, when the Sabres evened the score on a rocket of a shot by Brian Campbell. Due to the less-than-ideal conditions, the game evolved into a defensive struggle.

"The ice was a little more fresh earlier in the game, so you didn't notice it as much," Crosby said. "But after the first [period], you could tell it was going to be tough to carry the puck a lot. You're pushing the puck and you're just trying to move it forward. You weren't even trying to stick-handle, chipping it in. It was pretty simple hockey. Even guys carrying it, it would just kind of pop up on them."

The contest was frequently interrupted to allow for repairs to the ice. Midway through each period, action was halted while the Zambonis performed their magic. The teams also switched ends so neither club would gain an advantage due to the elements or ice conditions.

With Miller and his Penguins counterpart, Ty Conklin, making save after save, the score remained knotted at 1–1 after 60 minutes of play. Armstrong nearly wore the goat horns when he drew a hooking penalty as time expired to hand Buffalo a four-on-three advantage in overtime. Fortunately for the popular winger, his teammates bailed him out and forced a shootout.

"I had a lot of time to sit there [in the penalty box] and think about it while they were scrapping on the ice," he said. "It wasn't the most fun place to be. It's cold and lonely, for sure."

The stage was set for a dramatic finish. With the shootout knotted at 1–1, Sidney Crosby weaved through the driving snow and snapped the puck between Miller's pads to set off a wild victory celebration.

"I just tried to get a shot away," Sid explained. "The last thing I wanted to do was lose the puck or miss the net or something. I just wanted to give it a chance to go in."

"It couldn't have worked out any better for [NBC]," Pens defenseman Ryan Whitney said. "They got the snowfall, they got Sidney to end the game. That's just what they wanted."

33 The Geno Is Out of the Bottle

From the moment he first stepped onto an NHL rink, Evgeni Malkin seemed destined to establish himself as an elite player. After earning the Calder Trophy as the league's top rookie in 2006–07, the big Russian rolled up 106 points the following season to place second in the NHL scoring race. However, in the playoffs that spring Geno tailed off after a hot start, raising concerns about his ability to produce at crunch time.

Taking the criticism to heart, Malkin emerged as a more confident and mature player in 2008–09. Displaying remarkable poise and consistency, the 22-year-old center led the league in points virtually wire-to-wire en route to his first Art Ross Trophy.

Malkin shone like a diamond during the opening round of the 2009 playoffs, tallying nine points to help the Penguins down Philadelphia. The victory over the Flyers set up what proved to be an epic matchup with the Washington Capitals and his archrival Alexander Ovechkin in the Eastern Conference Semifinals.

Rarely have two players with such opposite personalities been so closely linked. In 2004 the twin sensations became the first Russians ever to be selected first and second in the National Hockey League Entry Draft. Four years later they became the first Russian duo to finish first and second in the NHL scoring race.

As always, Malkin played best man to Ovechkin's bridegroom. While his bold and brash countryman was constantly grabbing the headlines, Geno was content to go about his business with a quiet excellence.

A feud was festering between the two as well. In August of 2007 Ovechkin punched Malkin's Russian agent, Gennady Ushakov, at a Moscow night club. On the ice, the rambunctious Capital rarely missed an opportunity to deliver a big hit on his former Olympic team linemate, often in borderline fashion. Although they appeared to settle their differences at the 2009 NHL All-Star Game, Malkin was no less determined to emerge from his rival's shadow.

Ovechkin held the upper hand during the first two games of the series. He scored four goals and fired off an astounding 21 shots, far outdistancing Malkin's eight shots and two assists. Worse yet, Geno drew a tripping penalty that led to Ovechkin's game winner in the second contest.

A Star Is Born

When HBO filmed a segment of its *24/7* documentary in preparation for the 2011 Winter Classic, Penguins center Evgeni Malkin did his best to put on a good show. He playfully teased his teammates, mugged for the camera, and engaged in various forms of hijinks.

"I tried," Malkin said, with a smile. "I had a microphone on my jersey, and I was talking with my teammates. Next show, maybe they'll show me more."

It was a far cry from his early years in the Steel City. Speaking little English, the big Russian shunned the spotlight while relying on former teammate Sergei Gonchar and Penguins staffer George Birman to translate for him. However, Geno's fun-loving personality began to emerge as he gradually became more comfortable with the language.

"We enjoy playing with him, and we enjoy his character," said Chris Kunitz, one of Geno's favorite targets. "Anytime [Malkin] is around, we know he likes to play jokes, likes to talk and 'chirp' guys just like anyone else."

"You're going to see that he's not so shy," Max Talbot added. "He's a smart guy, a funny guy. He's great to be around."

Malkin seemed perfectly at ease with revealing his lighthearted nature before a national TV audience.

"Of course. It's not a big secret," he said. "I'm a good guy. I try to speak with my teammates, joke. It's a young team, and everyone likes jokes."

It was a pivotal moment for Malkin, the kind that can make or break a champion. With his team's Stanley Cup hopes hanging in the balance, Geno stepped forward in Game 3 with arguably the finest performance of his career. No one—not Ovechkin nor Penguins teammate Sidney Crosby—would match him on this night. Playing both ends of the ice with a singular brilliance, he dominated the action, unleashing a game-high nine shots and scoring the Penguins' second goal.

"He was at a different level," Penguins coach Dan Bylsma said. "Another level."

Geno's game remained at another level for the remainder of the playoffs. He torched All-Star goalie Cam Ward for six goals during the Pens' four-game sweep of Carolina in the Eastern Conference Finals, including an electrifying tally in Game 2 that was instantly dubbed "the Geno."

Working a set play, Malkin won a face-off deep in the Carolina end and snapped the puck to the end boards. As Hurricanes defenseman Dennis Seidenberg chased after him in hot pursuit, Geno regained the puck and quickly circled behind the cage. With his back to the net, he suddenly wheeled and whipped a seeing-eye backhander over Ward's shoulder.

After witnessing the stunning display of skill, Versus hockey analyst Brian Engblom remarked, "The Geno is out of the bottle."

Malkin continued his extraordinary play during the Penguins' hard-fought Finals matchup with Detroit. He paced all black-and-gold scorers with eight points to help lead the team to its third Stanley Cup. In all, the big center piled up 36 points—the second highest total in Penguins playoff history—to earn the Conn Smythe Trophy.

"He told us before the playoffs that he was going to lead us to the Stanley Cup," Bill Guerin said. "He's an amazing competitor, an amazing player."

34 Jack Lambert on Skates

On a team not noted for employing physical defensemen, Ulf Samuelsson stands out as a glaring exception to the rule. In many ways he was a dinosaur, a throwback to an earlier time when rugged rearguards like Bashin' Bill Barilko, Bobby Baun, and Leo Boivin

Dean of Mean

During his 16 seasons in the NHL, Ulf Samuelsson carved out a reputation as a relentless competitor who would high-stick his own grandmother if it meant preventing a goal. Even friends and former teammates hated facing the ornery defenseman.

"I never liked playing against him," Kevin Stevens said. "He hits you head-on, and every time you turn around, he's right in your face. You love him when he's on your team, and you hate him when he's not. He can make you cringe, even when he's playing with you. He just plays with such reckless abandon."

"He's got a junkyard-dog mentality, he's tougher than nails, and he's got a terrifically high threshold of pain," said color commentator Bill Clement, a onetime member of the Philadelphia Flyers' Broad Street Bullies. "He would have fit right in with the Flyers of the '70s, beside guys like Eddie Van Impe and Moose Dupont. He's crude, but Dick Butkus was crude, and he's in the Pro Football Hall of Fame. To me, Samuelsson is like a linebacker on skates."

Others were far less charitable.

"If they had a poll of players, he'd win as the dirtiest player in the league," said forward Bernie Nicholls, who once engaged Samuelsson in a stick-swinging duel. "Nobody else is close. I hate the guy."

In October of 1995, *Sports Illustrated* made it official. In a poll conducted to name the NHL's dirtiest player, Samuelsson won in a landslide, garnering votes from 26 of the 56 respondents to earn the title "Dean of Mean."

put the fear of God into opposing forwards with their brutally efficient physical play.

There was nothing subtle about Samuelsson's game. Although hardly a heavyweight, the Swedish-born defender employed an edgy, in-your-face style that delighted his teammates and infuriated opponents.

The slot was Ulfie's turf. Opposing forwards who had the nerve to venture in were treated like trespassers. He used every weapon in his considerable arsenal—body checks, cross checks, slashes,

*Old-school defenseman
Ulf Samuelsson provided
a physical presence to the
Penguins' back-to-back
Stanley Cup champions in
1991–92.*

elbows, rabbit punches, and the occasional face wash—to make sure they didn't linger.

"I do whatever it takes," he said. "Whatever it takes to stop the other guy."

Ulf spent his formative years playing in his native Sweden, where he starred as a teenager for Leksands of the fast Swedish Elite League. Attracted by the youngster's spirited, physical brand of defense, the Hartford Whalers made him their fourth choice in the 1982 Entry Draft. For nearly seven seasons he patrolled the Whalers' blue line, banging bodies and making enemies at a rapid rate.

"No, I didn't like him," future teammate Rick Tocchet said. "In fact, like most people who don't know him, I hated him."

By 1990–91 the Whalers were in turmoil. Armed with a mandate to shake up his team—or else—Whalers general manager Eddie Johnston sent Samuelsson, Ron Francis, and Grant Jennings to the Penguins in a blockbuster six-player trade.

Rejuvenated by the change of scenery, Ulf belted any opponent who had the temerity to cross his path. He quickly became a favorite of the Mellon Arena faithful who loved his take-no-prisoners style.

"I nicknamed Ulfie 'Jack Lambert on skates' because he was crushing people one night in Philly," color man Paul Steigerwald said. "When we saw Ulfie hitting guys in Philadelphia, that was the first sign he was someone who was going to make a big difference."

Samuelsson cemented his physical reputation against the Bruins during the bitterly fought 1991 Wales Conference Finals. He went head-to-head with Cam Neely, an old foe from his days as a Whaler. A 6'1", 210-pound slab of granite, Neely was considered far and away the top power forward in the league—as equally adept at delivering pulverizing body checks as he was at scoring goals.

"Cam Neely was a big, strong winger and he was very difficult to play against," the late Bob Johnson recalled in the highlight video, *One From the Heart*. "A lot of players couldn't handle him— he just physically overpowered them. Ulf accepted the challenge. He's the toughest guy I've ever been around."

Through three emotionally charged contests Samuelsson and Neely hammered away at each other. Like a pit bull terrier, Ulfie kept coming after the imposing Bruin.

The turning point of the series came late in Game 3. With the Penguins protecting a two-goal lead in a must-win game, Samuelsson lined up Neely once more. At the last second the Boston strongman took evasive action, but the tough defenseman instinctively stuck out a knee to block his path. Neely went down in a heap.

Out for blood in Game 4, the revenge-minded Bruins came at Ulfie with a bare-knuckled fury. He never wavered. Like a spent bullet, Boston faded while the Pens went on to capture their first Stanley Cup.

Over the next four seasons, the rugged Swede was at his head-knocking best. He played some of the finest hockey of his career during the Penguins' march to a second Cup in 1992. The following season he logged a sterling plus/minus rating of plus-36 while helping to lead the team to a stunning 56-win season and the President's Trophy.

Penguins fans hoped Ulfie would finish his career in Pittsburgh. Sadly, it was not to be. During the summer of 1995 he was traded to the Rangers in a big four-player swap, ending his run in the Steel City. He departed as one of the most popular players in team history.

35 Tommy B

During his senior year at Acton-Boxborough High School, Tom Barrasso's dad noticed his son didn't order a class ring like all the other kids.

"Why aren't you going to order a ring?" Barrasso's father asked.

"Dad," Tom replied, "the only ring I want to wear has the Stanley Cup on it."

Barrasso would get his wish. Over the course of an exemplary 19-year career that spanned three decades, he recorded 369 victories—the most of any American-born goalie—and won two Stanley Cups.

In 1983–84 Barrasso burst onto the NHL scene like a meteor. Selected with the fifth overall pick by Buffalo, the 18-year-old netminder brushed aside the competition to claim the Sabres' starting job. Playing with the poise of a seasoned veteran, he captured the Calder Trophy and Vezina Trophy (awarded to the league's top goaltender) while becoming the only goalie in history to make the jump directly from high school to the NHL.

"Tom was very confident of his ability," said his high school coach Tom Fleming. "We went 80–4–1 over the four years Tom played goal."

After earning All-Star honors in each of his first two seasons, Barrasso's career hit a speed bump. Following a rocky start in 1988–89, he lost his starting job to Darren Puppa. Seeking a No. 1 goalie to backstop his high-octane but porous team, Penguins GM Tony Esposito acquired Barrasso on November 12, 1988, for talented young defenseman Doug Bodger and first-round draft pick Darrin Shannon.

With Barrasso guarding the net, the Pens nailed down their first playoff berth in seven years. Poised for another big season in 1989–90, his world was turned upside down when his young daughter, Ashley, was stricken with cancer.

"I found out what life is about," Barrasso told Jon Scher of *Sports Illustrated*. "Life is not about playing hockey. My daughter was in a situation where it didn't look like she was going to see age three. That's something that gives you tremendous perspective on your life."

The Penguins granted Barrasso a leave of absence to care for Ashley.

"Tom belongs with his family right now," said Penguins general manager Craig Patrick.

Thankfully, Ashley beat the disease. With his daughter's cancer in full remission, Barrasso reclaimed the Pens' starting job in 1990–91. More intense and focused than ever before, he won 27 games and led the club to its first division title. Displaying marvelous consistency and coolness under fire, he paced all playoff goaltenders with a 2.60 goals-against average and helped pave the way to the Pens' first Stanley Cup.

Barrasso was even better the following season. When Mario Lemieux was sidelined with a broken hand during the 1992

Rebel Without a Cause

Entering the 1976–77 season, the Penguins were pinning their playoff hopes on the young goaltending tandem of Denis Herron and Gord Laxton. The duo performed well during the preseason, backstopping the Pens to a 7–3 record in exhibition play.

However, disaster struck during a season-opening victory over Vancouver. Herron, who was expected to carry the bulk of the netminding chores, suffered a broken left arm. Thrust into the starting job, the 21-year-old Laxton was strafed for 10 goals in a humiliating loss to the powerhouse Canadiens.

Duly alarmed, Pens general manager Wren Blair scurried to find an experienced goaltender. The New York Rangers were only too happy to oblige. The next day they peddled problem child Dunc Wilson to the Penguins for a fourth-round choice in the 1978 Amateur Draft.

Playing a position that produced more than its share of flakes, Duncan Shepherd Wilson seemed to take quirkiness to a new level. While playing for Vancouver in the early 1970s, he grew his hair to shoulder length and wore a headband under his goalie mask. Unlike many of his contemporaries, Wilson shrugged off losses with a smile or a joke.

"I can't go around being serious all the time and looking down in the dumps at the appropriate times," he said.

Wilson's attitude hardly endeared him to his coaches. He even ran afoul of Red Kelly, normally an easygoing skipper, during a stint with the Maple Leafs. Following a disastrous West Coast road trip and some hard partying with his teammates, a reporter asked Dunc if he expected a warm reception back in Toronto.

"I doubt it," he smiled. "But the boys from the North Vancouver booze store undoubtedly will call."

Despite his carefree reputation, the Penguins had little choice but to hand Wilson the goaltending reins. Much to the delight and amazement of Blair and coach Ken Schinkel, he thrived. Sporting a distinctive goaltending mask that featured the stars and bars of the Confederate flag, the rebel without a cause posted a sparkling 2.95 goals-against average and five shutouts. Thanks largely to Wilson's heroics, the Penguins nailed down their third consecutive playoff berth.

It proved to be the colorful goalie's swan song. He endured a miserable season as the Pens' backup in 1977–78, registering a career-worst goals-against average of 4.83. Wilson's sorry performance could at least partly be attributed to his carousing.

"He smoked, he drank, he broke curfew," teammate Dave Schultz recalled. "You name it, Dunc had done it."

playoffs, he took charge and won 11 straight games during the march to a second Stanley Cup.

"Tom Barrasso was magnificent," play-by-play announcer Mike Lange said.

"It seems that for the saves you absolutely have to have, in the games you absolutely have to win, he's there," said teammate Rick Tocchet. "He makes the big saves."

Barrasso continued to make the big saves in Pittsburgh for eight more seasons. In 1992–93 he topped the NHL with 43 wins to earn Second Team NHL All-Star honors. After sitting out virtually the entire 1996–97 campaign due to a shoulder injury, he returned with a vengeance in 1997–98 to enjoy perhaps his finest year. Appearing in 63 games, he posted a sparkling 2.07 goals-against average and a club-record seven shutouts.

By the spring of 2000, however, age and injuries had begun to creep up on Barrasso. With his play slipping noticeably, Craig Patrick dealt the winningest goalie in franchise history to Ottawa for Ron Tugnutt.

Barrasso played two more seasons before hanging up his skates. In June of 2003, Patrick quietly signed him as a free agent so he could retire as a Penguin. It was a fitting end to the career of a man who had been instrumental in leading the team to two Stanley Cups.

36 Good-bye, My Friend

For the Pittsburgh Penguins, the summer of 1991 was the best of times and the worst of times. In May, the team celebrated its first-ever Stanley Cup. Weeks later they visited the White House. However, the festive mood was shattered in late August with the announcement that the team's beloved coach, Bob Johnson, had two brain tumors.

Doctors performed emergency surgery to remove one of the tumors, but the second was deemed inoperable. Although the prognosis was grim, Badger Bob fought his illness with the heart of a lion. Still passionate about the Penguins and the game he loved, he vowed to return to Pittsburgh for the raising of the championship banner in October.

"The fire of coaching still burns inside me—I will be back," he said in a statement released through his son-in-law, Tim McConnell. "When I return, it will be my greatest day in coaching."

Johnson attended an exhibition game in Denver to watch the Pens take on his former team, the Calgary Flames. However, his condition worsened dramatically through the opening weeks of the season. Following a courageous three-month fight, Johnson tragically passed away on November 26, 1991. Pens general manager Craig Patrick broke the news to the team after a practice session.

"The way Craig explained it to the players, Bob fought a real tough battle," interim coach Scotty Bowman said. "The last couple of weeks were real difficult, but he just wouldn't give in until now. We just have to stick together and help each other out. A big part of us is gone now."

The Penguins had precious little time to cope. The following evening they were slated to play the New Jersey Devils at the Civic Arena.

To honor their fallen coach, the team held a candlelight vigil prior to the game. With the lights dimmed low, the Penguins stood with heads bowed at center ice while the Karla Bonoff song, "Goodbye My Friend," poured out over the Arena. The players struggled to choke back their emotions.

"It was really tough," Ron Francis said. "To see everybody in the stands with the [candle] lights up, knowing the kind of person Bob was…it was very emotional for all us."

Then, abruptly, the overhead lights came on. Officials gathered the teams at center ice for the opening face-off. Somehow, the Penguins had to find it in themselves to play a game.

"It was an amazing situation," Kevin Stevens said, "because everyone's sitting there with tears in their eyes and all of a sudden the lights come on and we've got to drop the puck and play hockey. It just didn't feel right to go out and try and play a hockey game after that."

Remarkably, the Penguins regained their focus and came out smoking. At 9:56 of the opening period, Francis whirled around Alexei Kasatonov and squeezed the puck between goalie Chris Terreri's pads. Less than two minutes later Jamie Leach rifled a shot past Terreri from the right hash mark. Phil Bourque, one of Johnson's favorite players, capped off an extraordinary period with a booming 35-foot slap shot to stake the Pens to a 3–0 lead.

In the second period, however, the intense emotions of the evening took a toll. Understandably drained, the Penguins watched as the Devils struck for three straight goals to even the score.

Determined to win the game for Badger Bob, the team regrouped for a final charge. Mark Recchi scored late in the second period to restore the Pens' lead. Early in the third period, defenseman Grant Jennings ventured deep into the New Jersey zone to convert a pass from Mario Lemieux. After the Devils closed the gap to one, Paul Coffey beat Terreri at 10:44 with a laser from the left circle. Lemieux and Francis put the finishing touches on a resounding 8–4 win.

As the Penguins gathered to celebrate their victory one couldn't help but notice that Johnson's favorite saying, "It's a Great Day for Hockey," was emblazoned on the ice.

"That would have been him, saying it's a great day for hockey, saying we have to move on," Francis said.

37 Bone Rack

Playing in an era when offensive-minded defensemen such as Bobby Orr, Brad Park, and Denis Potvin were revolutionizing the game, Dave Burrows was a throwback to earlier times. Caring little about his point totals—he scored only 24 goals during his Penguins career—Burrows focused his energy on protecting his goaltender and preventing goals. Few have done it better.

The foundation of Burrows' game was his skating. Blessed with outstanding speed and agility, he could skate backward faster than many players of his day could skate forward, which allowed him to keep the play in front of him at all times.

"I took a lot of pride in being able to move laterally and backward with great ease," he said. "It took a lot of practice, but it was something I enjoyed doing."

A born-again Christian, Burrows played the game hard but clean. Using his skating ability and 6'1" frame to their fullest advantage, he excelled at angling the puck carrier away from the net and into the boards. He also was an outstanding shot blocker who selflessly gave up his body time and time again to prevent scoring chances. His teammates teased him about his legs, which were perpetually bruised. Dubbed "Bone Rack" for his lean physique, Burrows didn't seem to mind.

"I knew I wasn't an offensive threat; I wasn't a goal scorer," he recalled in Jim O'Brien's book, *Penguin Profiles*. "I always got a thrill out of breaking up a two-on-one break. I was a stay-at-home defenseman. I was happy with that role. You have to use the ability God gives you."

As a youngster growing up in Toronto, Burrows idolized the Maples Leafs' great defenseman Tim Horton. Ironically, when the Penguins claimed Burrows from Chicago in the 1971 Intra-League Draft, they picked up Horton from the Rangers. Needless to say, it was a delight for the 22-year-old Burrows to play on the same team as his idol.

"The biggest thrill of my career was playing defense with Tim when we were together in Pittsburgh," he said. "He helped me out with a lot of little things in my game. He's a man I'll never forget. I owe him a lot."

Despite his less-than-gaudy point totals, Burrows quickly earned the respect of his peers for his sound positioning and rock-solid defensive play. In 1973–74 he was named to the West Division All-Star Team. Playing in Chicago, he helped his team earn a 6–4 victory over the powerful East Division squad. However, he sustained a dislocated shoulder, an injury that would trouble him for the rest of his career.

Still, Burrows remained the Penguins' top defenseman for the next four seasons. In 1975–76 he enjoyed the finest season of his career, topping a talented Pens squad with a plus/minus rating of plus-27. He flashed a little offense as well, registering career highs in goals (seven) and points (29).

In June of 1978 the Penguins traded the reliable defenseman to Toronto for Randy Carlyle and George Ferguson. As fate would have it, he played his first game in a Maple Leafs uniform against the Penguins at the Civic Arena.

"It was weird, going to the locker room at the other end of the ice," he recalled. "I was in the starting lineup, and when I was introduced over the PA system I received a standing ovation from the crowd. I remember that like it was yesterday. It's one of those times you'll never forget. It was very moving. It made me feel so good."

Playing for Toronto should've been the realization of a boyhood dream, but Burrows missed Pittsburgh. Fortunately, the Penguins reacquired him in November of 1980, enabling him to finish his career in the Steel City.

The bedrock defender is currently seventh on the team's all-time list of games played (573), second among defenseman to his former teammate Ron Stackhouse. In 1996 Burrows was inducted into the Penguins Hall of Fame. Fourteen years later he was voted to the Penguins All-Time Team.

38 Mr. D

Unlike other Penguins owners, Edward J. DeBartolo Sr. never intended to own a hockey team. He knew little about the sport and cared even less about it. However, he was friends with Al Savill, who owned a share of the Penguins. The Columbus investment broker was seeking a new investor to replace Wren Blair.

In February of 1977 Savill convinced DeBartolo, who had amassed a fortune through his construction company, to purchase a one-third interest in the team. By April 5, 1978, the Youngstown, Ohio, native had assumed complete control of the team. It marked the beginning of 14 years of stable ownership.

A true American success story, DeBartolo was born on May 17, 1909, to Italian immigrants Anthony Paonessa and Rose Villani. He never knew his biological father, who died suddenly before his birth. After Anthony passed away, his mother married Michael DeBartolo, who also had emigrated from Italy. Young Edward took his stepfather's name.

As a teenager, Edward transcribed paving contracts for Michael while learning the construction industry trade. The lessons would serve him well following World War II, when he and his wife, Marie, formed the Edward J. DeBartolo Corporation. By 1971, Edward's company ranked 47th in the nation among construction contractors.

The Penguins were not a good hockey team when DeBartolo arrived on the scene. After a few modestly successful seasons, the club collapsed in the early 1980s. As the team's performance worsened, attendance plummeted to an average of fewer than 7,000 fans per game. The team was hemorrhaging millions of dollars. Rumors were swirling that the Penguins would relocate to Hamilton or Saskatoon following the 1983–84 season.

"You'd walk into the arena for a game and there would be 3,800 people in the place, and most of them were booing, and some of them had bags on their heads," Paul Steigerwald recalled in Tom McMillan's book, *The Penguins: Cellar to Summit.* "Hockey in Pittsburgh had reached the bottom, the absolute pits of professional sports. It was torture. You had to cry to keep from laughing."

One man who wasn't laughing was the boss. An intense, driven man, DeBartolo would phone the Penguins' offices from his headquarters in Youngstown each morning, demanding explanations.

"I remember a lot of days when no one wanted to be the first one in the office because no one wanted to have to answer the phone," said Tom Rooney, the team's vice president of advertising. "Especially after some horrible loss on the road."

In 1984 the Penguins' on-ice fortunes took a dramatic turn for the better when the club drafted Laval Voisin phenom Mario Lemieux. With Super Mario serving as the star attraction, the team's attendance soared. However, it would take several seasons and countless millions in losses before the Penguins developed into a competitive team.

Through it all, DeBartolo persevered. In 1991 his willingness to see the team through the lean years was finally rewarded. With Lemieux leading the way, the Penguins won the Stanley Cup. By his own estimation, it had cost DeBartolo some $25 million for the honor of hoisting Lord Stanley's chalice.

His moment in the sun was remarkably brief. In October of 1991 he sold the Penguins to a group headed by Howard Baldwin for $31 million. DeBartolo passed away three short years later at the age of 85. In his honor the Penguins created the Edward J. DeBartolo Community Service Award, which is given each year to the player who is most involved in community and charity projects. His legacy in Pittsburgh will never be forgotten.

"I don't think anyone should underestimate what DeBartolo and his family meant to hockey in Pittsburgh," Rooney said. "There's no question that Mario Lemieux was the savior of the franchise, but Mr. D had to keep it alive just to let him be the savior. He took a tremendous financial beating all those years. And if it wasn't for his hard-headedness...hey, Mario might have been saving the *Saskatchewan* Penguins. Think of that."

39 Pepto-Bylsma

When Dan Bylsma assumed the Penguins' coaching reins from Michel Therrien on February 15, 2009, the club was in dire straits. Only eight months removed from a trip to the Stanley Cup Finals, the Pens were in real danger of slipping from playoff contention.

Despite a talented core that included superstars Sidney Crosby and Evgeni Malkin, the club had grown increasingly stale and lifeless.

"Guys just weren't having fun," Max Talbot said. "It was like no one wanted to come to the rink."

Hired on an interim basis, Bylsma seized his chance. Although the Penguins dropped a 3–2 shootout to the Islanders in his first game, the Bowling Green grad made an impression.

"After his first game, we sat down and talked for about an hour," Pens GM Ray Shero recalled. "He was so impressive. I remember calling [former president] Ken Sawyer and saying, 'I think this guy is impressive. We'll see how he does.' And we saw how he did."

A former NHL player who had carved out a career as a gritty defensive specialist, Bylsma proved to be just the right tonic. Eschewing Therrien's trap-oriented system, the new coach preached an up-tempo style that emphasized speed and puck possession. The team immediately responded.

"We had been playing cautiously, playing not to make a mistake, which was a disaster," Brooks Orpik recalled. "But after we won a few in a row, we grew confident and we started to be aggressive. Things just came together."

Dan-dy

It took Dan Bylsma just a few short months to accomplish what most coaches never achieve in a lifetime. Displaying the poise, acumen, and presence of a man far beyond his years, he won a Stanley Cup in his first season behind an NHL bench.

Addressing an adoring crowd at the Penguins' triumphant Stanley Cup victory parade on June 15, 2009, general manager Ray Shero singled out the rookie coach for praise.

"Raise your hand if you knew who Dan Bylsma was before February 15," he said before the huge throng.

Standing in the wings, Bylsma smiled and raised the hand of his young son Bryan.

In a turnaround that bordered on the miraculous, the club ripped through the homestretch at an incendiary 18–3–4 clip. The players were quick to credit Bylsma.

"Obviously, I think he's a great Xs and Os coach," then-Penguins defenseman Hal Gill said. "He does the little things right. But, more importantly, I think our attitude changed. We came to the rink excited to play. We had fun."

During the cauldron of the Stanley Cup playoffs the unflappable 38-year-old skipper continued to push the right buttons. After leading the Penguins past the Flyers, Capitals, and Hurricanes, Bylsma guided the team to a pulsating come-from-behind victory over Detroit in the Finals. Along the way he became a folk hero in the Steel City.

"I've only been in Pittsburgh for four and a half months," Bylsma told the crowd at the team's victory parade. "But it was only about two months in that I knew I was 'from' Pittsburgh."

Although the Penguins fell short in their quest for a second straight Cup in 2009–10, the energetic coach remained as popular as ever with his players.

"He brings an enthusiasm to the rink, and something new every day," Dustin Jeffrey said. "When you see a guy who's

Dan Bylsma took over the Penguins' helm in February of 2009 and led the franchise to its third Stanley Cup victory four months later.

genuinely excited to be here every day to teach us, to be on the ice with us, I think it's contagious. You see with our team the way we play, it's almost a reflection of the way he carries himself and the way he brings himself to the rink."

The 2010–11 campaign proved to the most challenging of Bylsma's young coaching career. Following a piping-hot first half, the Penguins were decimated by injuries. Superstars Sidney Crosby and Evgeni Malkin were lost for the season. Key players such as Chris Kunitz, Brooks Orpik, and Jordan Staal also spent significant chunks of time on the disabled list.

Remarkably, Bylsma kept his bruised and battered club focused and on course. With a ragtag lineup that featured as many as eight call-ups from Wilkes-Barre Scranton, he guided the Pens to a 106-point season—the second-highest total in franchise history. As a reward for his fine work behind the bench, Shero inked Bylsma to a three-year contract extension.

At the NHL Awards banquet on June 22, 2011, Dan received the prestigious Jack Adams Award as coach of the year.

"I was very happy for him and his family," Shero said. "With Crosby and Malkin injured, people see what kind of coach Dan is. We're proud to have Dan as our coach. He's very deserving."

40 Winter Classic IV

In May of 2010 Penguins fans received a special treat when the NHL announced that Pittsburgh would play host to the fourth Winter Classic. Scheduled for New Year's Day 2011, it featured a dream matchup between Sidney Crosby and the Pens and their bitter rivals, Alexander Ovechkin and the Washington Capitals.

The buildup for the game was unlike any other. In anticipation, HBO contracted to film a special documentary titled *Road to the NHL Winter Classic*. While the players reveled in the spotlight, the Penguins unveiled a new alternate jersey designed especially for the game.

"I'm really looking forward to it," Pens winger Chris Kunitz said. "Just being able to play in a game of that magnitude during the season, not too many people have done that. It has a whole different element to the game. The majestic part of playing outdoors is going to be a fun part."

Unfortunately, the weather threatened to literally put a damper on the Classic. Almost on cue, a rare winter heat wave arrived in the Steel City the weekend of the contest. With the 50-degree temperatures and steady rain threatening the ice surface, the NHL wisely pushed the opening face-off back seven hours to 8:00 PM, making the fourth Winter Classic the first to be played at night.

Nonplussed, the Pens and the Caps put on a show for the 68,111 fans at Heinz Field. The feisty Ovechkin delivered a teeth-rattling check on Penguins defenseman Zbynek Michalek on the opening shift of the game, setting the tone for a chippy first period that featured a whopping 25 hits.

"It was close to the Stanley Cup Finals," Washington coach Bruce Boudreau said. "We don't deny it meant more than just two points. It was a fabulous game."

Early in the second period the home team drew first blood. Moments after Marc-Andre Fleury made a spectacular save to thwart Ovechkin, Kris Letang found Evgeni Malkin with a pretty lead pass off the sideboards. Geno gathered up the puck in full stride and ripped a shot past Washington goalie Semyon Varlamov.

For the Penguins, Malkin's electrifying tally would be the highlight of the evening. Minutes later the Capitals evened the score on a power-play tally by Mike Knuble. The momentum began to swing in favor of the red-and-white-clad visitors, who did a better job of adjusting to the less-than-ideal conditions.

"You needed to simplify a little more, and I don't know if we did that," said Pens forward Mike Rupp. "I think they did. They rimmed pucks around the boards, and when you do that, you know where the puck's going, and it's a lot more of a consistent game."

At 14:45 Washington grabbed the lead thanks to a puck-handling gaffe by Fleury. The Pens' goalie ventured behind his net to corral a loose puck but coughed it up to Marcus Johansson, who quickly slid the rubber to Eric Fehr. The Caps' winger made no mistake and whipped it into the wide-open net.

"I stopped and looked around, and the puck was gone," Fleury said glumly.

Down 2–1 entering the final period, the Penguins faced an uphill climb. Adding to their woes were high winds and a steady drizzle that created pronounced wet spots, especially on the south end of the rink. The puck left a trail of water as it skittered along the ice.

"It was the same conditions for both teams," Pens forward Max Talbot said, refusing to make excuses.

While the Penguins struggled to mount an attack, Fehr put the game out of reach at 11:59 with his second goal of the night. Washington survived a last-minute onslaught to prevail 3–1.

"It's frustrating," said Fleury, who made 29 saves in a losing cause. "There was so much buildup to the game. It's definitely disappointing to lose that one."

41 The Century Line

Throughout hockey history there have been many storied line combinations. The powerhouse Red Wings of the early 1950s boasted the "Production Line" of Gordie Howe, Sid Abel, and Ted Lindsay. Later in the decade Montreal rode the stellar play of "Rocket" Richard and his "Punch Line" mates to Stanley Cup glory.

Unlike their famous counterparts, the Penguins' first great line came together almost by accident. Each member was a cast-off from another team. Yet together they became one of the most dynamic combinations in team history.

The first to join the fold was right wing Jean Pronovost. The kid brother of Hall of Fame defenseman Marcel Pronovost, Jean was originally signed by the Boston Bruins. Following a strong season with the Oklahoma City Blazers in 1967–68, the Penguins acquired the 23-year-old from the talent-rich Bruins. Blessed with good speed and sure hands, Prony was named the Pens' Rookie of the Year in 1968–69.

Next on the scene was an oft-injured port-sider named Lowell MacDonald. Selected by Los Angeles in the 1967 Expansion Draft, he notched 21 goals for the Kings in 1967–68. However, a succession of knee injuries, coupled with a fear of flying, threatened to derail his career. MacDonald was on the scrap heap when the Penguins plucked him from the Kings in the 1970 Intra-League Draft.

The third and final piece of the puzzle arrived in a trade with the New York Rangers on January 26, 1971, in the form of center Syl Apps. Although he bore the same name as his legendary father, a Hall of Famer with Toronto in the 1930s and '40s, there was little to suggest that Apps was a star in the making. In half a season with the Rangers he had tallied one measly goal.

From the moment they were united by coach Ken Schinkel the trio made sweet music. Initially dubbed the "MAP Line"—a play on the first letters of their last names—they displayed an instinctive feel for each other.

"Syl and Prony and I just clicked," MacDonald said. "We roamed all over the place. It was more dangerous running into Prony and Apps than it was those guys like [Dave] Schultz on the Flyers. But we had a chemistry where we just knew where the other guys were going to be."

Taking full advantage of the Civic Arena's 207-by-92-foot ice surface, they employed the weaving, up-tempo style popularized by the Europeans.

"Lowell and I couldn't shoot the puck any more than 15 feet; that's why we did a lot of passing," Apps told Joe Starkey in *Tales from the Pittsburgh Penguins*. "Plus, Lowell couldn't see that far. I think he had a worse shot than I did, but, boy, could he pick his spot. We were a little bit of a throwback in that we didn't dump the puck and we used a lot of drop passes."

After the line piled up more than 100 goals during the 1973–74 campaign, team publicist Terry Schiffhauer came up with a bold new nickname—"the Century Line."

For the next two years the trio ranked among the most lethal combinations in the league. After tallying an impressive 94 goals in 1974–75, including a team-best 43 by Pronovost, the unit exploded for 114 goals in 1975–76. Pronovost (52 goals) and Apps (99 points) finished among the league's top 10 scorers, while MacDonald potted 30 goals.

"When Prony got his 50th goal, that was kind of special," Apps said. "When someone gets 50 goals, that's a product of a line. We were very proud of that moment. It was his goal but we shared in it. That was special."

Sadly, a knee injury to the classy MacDonald signaled the end of the Century Line. Apps was traded to Los Angeles in November of 1977, departing as the team's all-time assist leader. Pronovost soldiered on in 1977–78 to lead the Pens in goals (40) and points (65). Seeking a fresh start, he requested a trade the following summer and was dealt to Atlanta. Pronovost finished his Penguins career as the team's all-time leader in goals and points.

42 Lucky Pierre

Even as a fresh-faced kid straight from the junior ranks, Pierre Larouche didn't lack for confidence. When the storied Montreal Canadiens promised to make the Sorel scoring sensation a first-round pick in the 1974 Amateur Draft, Larouche told them not to bother.

"If you draft me, you'll send me right to the minor leagues," he said. "I'm good enough to play in the NHL now. If you draft me, I'll sign with the World Hockey Association."

Rebuffed, the Canadiens passed on Larouche. Penguins general manager Jack Button promptly snatched up the cocky youngster with the eighth overall pick.

"We had a lot of good steady hockey players, the guys you needed to win," Button said. "What we still didn't have was a player who would get the fans out of their seats."

Button was convinced Larouche could be "the guy." However, he wasn't sure if the 19-year-old was ready for the rigors of NHL competition.

Any lingering doubts were quickly erased during training camp. Placed on a line between rugged Bob "Battleship" Kelly and

Precocious

Upon his arrival in Pittsburgh in 1974, Pierre Larouche wasn't the least bit awed by his surroundings. In an era when rookies were seen and not heard, the brash youngster surprised onlookers by routinely trading barbs with his veteran teammates.

The tone was set when Pierre beat Vic Hadfield, an off-season golf pro, during the team's training camp golf tournament.

"Vic said I cheated, that I moved the ball with my foot in the rough," Larouche said. "So we played again, and I beat him again. He had another excuse that time but I forget what it was."

The teasing escalated during the regular season. One day Pierre's linemate, Bob "Battleship" Kelly, invited him to join the boys at the Jamestown Inn for post-practice drinks. When the waiter arrived at the table with a round of beers, Kelly warned him not to serve the teenager. Bob Paradise complained that the Penguins didn't practice until 2:00 PM because "Pierre doesn't get out of school until 1:30."

Larouche gave as good as he got. In response to some good-natured needling by Hadfield, Pierre shot back, "When I was a little kid, Vic, I used to watch you on television."

hard-shooting Chuck Arnason, the hotshot rookie immediately made his mark. Larouche enjoyed a terrific season in 1974–75, tallying 31 goals, 37 assists, and 68 points—all club records for a first-year player.

Larouche finished a close second to Atlanta's Eric Vail in the race for the Calder Trophy. Pierre left little doubt about who the real superstar was during his sophomore season. At the callow age of 20, he exploded for a remarkable 53 goals and 58 assists to place fifth in the NHL scoring race.

By the 1976–77 season the crafty young center had clearly emerged as the face of the franchise. However, some of his veteran teammates resented his brashness and penchant for self promotion.

"He wasn't quite in the same mold as everyone else," Syl Apps said. "No one else had the same sort of elite junior career he had in

Canada. He came in saying, 'I'm here.' Some people liked him for it, some people didn't."

With top scorers Vic Hadfield and Lowell MacDonald shelved due to injuries, coach Ken Schinkel was determined to tighten the reins. Never a bastion of back checking or self-discipline, Larouche chafed under the new restrictions.

"If you're on offense all the time, there's no way you can get in trouble on defense," he quipped.

Following a 7–1 victory over Los Angeles on November 2, Larouche arrived 45 minutes late to practice the next morning, drawing the ire of the normally easygoing Schinkel. After initially attempting to send him to Hershey—a move that Larouche promptly vetoed—general manager Baz Bastien suspended his prodigy for five days.

"A kid like that has to realize he's not bigger than the team," Bastien grumbled.

A penitent Pierre seemed to take the forced absence to heart.

"The suspension gave me a good time to think about things, he said. "I realized I was thinking too much about me and not enough about the rest of the guys."

After sitting out two games Larouche returned to the lineup. By season's end, however, Lucky Pierre's output had slipped below his rookie totals.

His attitude continued to deteriorate in 1977–78 along with his play. At wits' end, Bastien traded Pierre to Montreal on November 29 for a soon-to-be-over-the-hill Pete Mahovlich and green prospect Peter Lee.

"He just got around the wrong crowd," teammate Rick Kehoe said. "He got sidetracked, which is easy to do when you're young. The best thing that happened to him was to get traded to Montreal. He went there and scored 50 goals and he went to Hartford and then New York with the Rangers, and he nearly had 50 goals there.

Pierre Larouche topped 50 goals and 100 points in 1975–76, becoming the youngest player to do so at that time in NHL history.

He almost became the first player to score 50 goals for three teams in the National Hockey League."

Years later, a more mature Larouche mended fences with his old team. A close friend and confidant of Mario Lemieux, he's a fixture in the owner's box at the CONSOL Energy Center during Penguins games.

"One thing about Pittsburgh," Larouche said. "From the crew at the rink to the people on the street, I was treated No. 1."

Visit the Civic Arena

The Civic Arena sits across Centre Avenue from the newer CONSOL Energy Center, perched on a 95-acre tract of land like a crown jewel. The unique stainless steel dome, once the largest in the world, still glistens. However, after playing host to some 1,667 regular season Penguins games and another 135 postseason contests, it sits empty and idle, silently awaiting its fate.

The multipurpose venue was originally designed for a more refined form of entertainment. In 1944 department store magnate Edgar J. Kaufmann Sr. and councilman Abraham Wolk proposed an idea for a new memorial amphitheater to serve as a home for the city's most popular cultural diversion, the Civic Light Opera.

"What will you do if it rains?" a reporter asked Wolk.

"I had to think fast," Wolk recalled in an interview with the *Pittsburgh Press* in 1961. "I just put my arms over my head, moved around a little, and said that we are going to have a moveable roof."

It would take 17 years, countless redesigns, and a massive urban redevelopment program for Kaufmann and Wolk's vision to come to life. It was worth the wait. Completed in the summer of 1961 at a cost of $21.7 million, the new space-age arena featured a retractable stainless steel dome, 417 feet in diameter and 109 feet tall. The dome gave the building its signature appearance and led to its enduring nickname—the Igloo.

Initially dubbed the Civic Auditorium, the name was changed to the Civic Arena because it was easier to fit on signs. The new facility officially opened its doors on September 19, 1961, when it played host to the Ice Capades. Hockey made its debut a month later when the Pittsburgh Hornets took on the Buffalo Bisons.

"It was a beautiful rink," said future Penguins goalie Les Binkley, "because most of the American League arenas were smaller attendance wise. It was always bright, and you could see."

No fewer than 13 professional sports teams—including the Penguins—eventually graced the Civic Arena's playing surface. The Dapper Dan Roundball Classic, America's first high school all-star game, was held annually at the Arena from 1965 through 1992. The World Figure Skating Championships took center stage in 1983. On January 21, 1990, the Igloo hosted the 41st NHL All-Star Game. In 1991, 1992, 2008, and 2009 Penguins fans were treated to Stanley Cup Finals action.

While sports were undeniably the building's lifeblood, it also became a popular venue for performers and recording artists. The CLO called the Arena home until it moved into newly refurbished Heinz Hall in 1969. Top acts such as The Beatles, Bruce Springsteen, and Elvis Presley played before packed houses. A major motion picture, *Sudden Death*, was filmed at the Arena during the 1994–95 lockout season.

Driven by the demand for more seats, the Civic Arena underwent three major expansions during its lifetime. When the Penguins joined the National Hockey League in 1967, new sections were added to increase the capacity from 10,732 to 12,580. During the summer of 1975, E-level "end zone" balconies were constructed at the north and south ends, increasing capacity to 16,402. In 1993,

F-level balconies, luxury skyboxes, and privately catered club seats swelled the capacity by an additional 1,000 seats.

Despite its cramped quarters and lack of amenities, the Mellon Arena (renamed in 1999) was surprisingly popular among the players. Penguins captain Sidney Crosby was a big fan.

"Everything is pretty close," he said. "I know with a lot of newer buildings there's a restriction on the grade of the rink and the level of the stands. This one has that old feel to it where it's straight up and everyone's right on top of you. And when you score, you feel like you're in the middle of everyone. It's a great atmosphere in here."

After hosting its final Penguins game on May 12, 2010, the Igloo reassumed the name Civic Arena. Two months later it returned to its entertainment roots for a concert featuring James Taylor and Carole King. In a touching sendoff, the 1970s icons closed the show with the song, "You Can Close Your Eyes."

44 Toc

Given his rugged style of play, one would think Scarborough, Ontario, native Rick Tocchet grew up idolizing a power forward like Toronto's bruising Dan Maloney. Not true.

"I used to love Guy Lafleur," he confessed. "I can't play like him, he's incredible. He was a very dynamic guy. He could take the puck on his own, go down the wing, and score. I used to love watching him play."

Indeed, Tocchet's confrontational style was the polar opposite of Lafleur's. Upon joining the Flyers in 1984 he carved out a reputation as a mean, relentless fighter in the true Broad Street Bullies

Spinner

Years before Rick Tocchet wore the black and gold, another rugged player donned No. 22 for the Penguins.

Brian "Spinner" Spencer was a rambunctious winger who skated for the Pens in the late 1970s. Possessing modest ability but an enormous reservoir of energy and spunk, the whirling dervish charged around the ice and bounced into opponents like a crazed pinball.

Blessed with a muscular physique and a wild shock of sandy-brown hair, Spencer looked like a character straight from a Tarzan movie. He played the part off the ice as well. During the summer of 1978, he built a vehicle from the shell of an army convoy truck that resembled nothing seen on the road before or since. A teammate dubbed his creation "the Incredible Hulk."

Sadly, tragedy would stalk the colorful winger throughout his life. Early in his rookie season with Toronto in December of 1970, his father, Roy, died in a terribly unfortunate incident. Incensed when a CBC TV station chose not to televise his son's game, the elder Spencer drove two hours from Fort St. James and at gunpoint forced the station to broadcast the Leafs' game. He was killed in a subsequent shootout with the Royal Canadian Mounted Police.

Remarkably, Brian suited up the following evening for a game against Buffalo. "My father would have wanted me to play," he told Leafs captain Dave Keon. By all accounts, the 21-year-old rookie played an inspired game.

Years later Spencer would meet a similar tragic and untimely end. Following a drug deal on June 3, 1988, in Riviera Beach, Florida, he and a friend were victims of a stickup. Spencer was shot to death during the robbery attempt. He was just 38 years old.

"He gave everything of himself," said his twin brother, Byron. "That's the way he was. He loved life. He loved people. Maybe he was a little too outgoing."

tradition. Yet Tocchet also was a diamond in the rough. Possessing enormous drive and character, he willed himself to become one of the game's premier power forwards.

After scoring 153 goals over a four-year span, Tocchet found himself on the trading block. On February 19, 1992, the Penguins acquired the bristling 27-year-old winger in a blockbuster three-team deal.

"I was ecstatic," he said. "I was going to be playing with some of the greatest players in the world: Mario Lemieux, Kevin Stevens, Jaromir Jagr, Ronnie Francis, and Ulf Samuelsson. It was an unbelievable list and I was going to be with these guys."

"He said all he wanted was a chance to win," said good friend Paul Coffey. "He'll have that in Pittsburgh. He's a good player who won't disappoint anyone in this city. He has the heart the size of a building. He'll do what it takes to win."

Tocchet immediately put that heart on display. During a March 15 showdown with the Blackhawks he was struck on the jaw by an errant shot. After leaving the ice for repairs, he gamely returned in the third period sporting a makeshift face shield. With blood stains spattered on the front of his uniform, he scored two huge goals to ignite a Penguins rally. Afterward it was revealed that Tocchet had played with a fractured jaw.

"We were .500 at the time, you want to play, and you want to try to win," he said. "It's amazing when you have adrenaline. The next day I was obviously in pain, but during the game you just don't think about it."

From that moment on Tocchet became a treasured member of the team. Not coincidentally, the Pens began to resemble Stanley Cup champions again. Along the way there were many more examples of his legendary toughness, including fights with Kris King and Kevin Hatcher while his broken jaw was still on the mend, and an early return from a separated shoulder during the Patrick Division Finals when the club desperately needed his fire and physical presence. Tocchet contributed mightily on the score sheet as well, tallying six goals and 19 points in just 14 playoff games.

"Rick delivered when we needed it most," coach Scotty Bowman said. "He's versatile enough to beat you in a lot of ways: with his shot, with his savvy, and with his body."

The tough winger was never better than during the record-breaking 1992–93 campaign. He racked up 48 goals and 109 points along with a team-leading 252 penalty minutes. During a crucial late-season showdown against Montreal when the Pens were on the verge of tying the Islanders' record 15-game winning streak, he scored a hat trick to key a huge victory.

Extremely popular with teammates and fans, it appeared that Tocchet would have a long and eventful stay in Pittsburgh. Sadly it was not to be. Following an injury-plagued season in 1993–94, he was traded to Los Angeles for All-Star sniper Luc Robitaille.

The old warrior has fond memories of his time in the Steel City. Winning the Stanley Cup tops the list.

"It was the greatest thing that ever happened to me," he told Stan Fischler in an interview for *Hockey Player Magazine*. "I was on top of the world for a few days, not just one. We became the focal point of the whole city, especially when they had the parade. I'll always look at my Stanley Cup ring and remember those three or four days as something to cherish."

 **Ray**

After serving a 13-year apprenticeship as an assistant general manager for Ottawa and Nashville, Ray Shero was hired by the Penguins on May 25, 2006, to replace Hall of Fame GM Craig Patrick. Regarded as one of the brightest young executives in hockey, the son of former Flyers coach Fred Shero had his work cut out for him.

"I still have all my notes from the summer when I first got here," Shero said. "I was like, 'Holy cow, there were a lot of holes.'

You had Crosby, you had Malkin coming, you had Ryan Whitney on defense, and Marc-Andre Fleury."

Shero immediately began to fill in the missing pieces. He inked veteran free agents Mark Eaton, Mark Recchi, and abrasive Jarkko Ruutu to deals. Blessed with a keen eye for talent, he plucked 18-year-old center Jordan Staal from Peterborough in the Entry Draft. The Penguins responded with a stunning 47-point leap to grab their first playoff berth since 2001.

Never one to rest on his laurels, Shero continued to improve the club in 2007–08. With the team humming toward another 100-point season, he pulled off the biggest deal at the trade deadline, acquiring All-Star winger Marian Hossa and Pascal Dupuis from Atlanta for Erik Christensen and popular Colby Armstrong. The Pens made it all the way to the Stanley Cup Finals before bowing to Detroit in six games.

Shero would soon face his stiffest test. A host of key players, including Hossa and rising stars Ryan Malone and Brooks Orpik, were eligible for free agency. In addition, new deals needed to be negotiated for Malkin, Fleury, and Staal.

A consummate professional, Shero navigated the negotiating minefield with skill and poise. Focusing his attention of the team's young core, he signed Fleury, Malkin, Orpik, and Staal to long-term deals. When Hossa, the biggest fish of all, wriggled off the hook, Shero plugged the dike with experienced free agents Ruslan Fedotenko and Miroslav Satan.

After a decent start to the 2008–09 campaign the Penguins hit the skids. With the team slipping from playoff contention, Shero moved boldly. He replaced established coach Michel Therrien with Dan Bylsma and acquired scoring wingers Bill Guerin and Chris Kunitz. Rejuvenated, the Pens tore through the homestretch at an 18–3–4 clip to qualify for postseason play. In the playoffs they beat back the challenge of the defending champion Red Wings to capture the Stanley Cup.

On the Button

If one were to compile a list of the Penguins' most underrated executives, Jack Button's name would appear at the top. His term as general manager was brief—barely a season and a half. During that time he presided over the team's first winning season while posting a .543 winning percentage, second only to Ray Shero in franchise history.

When the 34-year-old Button was promoted to the post of general manager in January of 1974, he was faced with a daunting task.

"We were hardly an entertaining team," the new GM recalled. "We had Dave Burrows on defense and the line of Syl Apps, Jean Pronovost, and Lowell MacDonald. That was all."

A timid, underachieving bunch, the Penguins were badly in need of a shakeup. Button saw that they got it. During his first week on the job he made two huge trades. On January 17, he sent mainstays Greg Polis and Bryan Watson to St. Louis for tough guys Steve Durbano, Bob "Battleship" Kelly, and puck-moving defenseman Ab DeMarco. Later that day Button shipped starting goalie Jim Rutherford and Jack Lynch to Detroit for giant defenseman Ron Stackhouse. In one fell swoop he transformed the Pens from not-so-lovable losers into a lively, aggressive team.

Button's finest trades were yet to come. The following summer he acquired former 50-goal man Vic Hadfield from the Rangers for journeyman defender Nick Beverley. Next he pried promising young winger Rick Kehoe loose from Toronto. He added a third scorer— junior hockey sensation Pierre Larouche—in the Amateur Draft.

The Penguins responded with the finest season in their brief history. With newcomers Hadfield, Kehoe, and Larouche each topping the 30-goal mark, they posted a 37–28–15 record in 1974–75 to earn a berth in the Stanley Cup playoffs. However, a disastrous loss to the Islanders in the quarterfinals undermined the team's fragile finances and sent owner Tad Potter and his partners reeling into receivership.

The club was purchased over the summer by a group that included Wren Blair, the former general manager of the Minnesota North Stars. He clearly intended to run the team.

"It was obvious from the start that if Blair's group got the Penguins, there would be no room for me," Button said.

He would not be unemployed for long. Impressed by his work in the Steel City, the NHL immediately hired Button to serve as the first director of the newly formed Central Scouting service. He went on to enjoy a distinguished career as a scout and director of player personnel for the Washington Capitals before succumbing to leukemia on August 1, 1996.

Although the Pens failed to win a second straight Cup in 2009–10, they enjoyed another strong season. As a reward for his fine work, Shero received a five-year contract extension on September 20, 2010.

"This was an easy decision," said co-owners Mario Lemieux and Ron Burkle in a joint statement. "Ray has done a tremendous job with our hockey operation—not only leading us to the Stanley Cup in 2009 but also building a team that can continue to compete for the Cup year after year."

Buoyed by free-agent acquisitions Paul Martin and Zbynek Michalek, the Penguins once again were poised to make a run at the Stanley Cup in 2010–11. Following a strong first half, however, the team was decimated by injuries to superstars Sidney Crosby and Evgeni Malkin.

Thanks in no small part to the character-laden lineup assembled by Shero, the undermanned Penguins kept on plugging. Meanwhile, the 48-year-old GM coolly waited for an opportunity to make a "hockey trade" that would benefit the team for the present as well as the future. On February 21, 2011, he acquired promising young power forward James Neal and defenseman Matt Niskanen from Dallas for rearguard Alex Goligoski.

Three days later he sent a conditional pick to Ottawa for former Penguins sniper Alexei Kovalev.

Ignited by the trades, the Penguins finished the season with 106 points—the second-highest total in franchise history. Although Shero was quick to deflect praise to the players and coaching staff, he had done a superb job of reinforcing his team.

"Maybe the best thing Shero did was continue to believe in a team that many thought couldn't be competitive in the playoffs without Crosby and Malkin," wrote Ron Cook of the *Pittsburgh Post-Gazette*.

46 Making a Point

The 1989–90 campaign won't go down in Penguins lore as one of the team's banner years. Indeed, the club seemed to operate under the influence of an evil spell as it lurched through a season marred by turmoil and strife.

Likewise, it was not an especially good year for the team's reigning superstar, Mario Lemieux. Following on the heels of a pair of monster seasons, Lemieux suffered a herniated disc and lost his two-year grip on the Art Ross Trophy. Yet Mario would accomplish a feat topped only by his closest rival, Wayne Gretzky.

On October 31, 1989, No. 66 picked up a pair of assists during a lopsided 8–4 loss to Gretzky's Los Angeles Kings. Although no one realized it at the time, it was the start of a point-scoring streak that would reach epic proportions.

Off to a sluggish start by his lofty standards, the big center began to produce at a remarkably consistent pace. Over an eight-day stretch in late November, Mario registered three points in four straight games. On January 4, 1990, he ran his streak to 29 games, breaking his own club record.

Lemieux was in rare company. Only Gretzky had ever scored points in at least 30 straight games, a feat he'd accomplished three times. Mario pushed his streak to third-best all time on January 8, thanks to a four-goal eruption versus the Rangers. On February 2, Lemieux's run reached 40 consecutive games with a four-point effort against Gretzky's old team, the Oilers.

Now possessing the second-longest streak in NHL history, Mario took dead aim at the Great One's mark of 51 games. He notched a goal against the Flyers on February 11 to run his streak to 46 games. It seemed nothing could stop Super Mario from claiming the record—nothing except the throbbing lower back pain he'd been experiencing for two months. On Valentine's Day, the pain became too great and the Pens' captain was forced to remove himself from a contest with the Rangers after 40 minutes.

"The buzzer sounded and Mario Lemieux understood in his heart that more than the second period had ended," Joe Sexton wrote in *The New York Times*. "He pulled himself one more time to his feet and walked gingerly down the hallway underneath Madison Square Garden, slipping into the locker room and onto a training table."

Although Lemieux's quest was halted five games shy of the record, nothing could detract from the luster of his heroic achievement. Playing at considerably less than 100 percent, Mario piled up an eye-popping 103 points over the course of his 46-game streak. Perhaps more remarkably, he tallied at least one point in 55 of the 59 games he played that season.

Lemieux enjoyed two other noteworthy streaks during his Hall of Fame career. A month removed from treatments for Hodgkin's disease, he scored 51 points over a 16-game stretch in the spring of 1993. After sitting out an entire season, he returned with a vengeance to score in 28 straight games to start the 1995–96 campaign, a streak that isn't officially recognized by the NHL because Mario sat out four games during the stretch.

It would take a second-generation Penguins superstar to match the excitement of Mario's magnificent accomplishment. On November 5, 2010, Sidney Crosby notched a pair of goals in a losing effort against Anaheim. It was the start of a 25-game point-scoring streak, the longest in the NHL since Mats Sundin reached 30 games nearly two decades earlier, and the 11th-longest in league history.

During his red-hot roll, 23-year-old Sid struck for 26 goals and 50 points, including a pair of four-point games and two hat tricks. Not coincidentally, the Penguins reeled off a 12-game winning streak during Crosby's incredible run.

One observer was clearly impressed with Sid's exploits.

"He's an incredible player, an incredible person, and what he just did for those 25 games, all those points, that's pretty hard to do in this day and age," Lemieux said. "It's not the same as 20 years ago with the good goalies and defensive schemes that are there now."

47 Slippery Rock Joe

As goal scorers go, Joe Mullen wasn't especially pretty to watch. He didn't fly down the wing with the grace and élan of a Guy Lafleur, firing tracer bullets past terrified goalies. On the contrary, he scored most of his goals while twisting and driving through traffic, often releasing the puck from awkward angles as he was tumbling to the ice. But my, was he effective.

Following a distinguished collegiate career with Boston College, Mullen signed as a free agent with St. Louis. Initially there were concerns about his small stature and his skating. He had a choppy stride, a by-product of his roller hockey days on the streets of Manhattan. But Mullen possessed great balance and surprising strength, along with a nose for the net. After tearing up the Central League for two and a half seasons, he was called up by the Blues in 1981.

Mullen immediately established himself as a big-time scorer. In 1983–84 he banged home 41 goals, the first of six consecutive 40-plus goal seasons. However, on February 1, 1986, the Blues sent him to Calgary as part of a big six-player deal.

Skating for former Team USA coach Bob Johnson, Mullen flourished with the Flames. He enjoyed a career year in 1988–89, tallying 51 goals and registering a league-high plus-51 while leading the Flames to a Stanley Cup.

When Johnson took over the coaching reins in Pittsburgh in the summer of 1990, he prodded general manager Craig Patrick to inquire about Mullen. Much to Patrick's surprise and delight, the Flames were willing to part with the high-scoring winger for a second-round draft choice.

"Craig Patrick was the one who made the trade and I knew Craig," Mullen explained. "I knew if I was going with Craig Patrick, it would be good. I could see what he was doing. He traded for [Bryan] Trottier right before. He signed Bob Johnson that summer. That all happened before I got traded. When I heard I was traded, I was pretty happy."

With Mullen and Trottier on hand to provide veteran leadership, the Penguins suddenly had the look of a contender. After a solid first half, however, Joe underwent surgery to remove a herniated disc from his neck.

Many feared it was the end of the line for the 33-year-old winger. Displaying his trademark bulldog tenacity, Mullen beat the odds. He returned to action in the playoffs wearing a neck collar for protection and scored eight goals, including two in Game 6 of the Finals to help spark the Penguins to their first Stanley Cup.

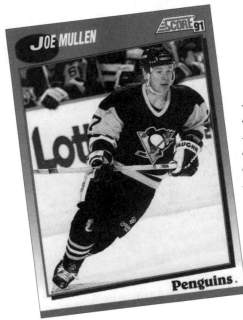

Acquired from Calgary for a second-round pick, Joe Mullen scored 153 goals and won two Stanley Cups during his six years in Pittsburgh.

"Going into that third period, I think we were up 6–0 at the time," Joe recalled. "Just watching that clock tick away, it took forever. As soon as the buzzer went, it was nice to see everybody celebrating. All those feelings from winning the first Cup in Calgary came rushing back. It was just great to win it again."

He was at his best during the adversity-strewn 1991–92 campaign. Seeing regular ice time alongside the great Mario Lemieux, he erupted for back-to-back four-goal games in late December. The hardworking winger finished the season with 42 goals, third-best on a talent-laden team.

Unfortunately, Mullen suffered another severe injury. In Game 2 of the Patrick Division Semifinals he absorbed a crushing hit from Rangers tough guy Kris King, resulting in torn knee ligaments. A week later he grudgingly submitted to season-ending surgery.

Again, there were doubts about whether Mullen could bounce back. Again, the gritty winger defied the odds, returning to score 33 goals in 1992–93 and 38 the next year to earn a spot on the Eastern Conference All-Star Team.

Following the lockout season of 1994–95, Mullen signed a one-year deal with Boston. Age finally seemed to creep up on the veteran winger as he tumbled to his lowest output as a pro.

At 39 years of age, it appeared he had finally reached the end of the line. But the Penguins missed his reliable two-way play and his penchant for scoring clutch goals. Returning to the Steel City for one last hurrah, the man Mike Lange dubbed "Slippery Rock Joe" potted his 500th career goal on March 14, 1997.

48 Dee-fense

During the 1970s, the Pittsburgh Steelers built a dynasty around their fabled Steel Curtain defense. Indeed, the chant of "Dee-fense" became a familiar chorus among the faithful at Three Rivers Stadium.

Fast-forward to the spring of 1992. Fresh off a Stanley Cup triumph the previous year, the Penguins were hoping to build a dynasty of their own. Unlike their football brethren, the Pens preferred a more offensive approach. Boasting elite scorers such as Art Ross Trophy winner Mario Lemieux, power forward Kevin Stevens, and 40-goal man Joe Mullen, the Pens overwhelmed the opposition with a full-throttle attack.

However, their first round opponent—the Washington Capitals—was proving to be a most formidable foe. Traditionally a defensive-oriented team that employed a clutch-and-grab style, the Capitals had evolved into an offensive power thanks to the big-time scoring of feisty Dino Ciccarelli and dynamic Peter Bondra.

Paced by Bondra, Ciccarelli, and offensive defensemen Kevin Hatcher and Al Iafrate, the Caps dominated the Pens through the early going. Worse yet, they were beating the defending champs at their own game. Following a dismal 7–2 loss at the Civic Arena in Game 4, the Penguins wisely changed tactics.

"Mario came to me the morning of the fifth game and said, 'Why don't we surprise them and play the game close to the vest. Tight, tight, tight,'" Pens coach Scotty Bowman recalled. "I'd never pushed a lot of defensive hockey on this team, but since it was Mario who suggested it…."

Lemieux and Ron Francis cooked up a scheme called the one-four delay. Bowman noted it was remarkably similar to a system legendary Montreal coach Toe Blake had devised for him some 30 years earlier.

Under the one-four delay, a lone forechecker would harass the puck carrier while the rest of the team waited to disrupt the Washington attack in the neutral zone. Ideally, this would frustrate the Capitals, who by this time believed that they could score at will, while opening up some chances on the counterattack.

"We knew if we could play that type of game and wait for our chances, we had the better team and we knew we could win," Mario said.

The defense-first strategy worked like a charm. The Pens surprised the overconfident Capitals by taking Games 5 and 6. However, another victory was needed to complete the comeback.

Washington coach Terry Murray had resisted the urge to make changes. However, with the series on the line he made a concerted effort to keep Ciccarelli away from Bob Errey, who had checked the scrappy winger to a standstill. In response to the way the Penguins were standing his team up at the blue line, Murray instructed the Capitals to play a more conservative dump-and-chase game.

The teams started slowly, like a pair of prizefighters probing for a weakness. The Caps got the first power-play opportunity midway through the first period, but their best chance missed by a fraction of an inch when Mike Ridley rang a shot off a goalpost. The puck ricocheted out to Larry Murphy, who sent Francis and Lemieux scurrying away on a two-on-one break.

Using Mario as a decoy, Francis carried the puck down the middle of the ice and drove a hard slap shot at Don Beaupre. The acrobatic goalie made the save, but he kicked the rubber right to Lemieux, who rifled it home.

Although the Capitals rallied to tie the score, the Penguins never wavered. Jaromir Jagr struck for a power-play goal and Mullen zipped in an empty netter to complete the improbable comeback.

"Washington never changed styles, they never adapted to what we were doing," Pens goaltender Tom Barrasso said. "It got to the point where they were really frustrated. They were always caught in-between and we were turning their defensemen on three-on-twos and two-on-ones."

EJ

During his 25 years of service with the Penguins, Eddie Johnston established himself as one of the team's most popular and beloved figures. Although his accomplishments are often overlooked, he remains far and away the winningest coach in franchise history with 232 victories to his credit.

"People ask me about Eddie Johnston," said his longtime assistant Rick Kehoe. "The best way to describe EJ is that he's in the middle of Scotty Bowman and Badger Bob Johnson. He's always talking hockey. We're coming off the ice together after a game and he's still talking hockey."

Following a long and distinguished NHL career, Johnston stepped behind the bench in 1979–80 and guided Chicago to the Smythe Division title. He was let go, however, following a dispute with Black Hawks GM Bob Pulford.

Numer Soixante-Six

Eddie Johnston will forever hold a special place in the hearts of Penguin fans for drafting Mario Lemieux. It took an enormous amount of perseverance, not to mention a bit of skullduggery, for the first-year general manager to ensure the Penguins would be in a position to draft the Laval phenom.

While the Pens didn't exactly tank games—at least by nobody's admission—Johnston made sure they didn't stray too far from the prescribed course. When promising young goalie Roberto Romano had the temerity to win consecutive games, he was sent to the minors in favor of Vincent Tremblay.

"We want to see what [Tremblay] can do," Johnston said.

Four games and 24 goals against later he had his answer, not to mention the top pick in the 1984 Entry Draft.

Other clubs did their best to pry the coveted pick from Johnston's grasp by wooing him with jaw-dropping packages of draft picks and veterans. Minnesota offered every pick they had in the draft. Montreal also made a big push.

Perhaps the most astounding proposal came from the Quebec Nordiques, who reportedly offered their all-star forward line of Peter, Anton, and Marian Stastny for the chance to draft Lemieux.

The Penguins' GM never wavered. On June 9, 1984, Lemieux became a Penguin.

"There was no way I was going to trade [the pick]," EJ told Ron Cook of the *Pittsburgh Post-Gazette*. "We were getting a guy who comes along once in a lifetime. Mellon Arena would be a parking lot now if not for Mario. There would be no hockey in Pittsburgh."

In the market for a bright young coach, the Penguins immediately hired Johnston. It was the start of a long and memorable relationship between EJ and the organization.

Although the Pens of the early 1980s were a less-than-imposing bunch, EJ kept the team competitive during his first go-around as coach. The key to the club's modest success was the power play. Using the basketball pick play, the Pens struck for a whopping 272 power-play goals over a three-year span.

"When I was with the Bruins, I'd have a few beers with [Celtics coach] Tommy Heinsohn at an oyster bar on the north shore, and we'd get to talking about 'picks' and how to set and use them," EJ said. "You can pick up a lot of things from basketball, how to screen for a guy to shoot, and so forth."

Following Baz Bastien's untimely death in 1983, Johnston assumed the role of general manager. In his first season on the job he earned lasting fame—and a permanent place in the hearts of Steel City fans—by ensuring the Pens would be in a position to draft Mario Lemieux.

"Drafting Mario; we wouldn't have a franchise here if we'd taken somebody else," he said.

EJ did a solid job during his five years as the team's GM. He drafted brilliantly, adding promising young players Doug Bodger, Craig Simpson, and Zarley Zalapski to the fold. In November of 1987, Johnston worked his magic a second time, acquiring Norris Trophy winner Paul Coffey in a blockbuster seven-player trade with Edmonton. Thanks to EJ, the building blocks for a future Stanley Cup champion were in place.

Unfortunately, he would not share in the triumph. After being demoted to assistant general manager, he left Pittsburgh in 1989 to take over as the Hartford Whalers' general manager. While serving with the Whalers, Johnston unintentionally provided the Penguins with the final pieces to their Stanley Cup puzzle by sending Ron

Francis and Ulf Samuelsson to the Steel City for John Cullen and Zarley Zalapski.

"That was such a great trade for the Penguins that they probably should've given me a small ring or something," he chuckled.

The Penguins went one better. In the summer of 1993 they brought Johnston back as a replacement for Scotty Bowman. Finally given a chance to coach a competitive club, the affable skipper led the Pens to a .600 winning percentage over three-plus seasons and a berth in the 1996 Eastern Conference Finals.

After being bumped upstairs to the post of assistant general manager in March of 1997, Johnston continued to serve the team in a variety of capacities. In 1999 he stepped behind the bench one last time as an assistant to coach Herb Brooks. Following the season he returned to the front office as a special advisor, a post he held through the team's Stanley Cup triumph in 2009.

The sight of the grandfatherly Johnston hoisting the Cup was truly one of the most heartwarming moments in team history. It also provided a perfect ending to a career that spanned more than 50 years.

"What a way for me to go out," he said. "It's time. They have such a great hockey staff in place now."

50 The Original Penguin

After watching Penguins goalie Les Binkley shut down the Flyers with a typically strong performance, Hugh Brown of the *Philadelphia Evening Bulletin* made an astute observation.

"Binkley looks somewhat like he sounds, meaning he could pass for a near-sighted, narrow-chested bird watcher," Brown wrote.

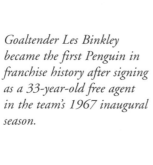

Goaltender Les Binkley became the first Penguin in franchise history after signing as a 33-year-old free agent in the team's 1967 inaugural season.

Binkley was, indeed, near-sighted, and narrow-chested to boot. Instead of watching birds flutter about in the summer breeze, however, the maskless goalie earned his keep by tracking down 100 miles-per-hour slap shots.

Back in the pre-expansion days of the Original Six, Binkley toiled in the minor leagues for 12 long seasons, stopping pucks in remote hockey outposts such as Charlotte, Toledo, and Ft. Wayne. It was a trial that would've discouraged a lesser man. But Binkley never gave up on his dream.

"I always hoped I would make it [to the NHL] someday," he said.

Binkley got his first big break in 1960. Cleveland Barons general manager Jim Heady offered him a job as a spare goalie and *trainer*. Although Bink knew nothing about training, the Barons played in the American Hockey League, the top minor pro circuit.

"I thought I might get a chance that way," Binkley said. "They couldn't afford two goalies."

The following year he took over as the team's starting goaltender. Over the next five seasons, he established himself as one of the premier puck stoppers in the AHL, earning All-Star honors while capturing the Dudley "Red" Garrett Memorial Award (rookie of the year) and the Harry "Hap" Holmes Memorial Award (top goalie).

Still, a call up to the big show never came.

"There were only six goalies' jobs in the National Hockey League, and you couldn't get them out of the nets," he said. "They were in there every night. Now those goalies are all in the Hockey Hall of Fame."

In addition to the stiff competition, Binkley had another strike against him. Due to his less-than-perfect vision, he wore contact lenses when he played.

"The contact lenses, that's what kept me back," he recalled. "[The managers] knew I had good reflexes, but they were afraid I couldn't see."

It wasn't until the NHL expanded to 12 teams in 1967 that Binkley got his chance to shine. He met with Penguins general manager Jack Riley at a restaurant to discuss a deal. Signing a contract scrawled on a paper napkin, he became the Original Penguin.

The 33-year-old rookie was sensational during the club's inaugural season. Appearing in 54 games, he posted a sterling 2.88 goals-against average and six shutouts while winning 20 games for a non-playoff team. On the night of January 28, 1968, Binkley enjoyed one of his finest games, stopping 33 shots against the powerhouse Bruins at the Boston Garden to earn a 1–0 shutout.

"It was one of those nights when you couldn't do anything wrong," he recalled in Jim O'Brien's book, *Penguin Profiles*. "There were some shifts we never got out of our end of the rink."

First Nation

During the summer of 1967, Penguins general manager Jack Riley was seeking additional talent to help bolster his roster. In August he signed free-agent forward Bill LeCaine to a contract. An aggressive left wing, LeCaine had racked up 643 points during eight seasons in the International Hockey League, mostly spent with the Port Huron Flags.

The 6'0", 172-pounder also was a member of the First Nation, and a rather prominent one at that.

"I was born on the Lakota Sioux Wood Mountain reserve in Saskatchewan, Canada, in 1938," he said. "I am a distant relative of Sitting Bull and a direct descendant of Chief Black Moon, who fought with Sitting Bull at the battle of the Little Big Horn."

Born into poverty, LeCaine rose above his humble beginnings. He became the first Native American to attend the University of North Dakota. In 1959–60 he joined the Minneapolis Millers of the IHL and emerged as a dangerous scorer, twice topping the 100-point mark.

After tallying 15 goals for the Baltimore Clippers in 1967–68, LeCaine was assigned to the Amarillo Wranglers. A month into the 1968–69 season the 30-year-old winger received one of his greatest thrills when was called up by the Penguins. On November 16, 1968, he became the first Native American ever to play in an NHL game.

LeCaine's stay in the Steel City was brief. After a four-game trial, the Pens sent him back to Amarillo for the balance of the year. Bill rejoined Port Huron in 1969–70 and enjoyed four strong seasons before hanging up his skates. He retired as one of the IHL's all-time leading scorers.

He fondly remembered another big game that season.

"In our first week, we beat Chicago 4–2," he said. "We were the first expansion team to beat an established team. And they had Bobby and Dennis Hull, and both had among the hardest shots in the league, and they had Stan Mikita."

The Penguins struggled mightily during the early years, missing the playoffs three out of their first five seasons. However, Binkley remained a veritable Rock of Gibraltar in goal, winning 58 games while posting a solid 3.12 goals-against average.

Following his playing days, Les returned to the Penguins organization in 1988. He was a member of the scouting staff when the Pens won two Stanley Cups in the early 1990s.

51 Mario's Amazing Streak

For Penguins superstar Mario Lemieux, the 1992–93 season represented the pits and the pinnacle of his career all wrapped into one. His balky back seemingly a thing of the past, the 27-year-old center bolted from the starting blocks at a scorching pace.

After piling up 101 points in just 38 games, Lemieux decided to have a doctor check a small lump on his neck early in the new year. Mario was stunned to learn that he'd contracted Hodgkin's disease, a form of cancer that attacks the lymph nodes.

"Just the word *cancer* scares you a lot," the Pens' captain recalled. "I didn't cry right at the time I was at the doctor's, but when I got in my car I actually started crying the whole way down to my house. That was probably the toughest day of my life."

Following surgery to remove the infected lymph node, Mario immediately began a battery of radiation treatments. While the prognosis for recovery was good, no one knew when—or if—he would be able to return to the lineup. At the very least, he seemed finished for the season.

"I was amazed when the doctors sat in my office and told me what they'd found," Penguins general manager Craig Patrick said.

"Then the more we learned about it, the more we heard about it, the more we understood about the disease, things were a little easier to swallow."

Lemieux responded well to his radiation treatments. Displaying recuperative abilities bordering on the superhuman, he made his triumphant return against the Flyers in the Spectrum on March 2, less than two months after learning of his illness.

Infamous as among the most hostile fans in all of sports, the Flyers' faithful stood in unison and gave Mario a warm, heartfelt ovation. Missing a patch of hair and wearing a protective collar to protect his singed neck, Lemieux remarkably notched a goal and an assist.

"It's unbelievable," his linemate Kevin Stevens said. "How can you even imagine what he did tonight? There's only one person in the world who could do it, and it's him."

It was then that No. 66 issued a staggering proclamation. He intended to surpass Buffalo's Pat LaFontaine in the scoring race.

"I felt that the scoring title was mine to lose," Mario would recall. "Even when I was sick, when I was going through the treatments, I always thought about coming back and winning the scoring title."

At the time, Lemieux trailed the Sabres' gifted center by a dozen points with only 19 games to play. Even his most ardent supporters gave Mario little or no chance. After all, he was barely a month removed from energy-sapping radiation treatments.

Lemieux would astonish the hockey world with perhaps the greatest athletic achievement of all time. Playing like a man possessed, he tallied *51 points* over a 16-game stretch, an astounding average of 3.19 points per game. During his unprecedented hot streak he recorded seven multiple-goal games, including back-to-back four-goal games and a five-goal effort against the Rangers. A veritable one-man wrecking crew, Mario scored or assisted on a whopping 55 percent of his team's goals over that span.

Mario's Amazing Streak

Date	Opponent	Goals	Assists	Points	Score	Result
Mar. 9	vs. Boston	0	1	1	3–2	Win
Mar. 11	vs. Los Angeles	1	3	4	4–3 (OT)	Win
Mar. 14	at NY Islanders	0	1	1	3–2	Win
Mar. 18	vs. Washington	4	2	6	7–5	Win
Mar. 20	vs. Philadelphia	4	1	5	9–3	Win
Mar. 21	at Edmonton	1	0	1	6–4	Win
Mar. 23	vs. San Jose	2	3	5	7–2	Win
Mar. 25	vs. New Jersey	1	3	4	4–3	Win
Mar. 27	at Boston	2	1	3	5–3	Win
Mar. 28	at Washington	1	2	3	4–1	Win
Mar. 30	vs. Ottawa	1	1	2	6–4	Win
Apr. 1	vs. Hartford	2	1	3	10–2	Win
Apr. 3	at Quebec	2	1	3	5–3	Win
Apr. 4	at New Jersey	1	2	3	5–2	Win
Apr. 7	vs. Montreal	0	2	2	4–3 (OT)	Win
Apr. 9	at NY Rangers	5	0	5	10–4	Win
Total		*27*	*24*	*51*		

Not only did he catch LaFontaine, but he also buried his rival by 12 points to capture his fourth Art Ross Trophy. Swept up in Lemieux's jet stream, the equally hot Penguins established an NHL record with 17 consecutive victories.

"He played so wonderfully that it makes you forget why he was out," said Penguins vice president Tom McMillan. "In comparison to the NBA, if Michael Jordan missed a third of the season, would he win the scoring title? No."

52 The Hatfields vs. the McCoys

In the spring of 1970, Stanley Cup fever had, quite unexpectedly, taken Pittsburgh by storm. Following two dreary seasons, the city's new National Hockey League entry had wrapped up second place in the West Division to earn a berth in the playoffs.

Led by their wily coach, Red Kelly, the Pesky Pens swept the Oakland Seals in four straight games to set up a semifinals matchup against the West Division champion St. Louis Blues.

The Penguins and the Blues were hardly kissin' cousins. During a contest at the Civic Arena on January 31, a jousting match between Pens policeman Bryan Watson and St. Louis bad boy Barclay Plager ignited a bench-clearing brawl that resulted in a key Penguins victory.

It took all of 19 seconds for the bitter rivals to renew hostilities. Boisterous Noel Picard squirted gasoline on the smoldering embers when he mugged peace-loving Pens winger Jean Pronovost in the St. Louis zone. Watson flew at Picard. Soon gloves and sticks littered the ice.

Although the Penguins were holding their own in the fisticuffs, St. Louis tallied three goals in a six-minute span of the second period to put the game out of reach. To set the tone for the next contest, Picard jumped willowy Michel Briere at the end of the game to spark yet another brawl that featured Tracy Pratt and Blues tough guy Bob Plager in the main event.

"They think they're going to kick the hell out of us, but they're not," declared defiant Penguins general manager Jack Riley.

In an effort to neutralize the Blues' intimidating defensive tandem of Picard and Bob Plager, Red Kelly started Game 2 with a makeshift forward line that featured two of his biggest and toughest players—Pratt and Dunc McCallum—alongside rugged Bryan Hextall.

The move backfired mightily as the Blues promptly scored on an odd-man break. St. Louis rolled up a three-goal first-period lead en route to a convincing 4–1 win.

Although they were down 2–0, the Penguins' spirited play had at long last captured the imagination of Steel City hockey fans. When the series shifted to Pittsburgh for Game 3, they turned out in droves. Suitably inspired, the Pens dominated the action from the opening face-off. Playing with a newfound confidence, they held the high-powered Blues in check and notched a 3–2 victory.

Suddenly the Penguins were the hottest ticket in town. A record throng of 12,962 jammed the Civic Arena to see if the Pens could even the series in Game 4. The fans in attendance were treated to another superb effort by their hometown heroes. Paced by Briere's game-winning goal, Pittsburgh triumphed 2–1 to knot the series at two games apiece.

What had seemed unthinkable—a berth in the Stanley Cup Finals—was now within the Penguins' grasp. Stoked to a fever pitch, they opened Game 5 in St. Louis hitting anything that moved. However, Hextall, Watson, and Glen Sather drew penalties in rapid succession. St. Louis cashed in on the power play and romped to an easy 5–0 win.

With their backs against the wall, the Penguins came out smoking in Game 6. Playing before another near-capacity crowd at the Civic Arena they grabbed the lead on goals by Duane Rupp and Ron Schock. Red Berenson scored in the second period to pull the Blues within one going into the final frame.

In the wildest finish of the series St. Louis tied the game at 5:26, only to watch Briere pot his fifth goal of the playoffs less than a minute later. The Pens had barely finished celebrating when the Blues' Tim Ecclestone evened the score again. The defenses stiffened until the 14-minute mark, when Larry Keenan fired the game winner past Al Smith to break the hearts of the Penguins and their fans.

"You feel bad about losing," Red Kelly said, "but you never feel bad when you've given everything you have, and that's what this team did. This club has more heart than any club in the world."

53 Mikey to the Rescue

Following disappointing playoff exits in each of the previous three seasons, the 1995–96 Penguins were poised for a run at the Stanley Cup. However, their first-round playoff opponents—the Washington Capitals—were proving to be a prickly foe.

Employing their physical, close-checking game to perfection, the Capitals stunned the heavily favored Penguins by sweeping the first two games in Pittsburgh. Thanks to the strong goaltending of Tom Barrasso, the Pens bounced back to take Game 3. They needed a victory in the pivotal Game 4 to keep their Cup hopes alive.

After falling behind 1–0, the Penguins received a jolt during the first intermission. Barrasso was suffering from back spasms and could not continue.

Fortunately, the team had an ace in the hole. Ken Wregget was widely regarded as the best backup goalie in the league. Nicknamed "Mikey" for his strong likeness to a child actor in the popular Life cereal commercials, he led the league in wins during the lockout-shortened 1994–95 season while filling in for the injured Barrasso.

A cross between a standup goalie and a flopper, Wregget wasn't the prettiest goaltender to watch. He had a curious habit of turning

The Flying Nedved

When Petr Nedved arrived in Pittsburgh during the summer of 1995 via a big trade with the Rangers, he had a reputation for contract squabbles and untapped potential.

Possessing a crackling wrist shot and good speed, Nedved blossomed in the Steel City. Skating on a high-octane second line with crafty veteran Ron Francis, he exploded for 45 goals, 54 assists, and 99 points in 1995–96, all career highs. During the playoffs that spring he tallied 10 goals and scored the game winner in the Pens' marathon overtime victory over the Capitals.

Nedved credited his countryman and housemate Jaromir Jagr for easing his transition.

"Having Jaromir on the team makes it that much more comfortable here," he said. "I knew him from back home, and now he's become one of my best friends. It's nice being around a fun guy like Jaromir."

Nicknamed "the Flying Nedved" by colorful play-by-play announcer Mike Lange, the Czech Republic native appeared to be set for a long and eventful run in Pittsburgh. Following a strong 33-goal

season, however, Nedved attempted to renegotiate his contract. Penguins general manager Craig Patrick refused to budge, and Petr sat out the entire 1997–98 campaign.

The impasse finally ended on November 25, 1998, when Patrick shipped Nedved back to New York for another burgeoning talent, Alexei Kovalev.

Petr Nedved scored 78 goals during his two-year Penguins career.

160

off-angle toward the post on face-offs, much like a batter in baseball with an extreme open stance. But he was very effective.

"Certainly it's an awkward style," said Pens goaltending coach Gilles Meloche, "but he'll come far out of the crease and let the puck hit him. He's got a great head on his shoulders."

"My philosophy is your style will find you," Wregget said. "The bottom line is to stop the puck, by whatever means necessary."

Just as important, Wregget had a history of coming up big in playoff competition. As a member of the Flyers, he stoned the Penguins in Game 7 of the 1989 Patrick Division Finals to lead his team to victory.

Still, Wregget hadn't seen action since suffering an embarrassing 6–2 loss to the Islanders during the final week of the regular season. While the rusty goalie struggled to get his bearings, explosive Peter Bondra scored to extend Washington's lead. But Wregget soon found his groove. While No. 31 slammed the door on the Caps, the Penguins rallied to send the game into overtime.

The Pens had dominated play through the first 60 minutes, outshooting Washington by a 2-to-1 margin. However, the home-standing Caps quickly took control in overtime. They poured into the Penguins' zone and peppered Wregget with shot after shot.

At his best in big games, the 32-year-old netminder warmed to the challenge. He made a spectacular glove save at 13:17 of the first overtime to rob Stefan Ustorf of a sure goal from point-blank range. Late in the second overtime Wregget thwarted a penalty-shot attempt by crafty Joey Juneau.

Undeterred, the opportunistic Capitals proceeded to throw everything but the proverbial kitchen sink at the Penguins' net. Again, the super sub stopped them cold. In all Wregget made 53 saves, including a whopping 42 in overtime.

Demoralized by the veteran goalie's brilliant play, the Caps finally began to fade. With 45 seconds remaining in the fourth overtime, Petr Nedved struck for the game winner at 2:16 AM. Thanks to Wregget's heroics, the Pens triumphed in what was then the third-longest game in NHL history.

Afterward, he shrugged off the accolades for his superhuman effort in typically modest fashion.

"I figured if this was my role, I was going to work hard and do everything I could at the rink to stay ready," Wregget said. "And if you're going to back up, this had to be the best place in the league to do it."

54 Sarge

As a youngster growing up in the Soviet Union, Sergei Gonchar had dreams of playing professional soccer. Noting that Sergei lacked the speed for the sport, his father encouraged him to play hockey instead. Soon Gonchar was starring for the local club, Traktor Chelyabinsk.

Following a strong showing in the European Junior Championships, he was selected by Washington with the 14th overall pick in the 1992 Entry Draft. One year later the Capitals invited the 19-year-old prodigy to training camp.

"I didn't speak any English," Gonchar recalled. "Going back to growing up [in Russia], you're playing for the team and they take care of everything—you live in the dormitory, there's food for you. You have to play hockey and nothing else. Now your life is changing completely, and you don't know what to do."

The 6'2", 211-pounder gradually adjusted to the North American lifestyle. Soon his game was in full bloom. Thanks to his deadly accurate wrist shot and outstanding mobility, Gonchar emerged as one of the finest defensemen in the league, twice earning NHL Second Team All-Star honors.

Following the lockout year of 2004–05, the Penguins signed the smooth-skating Russian to a lucrative five-year deal worth $25 million. However, Gonchar got off to a dreadful start, prompting one network analyst to ask, "Who's the impostor wearing No. 55?"

Determined to show the Penguins they had made a wise investment, Sarge whipped himself into top shape over the off-season. He jumped out of the starting blocks in 2006–07 at a sizzling pace to lead the resurgent Pens to their first playoff berth in six years.

Extremely popular with his teammates, he proved to be a wonderful leader and mentor.

"He's a quiet guy, so he probably doesn't get talked about as much for being a leader, but he's definitely an important leader on our team," Sidney Crosby said. "His calmness rubs off on everybody. It helps guys to settle down sometimes. He's got that quiet confidence. His game speaks pretty loud, but just the way he handles himself, that's contagious, too."

When Evgeni Malkin defected from Russia prior to the season, Gonchar moved the youngster into his Sewickley home and took him under his wing. Malkin responded with a fine 33-goal season to capture the Calder Trophy.

"I remember how tough it was for myself," Gonchar said. "I knew him from the lockout year when we played together [2004–05 in Magnitogorsk]. I knew he was a good kid. I just decided it would be the right thing to do."

By the 2007–08 campaign, the Penguins were ready to contend for the Stanley Cup. Gonchar played a prominent role. Enjoying a season worthy of Norris Trophy consideration, he tallied 12 goals and 65 points—second among NHL defensemen—while once again keying the Pens' deadly power play.

He earned further distinction that spring, not to mention the undying respect of his teammates. During the early stages of a do-or-die Game 5 against Detroit in the Stanley Cup Finals, Gonchar injured his back. Although he could barely skate, he returned to the ice for a power play in the third overtime and promptly set up the game winner by Petr Sykora.

"I was just trying to help the team any way I could," he said.

In 2008–09 Gonchar suffered a dislocated shoulder during the preseason and the team floundered in his absence. After missing 56 games, the ultra-smooth defenseman returned to lead the resurgent Penguins to a second-place finish in the Atlantic Division.

Once again, Sarge displayed his mettle in the postseason. In Game 4 of the Eastern Conference Semifinals, he absorbed a brutal knee-on-knee check from countryman Alexander Ovechkin. Expected to be out for the remainder of the playoffs, he returned after missing just two games. His winning goal in Game 3 of the Finals was a turning point, as the Penguins vanquished the Red Wings to capture the Stanley Cup.

With his contract up for renewal during the summer of 2010, the team decided to part ways with the 35-year-old defender. Gonchar promptly signed a three-year deal with Ottawa worth $5.5 million per year. He departed as the fifth-highest scoring defenseman in Penguins history.

55 Chico

Rick Kehoe was a wonderfully consistent goal-scorer through perhaps the most trying period in Penguins history. Enduring a nearly endless succession of rebuilding programs with a calm stoicism, he never scored fewer than 27 goals during a remarkable

The Fergie Flyer

George Ferguson was a versatile and valuable performer who typified the Penguins teams of the late 1970s and early 1980s. While not a star, he was an excellent two-way player who exhibited a team-first attitude and a penchant for scoring big goals.

Following six so-so seasons in Toronto, Ferguson got a new lease on life when he joined the Penguins in the summer of 1978. Given an expanded role by coach Johnny Wilson, the former first-round pick flourished in the Steel City.

"Pittsburgh is a tremendous place to play," he said. "I wish I could have played my whole career here."

Equally adept in an offensive or defensive role, Ferguson skated on the power play and became one of the team's top penalty killers. Taking full advantage of Fergie's adaptability, the Penguins used him at right wing and center. A model of consistency, the speedy forward tallied 89 goals and 195 points during his four seasons with the club.

Always a clutch playoff performer, Ferguson enjoyed his moment in the sun during Game 3 of the 1979 Preliminary Round series versus Buffalo. With the Penguins trailing the powerful Sabres 3–2, he notched the tying goal to send the game into overtime.

Early in the extra frame, the Fergie Flyer swooped into the Buffalo zone and drilled a 15-footer past Bob Sauve to give the Pens their first series victory in four years.

"On the winning goal, I noticed the left side of the rink was open," Ferguson said. "So I just took off, and when I thought I could score, I let it fly."

nine-season run, including five years of 30-plus goals and a career-best 55 tallies in 1980–81.

"I always dreamed of playing in the NHL, and I was doing it and doing it well," he said. "I was just thinking of playing the game, at the highest level. It came down to how you handled it."

His given name was Rick, but everyone called him Chico for his likeness to the late *Chico and the Man* TV star, Freddie Prinze. Indeed, with his swarthy complexion and signature mustache he resembled a bandito on the ice for the way he picked goaltenders' pockets.

Pens general manager Jack Button acquired Kehoe from Toronto in the summer of 1974. Playing on a line with veterans Ron Schock and Vic Hadfield, he made an immediate splash by pumping in 32 goals. In the playoffs, however, the sharp-shooting winger failed to find the net. It was a bugaboo that would haunt him throughout his otherwise distinguished career.

Kehoe had vivid memories of his second season in Pittsburgh, when he piled up 76 points while skating with phenom Pierre Larouche.

"I was on a line with him and Bob 'Battleship' Kelly when Larouche got 53 goals our second year with the team," he recalled. "Kelly was the guy who took care of everybody. He was our enforcer. Larouche had so much talent. Give him the puck around the net, and he could put it past anybody."

The Windsor, Ontario, native rolled along until the 1980–81 campaign, when Eddie Johnston took over as coach. A power-play wizard, EJ opened up the attack and Kehoe responded with a breakout year.

"I was pretty consistent around the 30-goal mark until '80–81, when I was fortunate enough to have a big year," he said. "It just seems that some years the puck goes in more than other years."

On the night of March 16, 1981, he beat Edmonton goalie Ed Mio to become only the third player in franchise history to score 50 goals in a season. At the postseason awards banquet he received the Lady Byng Trophy for his stellar and gentlemanly play.

Racking up 33 goals and a team-high 85 points, Kehoe enjoyed yet another strong season in 1981–82. In the playoffs the Pens squared off against the powerhouse New York Islanders in a best-of-five-series. Trailing the two-time defending Stanley Cup champs 2–0, the gritty Penguins managed to force Game 3 into overtime.

The stage was set for Kehoe's long-awaited moment of postseason glory. Just 4:14 into the extra frame he snapped off his laser of a wrist shot. The puck bounced through a tangle of players and past Islanders goalie Billy Smith.

With the monkey finally off his back, Kehoe struck again in Game 4 as the inspired Penguins knotted the series. They fought valiantly before succumbing to the Islanders in a pulsating deciding game.

Unfortunately, the talent-starved Penguins bottomed out the following season. Despite the dismal circumstances, Kehoe once again paced the team's scorers with 29 goals. He was chugging along toward a 10th straight 20-goal season when he was felled by a neck injury in February of 1984.

"I had a herniated disc," he said. "Back then, they weren't sure you could have an operation and correct it."

Playing with numbness in his right arm and risking permanent damage, the 33-year-old sniper hung up his skates early the following season as the team's all-time leading point scorer. As a special treat, he got a chance to play alongside the man who would eventually surpass him—Mario Lemieux.

Three years later he began his second career when he rejoined the team as an assistant coach. In perhaps his greatest contribution, Kehoe helped budding superstar Jaromir Jagr develop his lethal wrist shot.

His achievements were duly rewarded in 1992 when he was inducted into the Penguins Hall of Fame. Eighteen years later Kehoe was voted to the All-Time Penguins Team.

56 Pensational

Entering the 1992–93 season the Penguins seemed on the verge of blossoming into a full-fledged dynasty. Fresh off a second straight Stanley Cup, the team boasted one of the greatest collection of superstars ever assembled. No fewer than four of the club's players—Mario Lemieux, Ron Francis, Joe Mullen, and Larry Murphy—would gain induction into the Hockey Hall of Fame. A host of others, including power forwards Kevin Stevens and Rick Tocchet, whiz kid Jaromir Jagr, and goalie Tom Barrasso, were All-Star caliber performers.

Led by Lemieux, who bolted from the starting gate at a scorching pace, the Pens blazed to an 11–1–2 start. Even the most veteran observers were awed by the team's exploits, including the Penguins.

"This is by far the best team we've had in Pittsburgh," Stevens said. "It's a confident team, it's got great leaders, and it's got 25 guys pretty much on the same page. It's just a great team to play for. I don't know how we got this good."

Lemieux echoed his husky linemate's sentiments.

"This is the best team I ever played with," he said. "We have three lines that can score a lot of goals, a lot of guys who can put the puck in the net…It's pretty tough to find guys who score 30, 40, 50 goals, which we have on every line."

Entering the new year, it seemed that nothing could stop this juggernaut. But on January 13, 1993, the team received some crushing news: Lemieux was diagnosed with Hodgkin's disease.

"We're a team that can hardly lose a game, and all of a sudden the word *cancer*'s involved," defensive stalwart Ulf Samuelsson said.

Predictably, the team swooned in Mario's absence. Sans No. 66, the Pens staggered through the dog days of January and February at a pedestrian 11–10–2 pace. Thanks to its white-hot start, the club remained among the NHL elite. However, the Penguins clearly missed their captain.

Fortunately, the big center responded well to his treatments. Improbably, Mario was given the green light to return to action for a March 2 showdown with the Flyers. Wearing a collar to protect his neck, Lemieux remarkably notched a goal and an assist.

With Mario back in the lineup, the Penguins quickly regained their early-season form. On March 9 they edged the Bruins 3–2 at the Civic Arena to snap a two-game losing streak. It was the first in a stunning string of victories that would reach epic proportions.

On April 7, the Pens beat Montreal on Samuelsson's overtime winner to equal the New York Islanders' league record of 15 consecutive victories. Fueled by Mario's five-goal explosion and a Joe Mullen hat trick, they established a new mark two nights later by bombing the Rangers 10–4. The Pens ran their win streak to 17 games before settling for a tie with New Jersey in the season finale.

It truly was a season to behold. The Penguins finished the campaign with a record of 56–21–7 and 119 points, far and away the best mark in franchise history.

A third straight Stanley Cup appeared to be all but in the bag. The President's Trophy winners raced to a 3–0 series lead over the Devils to extend their league-record playoff winning streak to 14 games before tasting defeat.

In the second round, however, the powerhouse Pens ran full-force into a determined Islanders squad. After clawing their way to a 3–2 advantage, Pittsburgh dropped the final two games of the series. Following a heartbreaking overtime loss in Game 7 a headline in the *Pittsburgh Post-Gazette* blared, "THREE-PEATERED OUT."

"We put ourselves in a position where anything could happen, and the worst did," Barrasso said.

Although no one realized it at the time, the shocking defeat signaled the end of the Pens' mini-dynasty. It would take 17 long years and a new generation of superstars to reclaim Lord Stanley's coveted chalice.

57 Visit the Site of the Duquesne Gardens

For a true Pittsburgh hockey fan, no pilgrimage would be complete without visiting the site of the Duquesne Gardens. Located at 110 North Craig Street near Fifth Avenue, the old arena was home to the Steel City's earliest hockey teams. Although nothing remains of the Gardens, it served as the nerve center of Pittsburgh hockey for 57 years.

To fully appreciate the Gardens' significance, one must go back in time to the late 19th century. In 1896 a fire destroyed the Schenley Park Casino, the city's first indoor skating rink. It was truly a devastating event for Pittsburgh. The loss of the Casino left the city without a social gathering place and was a blow to the city's civic pride.

Fortunately, the city fathers were quick to react. A year earlier political heavyweight Christopher Magee had purchased a large red-brick structure on North Craig Street. Formerly the Duquesne Traction Company, it was built in 1890 to serve as a trolley barn.

Hastened by the loss of the Casino, Magee sank $500,000 into the purchase and renovation of the building, including the installation of a movie theater and a state-of-the-art ice skating rink. Rechristened the Duquesne Gardens, the multipurpose venue opened its doors for public skating on January 23, 1899. The following evening the Gardens hosted its first hockey game, a match between the Pittsburgh Athletic Club and Western University (later the University of Pittsburgh).

Trumpeted as "the Largest and Most Beautiful Skating Palace in the World," the Gardens was renowned for the quality and size of its artificial ice. Featuring a 250-foot-long ice surface (later shortened to 200 feet to meet NHL standards), it was constructed using the most up-to-date refrigeration technology of the day.

"Lester Patrick, Craig's grandfather, started a league on the Pacific Coast early in the 20th century," hockey writer Stan Fischler said. "To learn how to get proper ice refrigeration, he came to Pittsburgh to see how it was done."

With a brand-new arena, hockey flourished in Pittsburgh in the early 20th century. Nearly a dozen amateur, college, and professional teams played their home games at the Gardens—including the Pittsburgh Athletic Club and the Pittsburgh Pro HC. One of the earliest professional leagues—the Western Pennsylvania Hockey League—was formed in Pittsburgh. Players and teams from Canada flocked to the Steel City, often performing before sold-out crowds.

"Pittsburgh is hockey crazy," the manager of a Canadian team told the *Toronto Globe*. "Over 10,000 turned out for three games there. The general admission being 35 cents and 75 cents for a box seat...the Pittsburgh rink is a dream. What a marvelous place it is."

Big-league hockey made its debut at the Gardens on December 2, 1925. Packing the place to the rafters, 8,200 fans (some 2,600 over the official seating capacity) watched as the Pittsburgh Pirates lost to the New York Americans 2–1 in overtime.

During the early 1930s, teams such as the Yellow Jackets and the Shamrocks played their home games at the Gardens. Then, in 1936, local theater owner and founder of the Ice Capades, John

Harris, purchased the Detroit Olympics of the International-American Hockey League and moved them to Pittsburgh. He renamed the team the Hornets.

The arrival of the Hornets sparked a second golden age for the Gardens. Although the arena gradually fell into disrepair, it remained the Hornets' home for 20 years. During that span the team captured two Calder Cups.

"The building was not really heroic," said Frank Mathers, a defensive stalwart on the 1950s clubs. "It was an old car barn, but it was home. They claimed the rats there were the biggest in the league. [Trainer] Socko McCarey used to load up with pucks and fire away at the rats."

The Hornets played their final game at the Gardens on March 31, 1956, dropping a 6–4 decision to the Cleveland Barons. Within months the new Plaza Park Apartments and a Stouffer's Restaurant stood on the former site of the arena.

A piece of the Gardens still remains. Bricks that once served as the back wall to the visitors' dressing room were moved to the sparking new CONSOL Energy Center and installed in the Captain Morgan Club.

58 Marathon Men

Paced by brilliant young superstars Sidney Crosby and Evgeni Malkin, the 2007–08 Penguins seemed poised to bring the Stanley Cup back to Pittsburgh. After capturing the Atlantic Division crown thanks to a 102-point season, the Pens made short work of their Eastern Conference foes to capture the Prince of Wales Trophy.

However, their Stanley Cup Finals opponents, the battle-tested Detroit Red Wings, were proving to be a brick wall. The Red Wings dominated the first four games of the series to take a commanding 3–1 lead.

"We have to keep our chins up," said Penguins sniper Marian Hossa. "They have to win one more game, and we have to make it really tough on them."

Determined to claw their way back in Game 5, the Penguins responded with a strong opening period. Just past the eight-minute mark Hossa whipped his 11th goal of the postseason past Chris Osgood. At 14:41 Adam Hall was credited with a goal when a Niklas Kronwall clearing attempt deflected in off his skate.

Playing before their hometown fans at the Joe Louis Arena, the Red Wings mounted a withering comeback. Early in the second period Darren Helm scored to cut the Pens' lead in half. In the final frame, Pavel Datsyuk and Brian Rafalski beat a beleaguered Marc-Andre Fleury to give Detroit a 3–2 edge.

Awash in a sea of bright-red jerseys, the Penguins struggled to keep pace. To make matters worse, All-Star defenseman Sergei Gonchar was forced to the locker room with a back injury. Power forward Ryan Malone—already playing with a broken nose—caught a Hal Gill shot in the face.

As the game clock ticked down under a minute to play, Penguins coach Michel Therrien pulled Fleury in favor of an extra attacker. Acting on a hunch, he sent grinder Max Talbot over the boards.

The hustling winger made a beeline for the Detroit net. Setting up shop beside the cage, he gathered in a pretty pass from Hossa and slung the puck around the goalpost. No goal. He took another whack at the rubber. This time the red light flashed. Talbot had tied the game with 34.3 seconds to play.

The Red Wings were hardly fazed by Mad Max's last-minute heroics. During the first overtime they poured over the Penguins

Sykora Calls His Shot

During Game 5 of the 2008 Stanley Cup Finals the Penguins were locked in a titanic overtime struggle with Detroit for their playoff lives. Trailing the mighty Red Wings by two games, it was do or die for Pittsburgh. That's when slumping winger Petr Sykora issued a staggering proclamation.

"I think I've got one, guys," he said.

Color announcer Pierre McGuire, who was stationed between the benches, said Sykora pointed to himself as if to say, "I'm scoring the game winner."

"When a guy like that steps out and says, 'I've got one, guys,' you look at him and you hope he's saying the truth," Max Talbot said.

No false prophet, Sykora proceeded to back up his words with deeds. At 9:57 of the third overtime, he snapped the winning goal past Chris Osgood, just as he'd predicted.

in waves, outshooting their foe by a whopping 13–2 margin. But Fleury stopped them cold.

"That was the game of his life," Ryan Whitney said afterward.

Buoyed by Fleury's brilliance, the Pens skated on even terms with the Wings through a second overtime. However, it would take another superhuman effort for the Penguins to emerge with a victory.

At 9:21 of the third overtime, Detroit's Jiri Hudler drew a double minor for high-sticking Rob Scuderi. With the game on the line, Gonchar gamely returned to the ice to quarterback the power play.

"His back was killing him," Brooks Orpik said. "They asked him if he could push through it if we got a power play. He said he'd try. That was just a gutsy effort by him."

Manning his customary spot on the point, Gonchar fed the puck to Petr Sykora, who ripped off a shot. The rebound caromed to Malkin, who passed the puck back to Sykora. This time the Czech sniper found the range, beating Osgood with a blistering drive to give his team a hard-earned 4–3 victory.

It was a gritty, heroic effort by the Pens, one that signified the team's coming of age. Fleury stopped 55 of 58 shots in a virtuoso performance. With Gonchar hobbled, Whitney logged a mind-blowing 50 minutes of ice time. Malone skated the last half of the game with cotton packed in his nose to staunch the bleeding. Indeed, the entire team battled through adversity with the heart of a lion.

"We just didn't want our season to end," Scuderi said.

59 Lazarus

When Lowell MacDonald was awarded the Masterton Trophy in 1973, it was a case of quiet vindication for a player who had scaled some huge hurdles in order to pursue his hockey dreams. Indeed, the trophy seemed to have been created with MacDonald in mind. Few players in the history of the game have displayed more perseverance and dedication on the road to stardom.

Following a promising junior career that culminated in a Memorial Cup triumph for his Hamilton Red Wings, MacDonald began his pro career with Detroit. Although undeniably talented, the youngster had a difficult time cracking the Red Wings' experienced lineup. He enjoyed greater success with the team's AHL affiliate, the Pittsburgh Hornets. In three seasons with the minor league club Lowell scored 67 goals, including 31 during the 1963–64 campaign.

MacDonald finally became a full-time player in the NHL in 1967 when he was drafted by Los Angeles. He enjoyed a strong first season with the Kings, notching 21 goals. Although his production dipped the following year, MacDonald had established himself as a solid big-league performer.

There was, however, a downside to playing in Los Angeles. MacDonald hated flying.

"I had a major fear of flying; I was in really bad shape," he confessed. "My two years in Los Angeles really took its toll. We flew over 100,000 miles a year."

Preparing to leave training camp in 1969, MacDonald narrowly missed boarding a plane that was hijacked to Cuba. It was the last straw. At 28 years of age, Lowell decided to retire rather than endure the agony of flying.

Taking a year off to earn his bachelor's degree from St. Mary's University in Halifax, MacDonald played a handful of home games for the Kings' minor league affiliate in Springfield, Massachusetts.

The following summer MacDonald was contacted by Penguins general manager Red Kelly, his former Kings coach, about playing for the Penguins.

"He called me," MacDonald said. "He said they flew only 30,000 to 35,000 miles a year in Pittsburgh. I said I'd come if he wanted me. So Pittsburgh picked me up from Los Angeles in the 1970 Intra-League Draft."

Unfortunately, MacDonald injured his troublesome left knee in training camp. After skating a shift here and there, he submitted to season-ending surgery. The operation was performed by the Penguins' team physician, Dr. Charles Stone. MacDonald would credit Stone for saving his career.

For two years MacDonald stayed away from the game. He began to think his career was over until his wife, Joyce, encouraged him to give hockey one more try. Whipping himself into peak condition, he won a spot on the Penguins roster in 1972.

Acting on a hunch, Kelly placed the 31-year-old veteran on a line with rising stars Syl Apps and Al McDonough. Playing the off wing, MacDonald responded with a huge season. He racked up 34 goals and 41 assists while leading the team with a sparkling plus/minus rating of plus-37.

Those who doubted whether MacDonald could repeat his Lazarus-like performance were in for a surprise. In 1973–74 he enjoyed the finest season of his career. Skating on the explosive Century Line with Apps and Jean Pronovost, No. 18 tallied a club-record 43 goals and 82 points to garner his second straight West Division All-Star berth.

"Lowell was something, considering he couldn't see 20 feet in front of him," Apps said. "Yet he could find the corner of the nets with his shot."

Due in part to a more balanced attack, the veteran winger dipped to 27 goals in 1974–75. He returned to 30-goal form the following season.

Unfortunately, the injury bugaboo resurfaced late in MacDonald's career. After sitting out virtually all of the 1976–77 campaign following his seventh knee surgery, the classy old pro was limited to 19 games in 1977–78. At 37 years of age, MacDonald decided it was time to hang up his skates once and for all.

Lowell retired as the third-leading goal scorer in team history, behind his linemates Apps and Pronovost. It was a remarkable achievement given his relatively brief career. During the summer of 2010 he earned honorable mention in the voting for the Penguins All-Time Team.

60 Kitty

Over the course of five-plus seasons with the Penguins, Randy Carlyle appeared in 397 games and racked up the impressive totals of 66 goals, 257 assists, and 323 points. He appeared in two NHL All-Star Games and was named an NHL First Team All-Star in 1981.

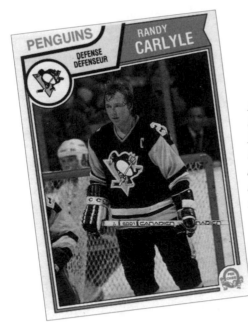

Randy Carlyle enjoyed a brilliant season for the Penguins in 1980–81, becoming the first defenseman from an expansion team to win the Norris Trophy.

Those achievements alone would be more than enough to place him among the team's all-time greats. However, in 1980–81 he accomplished something that no Penguins defenseman has done before or since. He won the Norris Trophy.

Penguins general manager Baz Bastien acquired Carlyle and versatile forward George Ferguson from Toronto on June 14, 1978, for All-Star Dave Burrows. While the Penguins were pleased with the return, they could not have imagined what was in store.

"A year later they were shocked by how good he was," Ferguson said. "Obviously, Baz Bastien made a good move. Randy was a good leader; he was made for that."

Given a free hand to join the rush by coach Johnny Wilson, Carlyle began to flash his offensive skills. Although a choppy skater, he possessed outstanding vision and excelled at leading the breakout. The man known as Kitty scored 13 goals his first season in the Steel City, along with a healthy 47 points.

Following a down year in 1979–80, Wilson was replaced behind the bench by Eddie Johnston. A former Boston mainstay, Johnston brought with him the secrets of the Bruins' imposing power play.

Thanks to his superb playmaking and puck-handling skills, Carlyle was ideally suited to serve as the quarterback. With the husky defender directing traffic from the point and dangerous scorers Paul Gardner and Rick Kehoe serving as the triggermen, the Pens exploded for 92 power-play goals in 1980–81. Remarkably, Randy was on the ice for 75 of those goals.

"EJ made it all possible," he said. "He came in and gave us the leadership and direction."

Almost overnight, Carlyle blossomed into a scoring sensation, tallying 16 goals and 83 points, tops among NHL defensemen. Although his offensive performance outstripped his defensive play (minus-16), he became the first player from a 1967 expansion team to win the Norris Trophy.

Now serving as the Penguins' captain, Carlyle nearly repeated his Norris Trophy performance in 1981–82. Once again spearheading the team's deadly power play (99 goals), he registered 11 goals and 64 assists to lead the Pens to a playoff berth. Unfortunately, Carlyle was victimized by a bad bounce late in Game 5, and the Penguins fell to the Islanders in overtime.

Although Randy continued to post big numbers in 1982–83 (15 goals, 56 points), the team fell on hard times. The following season he was involved in one of the most controversial trades in NHL history. With the Penguins on a fast track to oblivion, Johnston traded the high-scoring defender to Winnipeg on March 5, 1984, for a first-round pick and future considerations.

Shorn of their best defenseman, the Pens stumbled to a miserable 2–11 finish, nudging out the equally putrid New Jersey Devils for the right to draft Mario Lemieux.

Easy Street Pete

One of the most exciting players to skate for the Penguins during the early years was center Peter Mahovlich. The younger brother of Hall of Famer Frank Mahovlich, Big Pete arrived in the big trade that sent Pierre Larouche to Montreal.

An accomplished player in his own right, Mahovlich had twice topped the 100-point mark while winning four Stanley Cups with the Canadiens. Dubbed "Easy Street Pete" by announcer Mike Lange, the hulking 6'5", 210-pounder wasted little time in making an impact. Putting his outstanding puck-handling skills to good use, Pete thrilled the Civic Arena faithful with his daring end-to-end rushes. He piled up 25 goals and 61 points in just 57 games while pacing the team with a plus-4.

Unfortunately, the 1977–78 Penguins weren't a very good team. After making the playoffs three years in a row, they failed to qualify for postseason play. The losing ate at Mahovlich.

"He had come to the Penguins in December 1977 from the Montreal Canadiens so he knew firsthand what pride was all about," wrote Dave Schultz in his biography, *The Hammer: Confessions of a Hockey Enforcer.*

Buoyed by key acquisitions Randy Carlyle, George Ferguson, and Orest Kindrachuk, the Pens rebounded to make the playoffs the following season. Playing on aching knees, the 32-year-old Mahovlich contributed as best he could, tallying 53 points in 60 games. However, Pete was nearing the end of the line. During the summer of 1979 he was traded to Detroit for Nick Libett.

As for Carlyle, he continued his strong production for the Jets, averaging 15 goals and 50 points per year over the next four seasons. Although advancing age and weight problems began to take their toll in the late 1980s, Carlyle played on through the 1992–93 season before retiring.

The former Pens captain has fond memories of his time in Pittsburgh.

"I think I was fortune enough to play for this hockey club," he said. "It's not like we had a lot of people in the building but our teams, we played hard. We had a good time doing it. It was a lot of fun to play hockey in Pittsburgh. I just wish we had more success."

61 The Recchin' Ball

Mark Recchi still remembers his first NHL shift as if it were yesterday. On September 17, 1988, the Penguins were facing the New York Rangers in an exhibition game. As the 20-year-old rookie took his first strides he noticed he was sharing the ice with Rangers superstars Marcel Dionne and Guy Lafleur. Little did he dream that one day his scoring totals would reach the same epic proportions as those of the two Hall of Famers.

"I thought that if I could get 10 years in [the league], that would have been unbelievable," Recchi said. "Twenty-one years later, I'm still enjoying it. It's been great."

Following a sensational 154-point season with Kamloops, the Penguins selected Recchi with their fourth pick in the 1988 Entry Draft. The hardworking youngster earned a spot on the team in 1989–90 and enjoyed a wonderful rookie season, potting 30 goals.

Playing on the Option Line with fellow rising stars John Cullen and Kevin Stevens, Recchi burst into prominence in 1990–91. With Mario Lemieux missing a huge chunk of the season, the 22-year-old right wing paced the Pens in points (113) while tying Stevens for the goal-scoring lead (40). In the playoffs Recchi shone like a diamond, tallying 34 points to help lead the Penguins to a Stanley Cup.

Dubbed "the Recchin' Ball" by play-by-play announcer Mike Lange, he displayed a curious skating style. At times he appeared to be running on his blades as he dashed along the ice. However, Recchi was a dangerous scorer, especially off the rush, catching goalies off-balance with his lightning-quick release and hard, accurate shot.

Recchi bolted to a fine start in 1991–92, piling up 70 points in 58 games. The Penguins, however, were struggling to keep pace in the playoff chase. In February of 1992, general manager Craig Patrick pulled off a blockbuster three-way trade, sending Recchi to Philadelphia as the center piece of a deal for Rick Tocchet, Kjell Samuelsson, and Ken Wregget.

Devastated by the trade, Recchi responded the only way he knew how. Digging deep into his enormous reservoir of character, he enjoyed a huge 53-goal, 123-point season with Philadelphia in 1992–93. During the next 11 years he averaged 72 points per season and appeared in six NHL All-Star Games.

Seeking a veteran leader for his improving young team, Craig Patrick righted an old wrong by signing Recchi to a free-agent deal during the summer of 2004. The move was lauded in the Steel City, where the Recchin' Ball remained a revered and popular player.

"He plays with so much energy and fire every single night," Patrick said. "It's good news for us."

Showing he still had plenty of juice left in his legs, the 37-year-old averaged nearly a point per game. Taking note, the Carolina Hurricanes came knocking on Patrick's door in March of 2006. With Recchi's blessing, the Pens' GM traded him to Carolina, where he at long last won his elusive second Stanley Cup.

The gritty winger returned to Pittsburgh for his third tour of duty in 2006–07. Playing like a kid half his age, he flung himself into the corners and battled for loose pucks while setting a sterling example for his youthful teammates. On January 26, 2007, the grizzled old pro notched his 500th goal against the Dallas Stars. He scored 24 goals and 68 points while leading the Pens to their first playoff berth in six years.

Recchi hoped to finish his career in Pittsburgh. Sadly, it didn't work out. Following a slow start to the 2007–08 campaign, he was unceremoniously placed on waivers.

"He still has a lot of hockey left in him," buddy Gary Roberts said. "I still think Mark Recchi's a top-six forward on any team. Unfortunately, [the Penguins] didn't think so."

Roberts proved to be prophetic. In 2010–11 the 43-year-old winger tallied 48 points to help Boston win the Stanley Cup.

"This is it for me," said Recchi after hoisting the Cup for a third time. "[The Stanley Cups are] all special and they all mean the same to me. It's kind of nice that this is the last one and you're going out on top."

62 Hall of Fame Game

As part of the festivities, the 2011 Winter Classic featured an NHL Legends Game between Penguins old-timers and former members of the Washington Capitals.

"We all grew up playing on outdoor rinks, so we're really looking forward to having this chance to skate on the Winter Classic rink at Heinz Field," Mario Lemieux said. "There is so much history between the Penguins and Capitals and it will be good to get together and see friends on both benches."

With no shortage of talent to draw upon, the Pens' roster read like a veritable "Who's Who" in hockey. Their lineup featured five Hall of Famers, including Lemieux, Paul Coffey, Ron Francis, Larry Murphy, and Bryan Trottier, not to mention former All-Stars Rob Brown, Kevin Stevens, and Rick Tocchet.

Legends Game Rosters

Penguins

Phil Bourque, Rob Brown, Rod Buskas, Jay Caufield, Paul Coffey, Bob Errey, Ron Francis, Bill Guerin, Dave Hannan, Mario Lemieux, Francois Leroux, Troy Loney, Greg Malone, Gilles Meloche, Larry Murphy, Frank Pietrangelo, Gary Rissling, Gary Roberts, Craig Simpson, Kevin Stevens, Peter Taglianetti, Bryan Trottier, Rick Tocchet, and Warren Young

Coaches: Randy Hillier, Eddie Johnston, and Pierre Larouche
Honorary GM: Jack Riley

Capitals

Greg Adams, Don Beaupre, Peter Bondra, Sylvain Cote, Dino Ciccarelli, John Druce, Dean Evason, Alan Hangsleben, Nick Kypreos, Yvon Labre, Gord Lane, Craig Laughlin, Mark Lofthouse, Dennis Maruk, Alan May, Paul Mulvey, Robert Picard, Michal Pivonka, Errol Rausse, J.R. Reich, Pat Ribble, Ken Sabourin, Blair Stewart, and Scott Walker

Coaches: Granny Grant, Joe Reekie, and Bucky Gallagher

The game provided a wonderful opportunity for the former teammates to renew old acquaintances and engage in some good-natured banter.

"Are you going to be up the middle for the long pass?" Coffey asked Lemieux.

"I'm not going to be as fast as I used to be," Mario replied.

"Well, the pass is probably not going to be on your blade, either," Coffey joked.

Not surprisingly, the exhibition match drew nearly as much attention as the Winter Classic. A healthy crowd of 10,000 turned out at Heinz Field on New Year's Eve to watch Mario and his mates weave a little magic.

Naturally, much of the attention focused on No. 66. Early in the first period the big center set up former linemate Brown for the game-opening goal.

"The pass was a little higher than usual," Brown said in mock critique. "Usually, he puts it nice and flat."

"It was great to play with him, Bob Errey, Rick Tocchet, Kevin Stevens…all my old linemates over the years," Mario said with a smile. "It was a little slower, but a lot of fun."

Lemieux picked up his second assist at 14:22 of the final period while working on a vintage power-play unit that featured Francis and Stevens up front, with Coffey and Murphy manning the points. The old pros flashed some of their latent skills with a series of tape-to-tape passes that led to a tap-in by Francis.

"A lot of fun," Francis said.

"Yeah, it looked like we knew what we were doing," Lemieux offered. "Pretty much the same setup we had 20 years ago."

The superstars weren't the only ones to contribute. Former Penguins tough guys Rod Buskas and Jay Caufield lit the lamp, as did their Capitals counterparts Alan May and Paul Mulvey. Agitator Gary Rissling shared the ice with Lemieux on numerous occasions.

"I just want to thank coach Eddie Johnston," he said. "I had more shifts on the first line than I did in my whole pro career."

The game ended in a 5–5 tie, but not before some drama in the waning moments. With two minutes left to play Murphy notched what appeared to be the clinching tally for the Pens. However, the goal was disallowed because Stevens fell on top of Caps goalie Don Beaupre.

"I'm used to falling on him," said the hulking power forward, who admitted to gaining "five or six pounds" since his playing days. "I didn't feel like getting up."

Some spectators were upset that the game didn't feature a shootout.

"I think everybody's a little disappointed that we didn't get to the shootout, because it would have been great to see Mario,"

Penguins defenseman Phil Bourque said. "We would have gone with all Hall of Famers, of course, in our shootout group."

Others were happy to make it through the affair unscathed.

"Glad it's over," Lemieux said with a smile.

63 Divine Intervention

The year 1972 will forever be etched in Steel City lore as the year of the "Immaculate Reception." Eight months earlier, however, the Penguins enjoyed their own slice of divine intervention.

Following a disappointing season in 1970–71, the Penguins seemed poised to turn the corner. The club was purchased by a group of bright and enthusiastic Pittsburgh investors headed by Tad Potter. Thanks to a trade with the Rangers in January of 1971, coach/general manager Red Kelly had constructed a promising young line featuring Syl Apps, Jean Pronovost, and West Division All-Star Greg Polis.

Determined to make a break with the team's sorry past, Kelly initiated a youth movement. Grizzled veterans such as Bob Blackburn, Dunc McCallum, Jim Morrison, and Dean Prentice were replaced with fresh legs. Rookie defensemen Darryl Edestrand and Sheldon Kannegiesser earned promotions from Hershey. Twenty-year-old Joe Noris—the club's second pick in the Amateur Draft—also made the squad.

Kelly performed wonders through the Intra-League Draft. He plucked budding All-Star Dave Burrows from Chicago and claimed speedy young forward Rene Robert from Buffalo. When the Red Wings selected hard-luck netminder Al Smith, he snapped up 22-year-old goalie Jim Rutherford.

The Entertainer

He wasn't the best player ever to don a Penguins jersey. Not by a long shot. But few players in the history of the National Hockey League ever generated more press—or cultivated a more loyal following—than Edward Steven Phillip Shack.

Projected to be a star following a productive junior career, Shack evolved into a third-line agitator who occasionally contributed on the score sheet. Eddie gained folk hero status in Toronto, where he was an underrated cog on four Stanley Cup winners. Nicknamed "the Entertainer" for his spirited style of play, he was the subject of a novelty song titled, "Clear the Track, Here Comes Shack." The tune shot to No. 1 on the Canadian pop charts.

With his team struggling to keep pace in the chase for a playoff berth in 1972, Penguins coach Red Kelly felt the club needed a shot of adrenalin. Convinced that Shack was the man to provide it, Kelly urged Jack Riley to swing a deal for his old teammate. The Pens GM complied, shuffling promising young right wing Rene Robert off to Buffalo in exchange for the Entertainer.

The trade provided an immediate spark, just as Kelly had hoped. Teamed with Ron Schock and Ken Schinkel on the tongue-twisting Schink-Schock-Shack Line, the colorful winger caught fire and tallied five goals and nine assists in just 18 games.

However, Robert had enormous potential. He would blossom into a star as a member of the Sabres' famed French Connection Line.

To serve as unofficial playing coach for his kiddie corps of defensemen, Kelly claimed Tim Horton, a former teammate on Toronto's great Stanley Cup champions. The 41-year-old strongman had long been regarded as one of the league's top defenders.

Buoyed by the infusion of new blood, the Penguins won five of their first six games, including a club record three straight on the road. However, Horton sustained a broken ankle and the young defensive corps struggled during his absence.

The Pens soon fell back into the pack. They spent most of the season chasing St. Louis and Philadelphia for the final playoff spot.

As the season wore on, Kelly began to rely more heavily on his veterans. Horton returned to the lineup at midseason, and steady Duane Rupp was recalled from Hershey. Club president Jack Riley reassumed the GM duties in January and promptly dealt Robert to Buffalo for another former teammate of Kelly's, winger Eddie Shack.

With the defense stabilized and the rugged Shack providing a much-needed spark, the Penguins rallied sharply down the home-stretch, compiling a 5–1–5 record in their last 11 games.

The chase for the fourth and final playoff spot came down to the final night of the season. Needing a victory over bitter rival St. Louis, coupled with a Flyers loss to Buffalo, the Pens rose to the occasion and bombed the Blues 6–2 at the Civic Arena.

"They sure were inspired," said St. Louis coach Al Arbour. "They must have had jets on their skates. We couldn't do anything right. We just stood around and watched Pittsburgh skate."

"I told my guys Buffalo was ahead 2–1 after two periods," Kelly said. "I wasn't taking any chances."

In reality, the Flyers were in the process of closing out a 2–2 tie with the Sabres, which would've clinched a postseason berth for Philly. However, with only four seconds left on the clock former Flyer Gerry Meehan skated down the left side and unleashed a 60-footer that sailed over goalie Doug Favell's left shoulder and into the net. Suddenly, the Pens were in the playoffs.

The Penguins were understandably elated—and relieved—by their stroke of good fortune.

"It's a terrible feeling to rely on someone else like we had to do," Bryan Watson said. "I was very pessimistic. I thought Philadelphia would win."

Teammate Bryan Hextall was more upbeat.

"I really figured Buffalo was going to win," Hextall said. "Buffalo was sitting there waiting for Philadelphia. They didn't play Saturday night, and the Flyers had played five times in eight days."

64 Look Out Loretta

"It's a *hockey night* in Pittsburgh." For more than 30 seasons, play-by-play announcer Mike Lange has welcomed Penguins fans to broadcasts with this simple but eloquent greeting. He became *the* voice of the Penguins, much as the late Bob Prince was the voice of the Pittsburgh Pirates.

The Sacramento, California, native started doing radio play-by-play for the Phoenix Roadrunners of the old Western Hockey League. He got his break in 1974 when the Penguins hired him to replace Joe Starkey.

"The World Hockey Association came in and the Western Hockey League went defunct, and the general manager there was a big help and he helped me get some contacts," Lange recalled. "Then KDKA hired me and I worked for the Penguins, and that's how it came about."

His arrival coincided with the team's first winning season. Lange's dramatic and colorful style added an extra level of excitement to the broadcasts. He punctuated each Penguins goal with his signature call, "Heeeeeee shoots and scores!"

Lange was influenced by Prince, who did the Penguins' TV play-by-play in 1977–78.

"I learned an awful lot from Bob," he said. "He taught me what people would like. He was unbelievable. He had the respect of everybody in the business. He was one of those guys who went out of their way to help young people find their way."

Encouraged by Prince, Lange started to expand on his repertoire of colorful catchphrases. Distinctive expressions such as "You'd have to be here to believe it," "Scratch my back with a hacksaw," and "He beat him like a rented mule" became as much a part of Penguins hockey lore as Mario Lemieux's highlight-reel goals.

Lange began doing simulcasts for TV and radio in 1979. He was at the microphone for every game during the team's rise from the ashes of the early 1980s through the glory of the Stanley Cup years. Not surprisingly, his favorite call came on a goal by Lemieux.

"There's so many things I've called over the years," Lange said. "But it definitely has to be Mario's goal against Chicago in Game 1 of the Stanley Cup Finals in 1992 to cap that big comeback. That was as exhilarating a goal as has ever been scored."

Play-by-play man Mike Lange has been broadcasting Penguins hockey for more than 30 seasons.

In 2001 Lange received the Hockey Hall of Fame's Foster Hewitt Memorial Award, given each year to a member of the radio and television industry who has made outstanding contributions to their profession and to the game of hockey. He was inducted into the Penguins Hall of Fame the same year. They were fitting tributes to the man who helped make hockey such a popular sport in Pittsburgh.

Sadly, in the summer of 2006 Lange was relieved of his TV play-by-play duties by Fox Sports Net. The dismissal set off a firestorm of criticism, the likes of which hadn't been seen since Prince was fired by KDKA some 30 years earlier.

The Penguins quickly hired the legendary broadcaster to do play-by-play on the radio.

"Mike is an extremely important guy in Penguins history," said Tom McMillan, the team's vice president of communications. "That's why we wanted to immediately offer him the job."

After a brief adjustment period, Lange settled comfortably into his new role. His radio partner, former Pens player Phil Bourque, clearly relishes the opportunity to work with the Hall of Famer.

"He doesn't try to force anything on me," the appreciative color man said, "but he tells me that there may be a better way to do that, or you might want to try this. So, in a way, he wants to always try to help me, but not help me too much. There's a nice balance between he and I."

65 Defection

In the spring of 2008, the hungry young Penguins were poised to take a run at the Stanley Cup. Noting that his club lacked a bona fide scoring winger to team with gifted young center Sidney

Crosby, second-year general manager Ray Shero stepped forward and swung a blockbuster deal at the trade deadline. In exchange for youngsters Colby Armstrong, Erik Christensen, Angelo Esposito, and a first-round pick, he acquired defensive specialist Pascal Dupuis and All-Star forward Marian Hossa from Atlanta.

The addition of Hossa was a major coup. Blessed with a strong, powerful stride and a rapier-like shot, the Slovakian sniper had long been regarded as one of the top wingers in all of hockey. No one-trick pony, he was an outstanding penalty killer who played a diligent two-way game.

However, the 29-year-old did have his detractors. Noting that Hossa struggled to produce in the playoffs, outspoken hockey analyst Mike Milbury dubbed him "Maid Marian."

Shrugging off the criticism, Hossa enjoyed a stellar postseason with the Pens. Blending with Crosby like peas and carrots, he racked up a team-high 12 goals, including two game winners. During a hotly contested Finals matchup against Detroit, the silky-smooth winger paced all Penguins scorers with seven points.

In the wake of his scintillating playoff performance, Shero offered Hossa a lucrative long-term contract reportedly worth $7 million per year. On the eve of free agency, however, the gifted winger spurned the Penguins' offer in favor of a one-year deal with Detroit. When asked why he'd turned down a better offer from the Penguins, Hossa gave a simple yet surprising answer.

"When I compared the two teams," he said, "I felt like I would have a better chance to win the Cup in Detroit."

Although Hossa's reason for jumping ship was understandable if not admirable, it cut his former teammates to the bone.

"There's anger," Penguins winger Max Talbot said. "You can't forget about something like that because everybody in the organization…we expected him to come back. We thought he was comfortable here, and he was really good with Sid."

Stung by the defection of their playoff hero, the Pens lurched through the opening months of the 2008–09 season. With his team struggling mightily at the two-thirds pole, Shero acquired a new set of wingers for Crosby—Bill Guerin and Chris Kunitz. While the Penguins scrambled to qualify for postseason play, the Red Wings—paced by Hossa's 40 goals—cruised to another banner year.

As the 2009 playoffs progressed, it was clear the two rivals were on a collision course. Privately, the Penguins were itching for a rematch with Hossa and his Motor City brethren.

"I was so happy when they defeated Chicago because I really wanted to play them," Talbot said. "And I remember just cheering for Detroit for one game."

From the opening drop of the puck the Penguins targeted their former teammate for special treatment. When Hossa skated through the neutral zone midway through the first period with his head down, Brooks Orpik rocked him with a huge hit.

Feeling added pressure to produce, Hossa failed to score during a hotly contested seven-game set. While the expatriate winger languished, the unheralded Talbot popped in two goals in the series finale to help his team win the Cup.

"Mad Max" relished the opportunity to greet his ex-teammate during the traditional post-series handshake.

"I just told him, 'Good job,'" Talbot said. "I think he knows he made the wrong choice, I don't have to tell him."

"It was his decision, a hard decision," Orpik added. "I've got nothing but respect for the guy. He was a great teammate. He's a really, really good person, too. He'll probably be a better person for it."

For Hossa, a third trip to the Finals proved to be a charm. After signing as a free agent with Chicago, the veteran winger hoisted the Stanley Cup in the spring of 2010.

66 Stacky

Following a dreadful start to the 1973–74 season, Penguins owner Tad Potter replaced longtime general manager Jack Riley with director of player personnel Jack Button. In one of his first moves, Button sent Jack Lynch and popular goalie Jim Rutherford to Detroit for defenseman Ron Stackhouse.

The trade came as a shock to Stackhouse, who thought he'd found a home in the Motor City. After a slow start to his career, the former California draft pick had shown steady improvement during his two-plus seasons with the Red Wings. A decent skater for a big man, he had developed into an offensive threat thanks to his low, hard shot.

Stackhouse also was an outstanding shot blocker. While skating for Peterborough in 1967–68, Petes coach Roger Neilson used him in place of a goalie to thwart penalty shot attempts. Thanks to his good size and large wingspan, the rangy defender stopped all six shots he faced.

Following his arrival in Pittsburgh, Stackhouse performed solidly while adjusting to his new team. Determined to prove his worth, he enjoyed a breakout season in 1974–75. Serving as the quarterback for the Pens' deadly power play, he set new club records for goals (15), assists (45), and points (60) by a defenseman. He tied an NHL record for blue-liners on March 8, 1975, by racking up six assists during an 8–2 demolition of the defending Stanley Cup champion Flyers. His outstanding performance earned him a share of the team's MVP award.

The following year the Haliburton, Ontario, native was even better. He broke his own club records with 60 assists and 71 points to go with a strong plus/minus rating of plus-19. On April

3, 1976, he fired off an incredible 14 shots during a game against Washington.

In 1977–78, Stackhouse suffered a separated shoulder and endured a subpar season. Although he was supplanted by Randy Carlyle as the team's top offensive defenseman, he bounced back to score 10 goals in 1978–79. The following season he made his first and only appearance in an NHL All-Star Game.

Sadly for Stackhouse, he never was fully appreciated in Pittsburgh. Standing 6'3" and weighing 210 pounds, he was a huge player for his day. Because of his stature, the Civic Arena faithful expected him to be a banger. Stackhouse was far from timid—he used his size effectively when the situation called for it—but he did not possess a mean streak. Perhaps no player in the history of the franchise endured more catcalls and verbal abuse.

"Maybe it was because of my style, or rather my lack of style," Stackhouse said.

Ironically, Stackhouse did play a more physical brand of hockey in the latter stages of his career. Early in the 1981–82 season, he stunned his teammates by chasing down and challenging Quebec's pugnacious Dale Hunter. He finished the campaign with 102 penalty minutes, the only time in his 12-year NHL career that he eclipsed the century mark.

Following the season, the big defenseman called it quits. While he had undeniably slowed a step, Stackhouse was only 33 years old and likely had a few more seasons left in him. However, the rough treatment he'd received from the Steel City fans no doubt hastened his departure from the game.

He retired as the all-time leading scorer among Penguins defensemen with 66 goals, 277 assists, and 343 points. To this day, Hall of Famers Paul Coffey and Larry Murphy are the only defenders to score more goals while wearing the black and gold; only Coffey has topped his point total. None have shown more perseverance.

As the old saying goes, time heals all wounds. On April 8, 2010, Stackhouse was among the 51 alumni who attended the Penguins' final regular season home game at the Mellon Arena. When Stacky was introduced to the overflow crowd during the pregame ceremony, he received a warm ovation. Months later the good-natured defenseman was given some long overdue recognition when he received honorable mention in the voting for the Penguins All-Time Team.

67 Handy Andy

During an NHL career that spanned almost 20 seasons, Andy Bathgate established himself as one of hockey's most dynamic stars. Blessed with good size, he was a strong, athletic skater who handled the puck with skill and creativity. Possessing a hard, accurate shot, he was one of the first players to employ the slap shot. It was a Bathgate blast that convinced Hall of Fame goalie Jacques Plante to don a mask.

From the start Bathgate had to overcome enormous adversity. He suffered a severe knee injury during his first shift in junior hockey, an injury that required a steel plate to be inserted into his left knee. For the rest of his career he wore heavy knee braces, which made his accomplishments all the more astonishing.

Bathgate hit his stride while playing for the Rangers. In 1958–59 he scored 40 goals and was awarded the Hart Trophy. Three years later he tied Chicago great Bobby Hull for the scoring title. Following a trade to Toronto in 1964, he helped the Leafs win the Stanley Cup. His stellar play earned him the respect of teammates and foes alike.

"When Bathgate is on, there isn't a better player in the league," Gordie Howe said.

By the 1966–67 season, however, Andy's star was waning. Mired in an uncharacteristic scoring slump, he was demoted to the Pittsburgh Hornets by Detroit.

"He just wasn't shooting the puck," teammate Leo Boivin said. "He'd get the puck like he used to, but instead of shooting he'd try to cut around the defense and work from in close. With his shot, he's got to shoot."

The former MVP quickly proved that he was too good for the American Hockey League. In six games with the Hornets, the classy old pro tallied four goals and 10 points to earn a quick recall by the Red Wings.

"I really never thought I lost it," he said. "It was just that they were playing me on the left wing, and I can't play that side. When I came back up, they had me at right wing on a line with Ted Hampson and Dean Prentice for a while, and we won eight of nine games."

That summer, however, the Red Wings unceremoniously exposed the future Hall of Famer in the Expansion Draft. Andy seriously contemplated retirement until the Penguins selected him with the 101st pick.

"Going into the 17th round I noticed that Andy Bathgate was still available," recalled Pens owner Jack McGregor. "He was expensive [$75,000], another reason why he had not been selected. But I felt he had a year or two left in him and should be worth the investment. I told Jack Riley, our general manager, 'Let's go for Andy Bathgate.'"

Their judgment was soon rewarded. On the night of October 11, 1967, Bathgate struck for the first goal in Penguins history. A week later he notched the team's first hat trick in a 3–3 tie with Minnesota. Skating on a line with fellow veterans Earl Ingarfield and Ab McDonald, he broke from the starting gate at a torrid

Fireplug

Although the Penguins missed the playoffs during their inaugural season, it was not for a lack of talent. Along with a cast of solid pros the team boasted two future Hall of Famers—Andy Bathgate and Leo Boivin.

Having spent the majority of his career in New York, Bathgate received plenty of press. But Boivin was a special player, too. Over the course of an NHL career that spanned 1,150 games, he established himself as one of the game's most fearsome open-ice hitters.

Squat and powerful, the 5'7", 190-pounder had a low center of gravity—perfect for hitting. His arsenal included the shoulder check and the hip check, often thrown with devastating results. Although he rarely put a stick, elbow, or knee into his checks, the Fireplug was one of the most feared men in the league.

"You better keep your head up at all times when that Boivin is cruising the blue line," Chicago's Doug Mohns said. "When he sticks a shoulder in your middle it's like being hit by a freight train."

New York Rangers forward Andy Hebenton agreed.

"The roughest I've played against is Leo Boivin," Hebenton said. "He throws the hardest body checks in hockey. A lot of players on other teams feel the same way I do about him. If he manages to catch you unaware, with your head down, his check really shakes you up in spite of all the padding. It's a thing you don't easily forget."

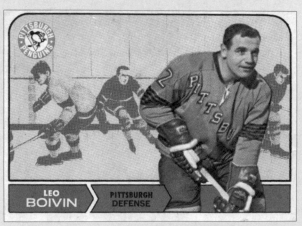

Leo Boivin played 19 seasons in the NHL and was inducted into the Hockey Hall of Fame in 1986.

> Eager to add some mustard to their blue-line corps, the Penguins claimed Boivin in the 1967 Expansion Draft. Although he enjoyed a solid season, pacing the team's defenders with nine goals, Leo's stay in the Steel City was relatively brief. On January 24, 1969, general manager Jack Riley traded him to Minnesota for Duane Rupp. The rock 'em, sock 'em rearguard played with the North Stars through the 1969–70 campaign before hanging up his skates.

clip, tallying eight goals and 16 points during the club's first 15 games.

"His legs may not be what they once were," said his coach Red Sullivan, "but Andy's still got that shot and that noggin."

Bathgate tailed off a bit following a knee injury to Ingarfield. Still, the veteran winger enjoyed a wonderful season, scoring 20 goals and pacing all West Division players with 59 points.

"He was the best 17th-round draft choice in sports history," Riley said.

Wishing to spend more time with his family, Bathgate arranged for the Penguins to loan him to Vancouver of the Western League. He starred for the Canucks for two seasons before making a surprise comeback with the Pens in 1970–71. Although 38 years old and playing on aching knees, Andy still was good enough to tally 44 points in his final NHL season.

68 Belly Up

Under the stewardship of Mario Lemieux and his partners, the Penguins have become one of the healthiest franchises in the NHL. It wasn't always so. For much of their 44-year-history the flightless waterfowl were perched on the edge of a precipice, one step away from tumbling into the abyss.

The Penguins' history of financial woes stretches all the way back to the original owners, a 21-man syndicate headed by founding fathers Peter Block and Pennsylvania senator Jack McGregor. Although the group boasted the crème de la crème of Pittsburgh business society, they quickly ran into problems.

"You knew it was shaky because [the Penguins] had so many investors," publicity director Joe Gordon recalled. "You had a lot of guys who didn't have a lot of cash lying around."

Toward the end of the team's inaugural season McGregor was forced to seek additional backing. He quickly found an interested party in Detroit bank executive Donald Parsons. Reassured that Parsons intended to keep the team in Pittsburgh, McGregor announced on March 21, 1968, that a substantial portion of the club's stock had been sold to the Michigan banker and his group.

Although generous to a fault, Parsons, too, lacked staying power. When the well ran dry, he turned control of the Penguins over to the National Hockey League on December 1, 1970. The league ran the club for the rest of the season while Parsons searched for a buyer.

"I've said it before and I'll say it again, the changes in ownership made it difficult on the hockey team," general manager Jack Riley said. "Everyone was well intentioned…but the philosophy kept changing."

In April of 1971 the Penguins were purchased by Pittsburgh businessmen Tad Potter, Peter Block, Peter Burchfield, and Elmore Keener. Perhaps no group of owners—with the exception of the Lemieux Group—cared more about bringing a winning team to the Steel City. The Penguin Partners worked hand-in-hand with Civic Arena manager Charles Strong to expand the Igloo's seating capacity. Players and coaches were rewarded with handsome contracts.

Unfortunately, Potter and his associates may have cared too much. Dreadfully overextended, they were forced into receivership following a catastrophic playoff loss to the New York Islanders in 1975.

"The next series against the Flyers, if there'd been one, would've bailed us out of our financial hole," Potter later explained. "Ownership would have stabilized. We were an organization which at that point was a couple of players away from being a real contender."

With the future of the franchise hanging precariously in the balance, a group spearheaded by Columbus, Ohio, investment broker Al Savill stepped in to save the Penguins from extinction. While the team was granted a stay of execution, the new owners hardly had deep pockets. Three years later Savill and his partners sold the Pens to Edward J. DeBartolo Sr.

It proved to be a major stroke of good fortune. One of the wealthiest men in America, DeBartolo absorbed enormous losses but doggedly stayed the course. Due largely to his patience and perseverance the Penguins evolved from a second-rate organization into Stanley Cup champions.

Having reached the pinnacle, DeBartolo sold the Penguins to Howard Baldwin and his partners, Morris Belzberg and Thomas Ruta, in the fall of 1991. Under the entrepreneurial Baldwin, the Pens won a second Stanley Cup and remained a perennial power. However, high operating costs and a revenue-draining lockout in 1994–95 combined to deliver a crippling one-two punch to the club's sagging finances. With debts exceeding $100 million, the Penguins became the second team in NHL history to file for bankruptcy under Chapter 11 on October 13, 1998.

Once more the club was skating on thin ice. The NHL Board of Governors considered shutting down the Penguins for the 1998–99 season. It appeared the team might have to liquidate in order to pay off its creditors.

Fortunately, a white knight was waiting just around the corner. On September 3, 1999, the Lemieux Group LP—which included wealthy California businessman Ron Burkle—rescued the team from bankruptcy and ushered in a second golden age in Penguins hockey.

69 When Irish Eyes Are Smiling

After winning his eighth Stanley Cup with Toronto in 1967, Leonard Patrick "Red" Kelly had nothing left to prove on the ice. Seeking a new challenge, the 40-year-old Hall of Famer negotiated a deal to become the first coach of the expansion Los Angeles Kings.

Nothing much was expected of the Kings, who were considered to be the weakest of the expansion teams. Although he had never coached on a professional level, Kelly surprised everyone by guiding the club to a pair of playoff berths.

Concerned about the way the Kings were being managed, Kelly left Los Angeles in the summer of 1969. He immediately was courted by Penguins general manager Jack Riley.

"I'd always thought Red did a great job in Los Angeles because his material really wasn't very good," recalled Riley. "I didn't know Red very well, but from where I sat I understood he was pretty fed up with things out there. When I talked to him in the springtime about coming to Pittsburgh, he said he was interested but that he needed some time to think things over. I just tried to impress upon him the fact that he'd have a free hand here."

After mulling things over, Kelly accepted Riley's offer on July 2, 1969.

"It all came down to the simple fact that I've spent practically my whole life in hockey," he said. "I've played every position except goal, and I think I know the game as well as anyone. It would have been pretty stupid of me, wouldn't it, to turn my back on something I'd been preparing myself for all along?"

Once again Kelly fooled the experts, piloting an undermanned but spirited Penguins club to a second-place finish and a berth in the semifinals. Although the Pesky Pens fell to the Blues in a hotly contested six-game set, Red's achievements earned him Coach of the Year honors.

As a reward for his fine work behind the bench, owner Donald Parsons handed the affable Irishman the dual role of coach and general manager while bumping Riley up to club president. It was a challenging job to be sure, but one that Red seemed wholly capable of handling.

Kelly, indeed, performed well during his brief tenure as general manager. On January 26, 1971, he engineered one of the best trades in club history, sending scrapper Glen Sather to the Rangers for Sheldon Kannegiesser and talented young center Syl Apps. He convinced veteran left wing Lowell MacDonald to end his premature retirement. Displaying a sharp eye for young talent, he traded for Al McDonough and picked up future stars Dave Burrows and Rene Robert in the Intra-League Draft.

Unfortunately, wearing two hats seemed to detract from Kelly's coaching. During his stint as general manager and skipper the team lost nearly twice as many games as it won. Seeking to ease Red's workload, new owner Tad Potter handed the GM duties back to Jack Riley on January 29, 1972.

The move worked like a charm. Free to concentrate on coaching, Kelly led the resurgent Pens to a 14–9–5 finish during the final two months of the 1971–72 season to qualify for postseason play.

Creative and resourceful, Kelly was exceedingly popular among his players. Lowell MacDonald, who also played for Red in Los Angeles, was a big fan.

"I never met a classier individual than Red Kelly," he recalled for Jim O'Brien in *Penguin Profiles*. "People said he was too easy, but when you look back only one thing counts—the decency of a human being."

However, popularity wasn't translating into wins, at least not enough to suit Riley. With the Penguins mired in a 2–7–3 slide and fading from playoff contention, he fired Kelly on January 10, 1973.

The genial redhead would have the last laugh. He returned to Toronto the next season to take over the Maple Leafs' helm. Outfoxing Ken Schinkel, the man who replaced him, Kelly guided the Leafs to first-round playoff victories over the Penguins in 1976 and 1977.

70 Bugsy

When Bryan Joseph Watson arrived in Pittsburgh in January 1969 as part of a big six-player trade with Oakland, the Penguins were mired in the West Division cellar and hopelessly out of playoff contention. They were reasonably skilled by expansion team standards, but sadly lacking in character and grit.

"Watson is the key," said Penguins general manager Jack Riley. "He's a tough little guy. He has the quality we want. He's a hockey player with spark."

A rambunctious little defenseman whose heart was several sizes bigger than his undersized body, Watson had made a name for himself during the 1966 Stanley Cup playoffs. Assigned the daunting task of shadowing Chicago superman Bobby Hull, the callow 23-year-old Red Wing resorted to tactics legal and illegal—including a liberal dose of stick work—to hold the Golden Jet in check.

"When I'm told to watch a guy, I watch him," Watson said with an impish grin.

Hull was less enthusiastic. When asked about his tormentor after the Black Hawks had been vanquished, the normally gracious Hull steamed, "Boy, does that guy bug me!" From then on Watson was known as "Bugsy."

Watson immediately established himself in the Steel City. Suddenly opponents who tried to take liberties with his less combative teammates found themselves nose to nose with the little roughneck. Not coincidentally, the Penguins rallied sharply and played nearly .500 hockey down the homestretch.

"He brought a different element to the team," Syl Apps said. "He was very supportive of everybody. He egged people on; he could get the best out of some guys one way or another."

Watson's confrontational style made him wildly popular in Pittsburgh. Although far from physically imposing and average with his dukes at best, he was nonetheless a very effective on-ice cop. With an arsenal that included trips, slashes, elbows, cross checks, butt-ends, and high-sticks—not to mention the quickest lip in the league—Bugsy would go to any length to stop an opponent.

"Pound for pound, he was the toughest and most hard-nosed player ever," said the late John Ferguson, a former Montreal teammate and NHL heavyweight champ.

Bugsy willingly paid the price for his indiscretions. Sporting a mass of scar tissue around his eyes and a nose flattened from countless battles, he had the look of a middleweight fighter.

"I'd better get married soon," he joked, "before I get any uglier."

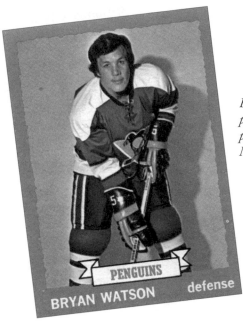

Bryan Watson scored 152 points and amassed 2,212 penalty minutes during his NHL career.

Although aggressive play was clearly his stock in trade, Watson worked hard to improve himself as a hockey player. In 1971–72 he enjoyed his finest season, tallying a career-best 20 points while piling up a league-leading 212 penalty minutes. The following season he paced the club's defensemen with a sparkling plus-18.

"Bryan had some great qualities," teammate Jean Pronovost said. "He was definitely a team man. He would do anything for the team. He wasn't the biggest guy, but he had a big heart. I liked his attitude. He was a player's player. He put the team first. He sacrificed his body to accomplish that. He was limited talentwise, but he lasted because he was willing to pay the price."

Bugsy also possessed a great sense of humor. During a road trip to Los Angeles in the early 1970s he famously hijacked a Marriott courtesy bus on a dare and took his teammates for a joy ride before returning them to the hotel safe and sound.

On another occasion, when the Penguins were being operated by the league, he needled NHL commissioner Clarence Campbell.

"Hey, Clarence," he quipped, "how do you think your club's doing tonight?"

Although always a Penguin at heart, Watson was traded to St. Louis in January of 1974. Despite his limited skills he played for five more seasons before hanging up his skates. True to form, Bugsy finished his NHL career with 2,212 penalty minutes.

71 Superstar

Through the years the Penguins have enjoyed tremendous success drafting centers of French Canadian descent. First came the late Michel Briere, then Pierre Larouche, and last but certainly not least, a big fellow who wore No. 66. So it was no great surprise when they selected feisty Hull Olympiques center Max Talbot in the eighth round of the 2002 Entry Draft.

Unlike his predecessors, Talbot was not projected to be a star. Although he tallied 202 points during his final two seasons with the Olympiques, he was neither big nor especially fast. But he possessed a ton of intangibles, including a winning attitude, underrated skills, and the heart of a lion.

Nicknamed "Mad Max" by his teammates for his colorful and irrepressible personality, he soon became a media darling. In 2007 he starred in a kitschy local TV commercial for A&L Motors with teammates Colby Armstrong, Sergei Gonchar, and Evgeni Malkin. Talbot stole the show, proclaiming, "I am the superstar." The new nickname stuck.

While nobody was confusing Talbot with Malkin or Sidney Crosby, he developed into a solid role player who displayed a penchant for producing in clutch situations. During Game 5 of the 2008 Stanley Cup Finals, he banged home the dramatic tying goal with 34 seconds remaining to propel his team to a triple-overtime victory over Detroit.

Talbot was even better during the 2009 Cup run. The Pens were trailing the surging Flyers 3–0 during the critical Game 6 of their opening-round series. Worse yet, Talbot had turned the puck over in his own end late in the opening frame, a gaffe that led directly to a Philadelphia goal.

With the series hanging in the balance, Mad Max turned the tide by taking on tough guy Daniel Carcillo, the NHL's reigning penalty king. In a spirited go, the rough-and-tumble Flyer quickly gained the upper hand and pounded an overmatched Talbot to the ice with a volley of hard rights.

While the victorious Carcillo pumped his fists to the roar of the Wachovia Center crowd, Talbot—beaten but unbowed—skated to the penalty box and raised his index finger to his mouth as if to shush the howling mob.

Talbot lost the battle, but he won the war. Fourteen seconds later Ruslan Fedotenko snaked the puck past Philly goalie Martin Biron to ignite a Penguins comeback. The Steel City sextet proceeded to torch the Flyers for five straight goals to advance to the second round. To a man, Talbot's teammates praised the peppery center for turning the game around.

"Max really stepped up," teammate Tyler Kennedy said afterward. "He showed a ton of guts."

Playing his gritty, hell-for-leather style, Talbot came up even bigger during the Stanley Cup Finals against Detroit. After scoring two key goals early in the series, Max shone like a diamond in the winner-take-all Game 7. Barely a minute into the second period of a tight scoreless battle, he corralled a loose puck at the right hash mark and snapped a low shot between Chris Osgood's pads.

Incredibly, Talbot struck again midway through the period. Gathering in a chip pass from Chris Kunitz, the little buzz saw raced into the Detroit end and ripped the puck over Osgood's shoulder. It proved to be the Stanley Cup–winning goal.

"It's the biggest day of my life," gushed a joyous Max during the victory celebration. "I wasn't trying to do anything special. I just wanted to win the Cup."

Weeks later it was revealed that he'd skated for much of the season with a dislocated shoulder, which made his feats all the more remarkable.

"He played hurt this year, even though it didn't look like it in Game 7," Talbot's agent, Pat Brisson said. "It shows how much character he has. That shoulder was popping in and out."

72 The Mad Hatter

His career with the Penguins was relatively brief, spanning only 152 games. During that time James Allison "Al" McDonough would achieve one of the most stunning feats in franchise history, earning him a colorful nickname and a permanent place in Penguins folklore.

Over the course of three seasons with the St. Catharines Black Hawks of the Ontario Hockey Association, McDonough established himself as a skilled and resourceful goal scorer. For a brief time, he would enjoy similar success in the National Hockey League.

Explosion

In the early 1970s, the Penguins and the St. Louis Blues were antagonists in one of the NHL's fiercest feuds. Contests between the teams invariably featured a liberal dose of brawling and rough play. Pens toughies Bryan "Bugsy" Watson and Bryan Hextall and the Blues' equally rugged Plager brothers, Barclay and Bob, were usually at the center of the mayhem.

A near-capacity crowd of more than 12,400 fans jammed the Civic Arena on a mid-November night in 1972 to watch the bitter rivals go at it. They were treated to fireworks of a different kind.

The archenemies stayed true to form during a nasty first period. Penguins winger Greg Polis engaged Mike Murphy in the obligatory fisticuffs, while feisty Blues center Garry Unger piled up 22 minutes in penalties. Thanks to some aggressive skating and checking, the Pens snatched a 3–1 lead.

Heading into the second period, the home team appeared to have the game well in hand. However, the Blues took advantage of sloppy defensive play to poke two pucks past Pens goalie Jim Rutherford. When St. Louis center Fran Huck scored barely a minute into the final frame, it appeared the game was slipping away.

Al McDonough immediately knotted the score for the Pens with his second goal of the evening. The game remained deadlocked until the nine-minute mark, when Hextall and Jean Pronovost set up Polis for the go-ahead goal.

That's when things really heated up. In rapid-fire succession, the Penguins hammered five goals past Blues netminder Wayne Stephenson in just over two minutes. Hextall tipped in a blast from the point for a power-play tally at 12:00. Eighteen seconds later, Pronovost beat the beleaguered goalie again. After a brief respite, McDonough lit the lamp at 13:40, followed in short order by Ken Schinkel (13:49) and Ron Schock (14:07).

The sudden outburst set two NHL records: the fastest five goals ever by one team (2:07), and the fastest seven goals ever by one team (12:13).

Following a strong 33-goal campaign with Springfield of the American Hockey League, McDonough earned a promotion to the Los Angeles Kings in 1971–72. Remarkably, the Kings gave up on the rookie after only 31 games, sending him to the Penguins for veteran defenseman Bob Woytowich.

Upon his arrival in Pittsburgh, the tall, slender right wing showed genuine promise as a scorer. In 37 games he tallied a respectable 18 points, including seven goals. One thing was certain—McDonough wasn't afraid to shoot the puck. He fired off 113 shots during his half-season with the Pens.

Penguins coach Red Kelly liked what he saw. During the 1972 training camp he moved McDonough to the top line with Syl Apps and Lowell MacDonald. While he was hoping for good things from the unit, even Kelly could not have anticipated what was in store.

Meshing beautifully with his new linemates, McDonough began to score goals in bunches. In the second game of the season he notched his first Penguins hat trick against Wayne Stephenson to key a 5–2 victory over archrival St. Louis.

McDonough was just warning up. On November 19, 1972, he exploded for his second hat trick of the young season as the Pens downed the Rangers 5–3 in Madison Square Garden. Three nights later the Penguins squared off for a return match with St. Louis at the Civic Arena. Victimizing Stephenson once again, Al connected three more times to pace a record-setting 10–4 demolition of the Blues.

In the process, he became the first player in team history to score hat tricks in back-to-back games, a feat that would not be equaled until Hall of Famer Joe Mullen registered consecutive four-goal games in December of 1991. He also earned a colorful new nickname—"the Mad Hatter."

"I guess three has to be my favorite number," he told Dan Donovan of the *Pittsburgh Press*. "I can't get past it."

McDonough would continue his hot scoring throughout the 1972–73 season. Although he failed to record another hat trick, the Mad Hatter enjoyed a breakout year, striking for a club-record 35 goals.

Coming off his big season, the 23-year-old winger appeared to have a bright future in the Steel City. But the Penguins bottomed out through the early stages of the 1973–74 campaign. Although McDonough remained productive—14 goals and a team-high 36 points through 37 games—his sometimes lackadaisical approach cast him in a poor light. On January 4, 1974, he was traded to Atlanta for Chuck Arnason and tough defenseman Bob Paradise. Ironically, he had just been named to the West Division All-Star Team.

McDonough never was the same player following the trade. Although he managed 10 goals in 35 games with the Flames, he was viewed as an underachiever. He jumped to the Cleveland Crusaders of the World Hockey Association in 1974–75 and scored 34 goals. However, his output gradually tailed off during three seasons in the WHA. Following a cup of coffee with the Detroit Red Wings in 1977–78, McDonough retired from the game at the age of 27.

73 Call into *The Mark Madden Show*

If you're a Penguins fan who likes your voice to be heard, then calling into the *The Mark Madden Show* is definitely something you should do. The show, described by one critic as "controlled chaos," airs on 105.9 The X from 3:00 PM to 6:00 PM every weekday.

Madden is brash, controversial, opinionated, and never, ever dull. Blessed with boundless energy, a deep intellect, and a strong knowledge of the game, the self-proclaimed "Super Genius" possesses an abiding passion for the Penguins. His unbridled enthusiasm for his favorite team is contagious. But be forewarned. Madden does not suffer fools, or foolish opinions, easily. Offer an "off-the-Mark" observation, and you're liable to be verbally sliced and diced on the air.

A fixture on the Steel City sports scene for nearly three decades, Mark worked as a journalist for the *Pittsburgh Post-Gazette* for 15 years, covering the Penguins and high school sports. An avid wrestling fan, he gained national notoriety as a TV commentator for World Championship Wrestling. During the early 2000s he began a highly successful run as a talk-show host for ESPN Radio 1250.

Madden's never been afraid to stir the pot. He once bet Mario Lemieux $66 (later upped to $6,600) that the iconic Penguins superstar couldn't score a goal from a face-off. During a game against Buffalo at Mellon Arena on December 23, 2002, Mario accomplished the feat. In one of the more colorful moments in franchise history, the big fellow wheeled around and looked up to the press box where he knew Madden was watching.

In November of 2006 Madden unceremoniously was fired from his job as a panelist on the WTAE-TV show *Action Sports Sunday*, reportedly for being too critical of the Steelers. An unrepentant Madden lashed out, stating, "The Steelers are like Pittsburgh's own version of the Kremlin."

Eighteen months later Madden made off-color remarks about terminally ill Masschusetts senator Ted Kennedy and was promptly fired by ESPN. Upon being released from his contract in October of 2008, the ratings king was back on the air with The X. As unapologetic and bombastic as ever, he quickly achieved cult hero status in Pittsburgh.

I had my own encounter with Mark in the fall of 2010. Shortly after my first book—*Total Penguins*—hit the bookstores, Triumph Books arranged for me to be a guest on Madden's show. Although

Big Mac

One night during the spring of 2004 I was out at a Pittsburgh night-club and happened to spot Penguins tough guy Steve McKenna near the bar. Standing 6'8" and sporting a shaved head and a goatee, Big Mac was kind of hard to miss.

I'd seen McKenna interviewed on TV countless times, and he always seemed friendly and approachable. I decided to introduce myself. He was every bit as good-natured and engaging as I'd anticipated. Soon we were talking hockey.

As our conversation grew more animated, I discovered McKenna had a habit of giving you a backhanded whap to the chest whenever he was making a point.

"You really cleaned [Buffalo enforcer] Eric Boulton's clock," I noted.

"Aw, he's just a little guy," McKenna responded. *Whap*.

"I think it's going to take the Pens five years to rebuild," I suggested.

"No, it's only going to take us three," he said. *Whap*.

And so it continued. I'd share my thoughts—he'd offer his opinion—and *whap*! While I'm no giant, I'm a lifelong weightlifter. But believe me, I was feeling those whaps. It gave me a new appreciation for how strong hockey players are...and how much it must hurt to get hit by a punch thrown with intent.

Finally I said, "You know, Mac, every time you whap me you just about knock me over."

He just laughed and said, "Aw, get out of here." *Whap*.

We wished each other luck, shook hands, and parted ways. I'll always have fond memories of my chance encounter with Big Mac. After all, I had the bruises as a keepsake.

I'd never spoken to Mark, I was keenly aware of his reputation. Given the fact that I'd never done a talk show before, I don't mind admitting that I was more than a bit nervous.

The morning of the show I ran a couple of miles through my neighborhood to take the edge off. Even that didn't help. I truly feared that Madden would chew me up and spit me out like a wad of stale gum.

My nerves were spiking as Mark introduced me to his radio audience, and I offered up a silent prayer that I'd make it through the show unscathed. Much to my relief, he made a joke about the size of *Total Penguins* (705 pages), claiming that it broke his coffee table. I got a good chuckle out of it and immediately felt at ease.

My initial fears proved unfounded. Madden was respectful, gracious, and engaging. He asked intelligent and thought-provoking questions, and I found myself thoroughly enjoying our banter. When my 15 minutes of fame drew to a close, I thanked Mark for having me on his show, grateful that it had gone so well.

While I can't guarantee your chat with Mark will be as pleasant as mine, calling into *The Mark Madden Show* is definitely worth the experience.

74 Battleship and Demolition Durby

The Penguins entered the 1973–74 season with high hopes. Although the club missed the playoffs by a scant three points the previous year, it registered the best record in team history to date. Armed with top-notch scorers Syl Apps, Al McDonough, and Lowell MacDonald and 24-year-old defensive stalwart Dave Burrows, better days seemed just around the corner.

There was, however, a glaring weakness. While the Pens were reasonably skilled, they were sadly lacking in muscle and grit. The point was pounded home during a preseason game against archrival St. Louis when the team's aging policemen—Bryan "Bugsy" Watson and Bryan Hextall—were overwhelmed by a legion of Blues tough guys.

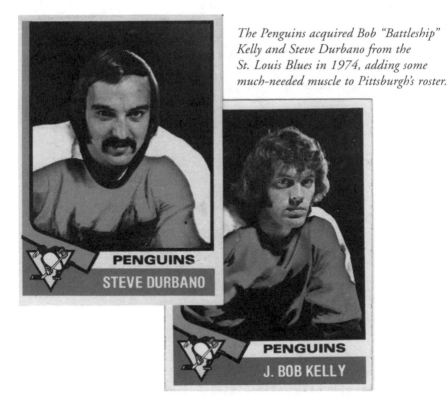

The Penguins acquired Bob "Battleship" Kelly and Steve Durbano from the St. Louis Blues in 1974, adding some much-needed muscle to Pittsburgh's roster.

PENGUINS
STEVE DURBANO

PENGUINS
J. BOB KELLY

Ill-equipped to handle such nasty foes, the paperweight Penguins sank like a stone. On the rare occasions when they fought back the results were dubious. After scoring a lopsided decision over Pens defenseman Jean-Guy Lagace, Philly bruiser Andre "Moose" Dupont chuckled, "Lagace should've gotten five minutes for *receiving.*"

Penguins owner Tad Potter had seen enough. On January 17, 1974, he shipped Watson, Greg Polis, and a second-round draft pick to the Blues for left wing Bob "Battleship" Kelly and defensemen Steve Durbano and Ab DeMarco.

The shakeup had a dramatic effect on the team. Standing 6'1" and weighing 210 pounds, the 22-year-old Durbano was a larger-than-life character who seemed plucked straight from the movie *Slap Shot.*

"Durbano doesn't check the condition of the ice before a game," said a St. Louis player. "He checks the condition of the seat in the penalty box."

Aptly described by a local sportswriter as a "hard fist of a defenseman," Durbano's appetite for mayhem had already reached legendary proportions. While skating for the Rangers' top farm club in Omaha in 1971–72 he set a professional hockey record with an astronomical 402 penalty minutes. As a member of the Toronto Marlboros junior team, Demolition Durby single-handedly wiped out the London Knights' top forward line during the opening shift of a playoff game.

"He went out on the first shift of the game and he speared Darryl Sittler, Gordie Brooks, and, I think, Gary Geldart," recalled teammate Mike Murphy. "There are these three guys, doubled over on the ice, lying there, and the crowd just wanted to kill us. I think we won the series right there."

Likewise, Kelly was coveted for his muscle. After all, he wasn't nicknamed "Battleship" for nothing. The tall, rangy winger had earned a reputation as one of the most fearsome fighters in hockey. His victims included the Flyers' notorious bad man, Dave "the Hammer" Schultz.

It was as if Wyatt Earp and Bat Masterton had suddenly ridden into town. With Durbano and Kelly riding shotgun the Penguins' skill players flourished once more. During a 6–2 triumph over Vancouver, Durbano scored the first goal of the game and broke Dave Dunn's nose with a roundhouse right.

Next the Pens visited Philadelphia on January 20 to take on the pugnacious Flyers. Prior to the game Kelly was interviewed on camera by a local sportscaster.

"You can play this interview in their locker room," Kelly said. "I don't care. I'm not afraid of anyone."

The Penguins won 5–3.

Three days later St. Louis arrived in town for a big post-trade grudge match. Early in the second period Durbano clashed

Tough Break

When the Penguins acquired Steve Durbano from St. Louis in January of 1974, they were well aware of his penchant for roughhouse play. However, Durbano's boisterous nature obscured the fact that he also was a talented defenseman. Hockey scribe Stan Fischler, for one, believed the former first-round pick of the Rangers had the makings of an All-Star.

Possessing a heavy shot and underrated skills, Demolition Durby enjoyed an outstanding first season with the Pens. In just 33 games he registered 18 points and a plus-17, not to mention 138 penalty minutes. However, his career took a sudden and irretrievable turn for the worse on October 19, 1974.

"We were playing Philadelphia and I was trying to avoid a hip check by Moose Dupont," he explained to writer Mike Hanley. "I put my hand out when I hit the ice and my elbow locked."

A bone from Durbano's arm was driven through his hand by the impact.

"The pain was unbelievable," he said. "When I pulled my glove off, I almost got sick. The doctor had a player sit on my arm while he yanked my hand back in place."

Despite numerous operations, Durbano never regained full use of his left hand.

"The timing was terrible," he said. "I felt like my game was just coming together. I couldn't lift weights with that hand. My arm started to shrivel. My fighting days were over, my shot was gone, and my career was starting to go downhill."

Reduced to the role of a sideshow performer, the volcanic defenseman was dealt to Kansas City on January 9, 1976, two short years after his arrival. Although his fighting ability was impaired, his infamous temper remained intact. He would *average* 5.12 penalty minutes per game over the course of his abbreviated NHL career, the highest mark in league history.

with the Blues' new enforcer, Bob Gassoff, while Kelly made short work of Barclay Plager. Following a pulsating 4–1 victory, the dynamic duo was named the game's co-No. 1 stars. As they skated onto the Civic Arena ice to the roar of the crowd, Durbano grabbed the sleeve of Kelly's jersey and hoisted his left arm high in the air.

"After that, the teams that used to run around all over the place against us all of a sudden weren't running around anymore," noted Apps.

75 Colossal Collapse

The 1974–75 Penguins were a team of immense promise. Possessing a near-perfect blend of youth, experience, toughness, and skill, the club boasted nine 20-goal scorers, the most in franchise history.

Optimism was high as the Pens opened the playoffs by sweeping archrival St. Louis in a best-of-three set. The quick kill set up a quarterfinals matchup with the plucky New York Islanders.

Under the watchful eye of bespectacled coach Al Arbour, the Islanders had made the playoffs in only their third year of existence. Featuring a curious blend of castoffs and rising young stars, the Islanders had melded into a spirited team that played a tight-checking game.

Undaunted, the Penguins' juggernaut rolled through the early stages of the series like a well-oiled machine. After toppling the Islanders in the first two games at the Civic Arena, the Pens prevailed 6–4 in a wide-open Game 3 on Long Island to snatch a commanding 3–0 series lead. Elated, owner Tad Potter threw a party for his team at the Salty Dog Saloon.

The revelry, while understandable, would prove to be incredibly premature. Acting on a hunch, Arbour replaced his harried starter, Billy Smith, with backup goalie Glenn "Chico" Resch in Game 4. The move worked like a charm. As the sharp-shooting

Penguins struggled to solve Resch, the Islanders ran off three straight wins to set up a deciding Game 7 in Pittsburgh.

"The Islanders are like a disease," grumbled Pens tough guy Bob "Battleship" Kelly. "You can't get rid of them. When they're down, they don't pull the rip cord and bail out. I like them but I don't like them. You know what I mean."

Noting that his erstwhile snipers had rattled no fewer than seven shots off of goalposts during the three losses, Penguins coach Marc Boileau called a mandatory practice the morning of Game 7 and instructed his players to shoot into an empty net.

"Resch has them all psyched out," he said. "We averaged more than four goals per game all year, but Resch has given us only four goals in three games. No goalie should be able to do that to us."

Determined to seize control, the Penguins came at the Islanders hard. Barely two minutes into the game Bob Paradise and Islanders heavyweight Clark Gillies engaged in a spirited slugging match. Later in the period Kelly bested Dave Lewis in a brisk dustup. Skating with purpose and fire, the home team peppered Resch with 25 shots through 40 minutes of play. The little goalie was up to the task.

"Resch repeatedly made the big saves," Arbour said.

The Pens had two great chances in the third period. Jean Pronovost thought he had a sure goal when he tipped a shot past Resch, but the puck bounced harmlessly off the iron. Moments later Pierre Larouche glided in on a breakaway and deked the Islanders goalie out of position. He missed a wide-open net and went crashing into the boards.

"[Denis] Potvin tripped me," he said. "I had the net open to me."

Two minutes later Bert Marshall lugged the puck over the blue line. As the Penguins swarmed to greet him, they left veteran Ed Westfall unattended in front of Gary Inness.

"All the Penguins went toward Bert so I yelled to him," Westfall said. "I held the puck for a second when I got it. [Inness] was leaning a little toward J.P. Parise coming in on his right side. So I put it up high and tried to get the puck in the eight inches he left open near the post."

"What could I do," Inness said. "He kept moving in from the side. I stayed as long as I could, then I had to move with him. The instant I did, he put it past me. Westfall's an old pro. He never panicked."

Demoralized by the sudden turn of events, the Penguins failed to register a shot during the final five minutes. They became the first team in 33 years to drop four straight playoff games after taking a 3–0 series lead.

"We got overconfident...definitely," Boileau said. "All they did was work for seven games."

76 Attend a Penguins Victory Celebration

Pittsburgh is a city that loves to celebrate. When the Pirates upset the mighty New York Yankees in the 1960 World Series to end a 35-year championship drought, an estimated 300,000 people flocked to downtown Pittsburgh to bask in the glow of victory. By 9:00 PM the area was so choked with merrymakers that local officials closed the two tunnels connecting the heavily populated South Hills to downtown.

Similar impromptu celebrations followed during the glorious decade of the 1970s, when the Steelers (four Super Bowls) and the Pirates (two World Series) earned Pittsburgh the nickname "City of Champions."

Through 24 mostly lean years, the city's long-suffering hockey fans waited for an opportunity to join in the revelry. Their moment

Tugger and Moose

Throughout the 1990s, the Penguins received stellar goaltending from the tandem of Tom Barrasso and Ken Wregget. By the spring of 2000, however, Wregget had been traded to Calgary, while age and injuries were finally creeping up on the 34-year-old Barrasso. No stranger to big swaps, on March 14, 2000, Penguins general manager Craig Patrick peddled Barrasso to Ottawa for defenseman Janne Laukkanen and goaltender Ron Tugnutt.

At first glance, Tugnutt hardly seemed to fit the bill of a big-time stopper. A fourth-round pick of Quebec in the 1986 Entry Draft, he bounced from team to team before finding a home in Ottawa. In 1998–99 Tugnutt led the NHL with a 1.79 goals-against average.

The little goalie wasted little time in establishing himself after arriving in Pittsburgh. Flashing his All-Star form, Tugger won four of six decisions down the homestretch while posting a sizzling .924 save percentage. During the Pens' opening-round upset of Washington, the unheralded goalie stopped 152 of 160 shots.

He was even better during the Eastern Conference Semifinals. With Tugnutt standing on his head the Penguins swept Games 1 and 2 in Philadelphia by scores of 2–0 and 4–1. Although the tougher, more talented Flyers rolled to four straight wins, Tugnutt was hardly to blame. He was superb during a marathon quadruple-overtime loss in Game 4, kicking out 70 of 72 shots. In 11 postseason contests, he registered a stunning 1.77 goals-against average and an extraordinary save percentage of .945, the finest marks in team playoff history.

Impressed by the veteran's exceptional play, the expansion Columbus Blue Jackets made Tugnutt an offer he couldn't refuse—$10 million over four years. Unable to offer him a comparable deal, the cash-strapped Penguins bid adieu to their playoff hero.

Fast-forward to the spring of 2001. Buoyed by return of superstar Mario Lemieux, the Penguins had the makings of a Stanley Cup contender. However, the club had received only so-so play between the pipes from Jean-Sebastien Aubin and Garth Snow.

Eschewing the big trade, Craig Patrick took a different approach to shore up the team's goaltending. In a minor deal he acquired Johan Hedberg from San Jose for defenseman Jeff Norton.

At the time of the trade, the 27-year-old Hedberg was toiling in relative anonymity for the Manitoba Moose of the American Hockey League. Indeed, his only claim to fame was being the kid brother of Swedish hockey legend Anders Hedberg. But Penguins assistant general manager Eddie Johnston had scouted the ultra-competitive goalie and liked what he saw.

Dubbed "the Moose" by announcer Mike Lange for the Bullwinkle-like image emblazoned on his mask, the unassuming Hedberg backstopped the Pens to a third-place finish in the Atlantic Division.

In the playoffs Hedberg led the Penguins past the Capitals and Sabres to a berth in the Eastern Conference Finals. While the Pens were vanquished by New Jersey in five games, it did nothing to detract from the rookie's stunning achievements.

Unlike Tugnutt, the Moose would go on to play two full seasons in the Steel City. In 2001–02 he was a tower of strength, appearing in 66 games while logging a 2.75 goals-against average and six shutouts, the second-highest total in club history.

in the sun finally came on Saturday, May 25, 1991, when their beloved Penguins vanquished the Minnesota North Stars 8–0 in Bloomington to capture the Stanley Cup.

Over two decades of abject frustration and misery were instantly dissolved in a wave of delirium. During the wee hours of May 26, some 25,000 championship-starved fans crammed Pittsburgh International Airport on a warm, muggy morning to greet their conquering heroes.

The Penguins and the city hastily organized a victory celebration to be held three days later at Point State Park. A throng of 80,000 strong jammed the site, while players, club executives, and local dignitaries such as Pittsburgh mayor Sophie Masloff took to the stage. When it was his turn at the microphone, Pens winger Phil Bourque hoisted the Cup overhead and famously bellowed, "What do you say we take this thing out on the river and party all summer!"

Steel City fans wouldn't have to wait long for another cel-ebration. The following spring, the team swept the Chicago Blackhawks to repeat as Stanley Cup champions. Again, the city and the Penguins set up a victory celebration, this time within the confines of Three Rivers Stadium on June 4, 1992.

Just when it seemed inclement weather would put a damper on the proceedings, Bryan Trottier grabbed Lord Stanley's chalice and took the venerable trophy for several slides on the rain-slicked tarpaulin that covered the field, much to the delight of the 40,000 in attendance.

It would take another 17 years and a new cast of superstars to return the Cup to Pittsburgh. Anticipating a crowd of 350,000, city officials opted to sponsor a victory parade and motorcade kicking off at noon on Monday, June 15, 2009. It proved to be a wise decision. Hundreds of thousands of fans lined the sidewalks and hung from the open windows of office buildings all along the parade route.

The air on the bright, cloudless day was electric as fans show-ered the Penguins with an outpouring of affection rarely seen in the annals of Pittsburgh sports history. The excitement intensi-fied when Bill Guerin, Jordan Staal, and Max Talbot hopped out of their cars on Grant Street and waded into the adoring throng, exchanging greetings, handshakes, and high fives with Cup-crazed fans.

Most in attendance were in their twenties and thirties, but the crowd was seasoned with a fair share of office workers. Everyone had a wonderful time.

"We lived in Maryland last time and couldn't be here for the parade, so we didn't want to miss it this time," said Beth Karos of Mars.

Danielle Hooks, clad in a homemade tank top displaying "71 Malkin" on the back, made the long drive from Vandergrift in Armstrong County "because [Evgeni] Malkin's my future husband."

Jennifer Lang of Plum brought her 13-month old son, Jacob.

"I wanted to be able to bring him out to see this," she said. "He's been clapping when everyone was clapping. A lot of people are here, and everyone's been so nice and polite."

77 History Lesson

In the fall of 1893 Pittsburgh power broker Christopher Magee decided to build a grand new gathering place for the city's residents that featured an indoor ice skating rink. The result was the magnificent Schenley Park Casino.

Open to the public on May 29, 1895, the Casino became a popular venue for hockey. Players and teams from across North America flocked to the Steel City to challenge the Pittsburgh Hockey Club and skate on the Casino's artificial ice surface, which was among the first of its kind.

Sadly, the Casino was destroyed by fire on December 17, 1896. Fortunately, a second arena—the Duquesne Gardens—was already in the works. The Gardens played host to its first hockey match on January 24, 1899.

Thanks to its brand-new home, Pittsburgh hockey enjoyed a period of unprecedented growth and popularity. Several amateur circuits sprang up, including a local banker's league. According to Pittsburgh sportswriter Paul Sullivan, the Bankers League may have been one of the first circuits to actively recruit and pay players.

"Some of the banks started a hockey league as a promotional stunt and brought Canadians down and gave them jobs in the banks," Sullivan recalled in an interview with Ed Bouchette of the *Pittsburgh Post-Gazette*. "They were down here to play hockey but in order to qualify and play for the bank they had to be an employee of the bank. I don't know what they gave them to do at the bank, but it wasn't much."

With a glut of players flooding in from across the country and Canada, a new semi-professional league formed in 1900—the Western Pennsylvania Hockey League.

"A gentleman named Garnet M. Sixsmith started hockey here, coming from Canada with several other players," said Jackie Powell, who served as a goal judge at the Civic Arena. "They were branded the first hockey professionals. Some people say that pro hockey had its origins right here in Pittsburgh."

In 1904 the WPHL ceased operations with the formation of the International Professional Hockey League. The Pittsburgh Pros competed against teams from Calumet, Michigan; Houghton-Portage Lakes, Michigan; Sault Ste. Marie, Michigan; and Sault Ste. Marie, Ontario.

Following the 1906–07 season professional leagues began to sprout up across Canada. Lured by the promise of bigger pay-checks, many players returned to their native country. When the IPHL folded, the WPHL resumed operations for two seasons before it, too, disbanded.

The demise of the WPHL left the city without a professional league. However, in 1915 the Pittsburgh Athletic Association joined the United States Amateur Hockey Association. Boasting big-time players such as Lionel Conacher and Roy Worters, the PAA—renamed the Yellow Jackets—captured USAHA titles in 1924 and 1925.

The Yellow Jackets joined the National Hockey League the next year. Renamed the Pirates, the team finished a strong third during its inaugural season.

"They were an amateur team one year and in the Stanley Cup Semifinals the next," Sullivan noted. "And they were barely nudged out."

Steel City Spectacle

During the decade of the Roaring Twenties, Pittsburgh dominated the national amateur hockey ranks. Paced by the likes of Lionel "Big Train" Conacher, Roy "Shrimp" Worters, and Harry Darragh, the Pittsburgh Yellow Jackets won the United States Amateur Hockey Association title in 1923–24.

Steel City fans were in for an even bigger treat the following season. A brand-new local club, the Fort Pitt Hornets, joined the USAHA. A strong team in their own right, the Hornets were paced by high-scoring defenseman Johnny McKinnon, who led the league with 24 goals, and goalie Joe Miller, who posted a sparkling 1.72 goals-against average. Many of the team's players, including McKinnon, Miller, Bernie Brophy, Charles "Bonner" Larose, Hec Lepine, and player-coach Rennison "Dinny" Manners, went on to play in the NHL.

As if scripted, the Hornets captured the East Division title and the Yellow Jackets won the West to set up an all-Pittsburgh championship series.

The hometown rivals opened the four-game set on April 3, 1925, before a packed house at Duquesne Gardens. Fort Pitt's pepper-pot captain, Arthur "Paddy" Sullivan, beat Worters six minutes into the first period to draw first blood. Darragh countered for the Yellow Jackets five minutes later, and the game settled into a knockdown, drag-out affair. Four minutes into overtime, Conacher sped into the Fort Pitt zone and beat Miller for the game winner.

Buoyed by their captain's efforts, the Yellow Jackets topped the Hornets 3–1 in Game 2 and battled them to a 2–2 tie in Game 3. On April 11, they eclipsed the East Division champs 2–1 to capture their second straight USAHA crown.

After enjoying a measure of success during their first three seasons, the cash-strapped Pirates hit the skids. Following a pair of dismal last-place finishes the club moved across the state to Philadelphia in 1930.

Despite the loss of the Pirates, the decade of the Great Depression ushered in a second golden age in Pittsburgh hockey. The Yellow Jackets reformed and skated for several more seasons. Two of the team's brightest stars, Frank Brimsek and Gordie

Drillon, went on to enjoy Hall of Fame careers. The colorfully named Pittsburgh Shamrocks competed in the International-American Hockey League in 1935–36.

In October of 1936 local theater owner John Harris purchased the Detroit Olympics and brought them to Pittsburgh. Rechristened the Hornets, the club became a perennial American Hockey League power. Stocked with future Hall of Famers George Armstrong and Tim Horton and flashy scoring champion Sid Smith, the team affectionately known as the Wasps captured Calder Cups in 1952 and 1955.

After the rickety Duquesne Gardens was torn down in 1956, the team was forced to suspend operations for five seasons. Upon completion of the sparkling-new Civic Arena, the Hornets rejoined the AHL in 1961–62. In a storybook finish, the Hornets won a third Calder Cup in 1966–67—their final year of existence.

78 Check Out PittsburghHockey.Net

For every true Penguins fan, no online surfing session would be complete without visiting the PittsburghHockey.net website. The Internet's version of *Total Penguins*, it's touted as "Pittsburgh's Online Hockey Museum" for a reason. It truly is an awesome resource.

"This site was developed because we had hundreds of bookmarks related to Pittsburgh hockey and we wanted to bring everything together under one umbrella (or retractable dome!) and make it accessible, free, and interesting to view," wrote the site's developers.

Boy, did they ever succeed. Virtually anything and everything a Pens fan could want to know about Steel City hockey can be found in "the museum." The site features nine main "exhibits," including Timeline; By the Decade; Arenas; Pirates; Hornets; Other Teams; Features; Jersey Rack; and last but certainly not least—Penguins. The individual exhibits house as many as 13 different "rooms," each containing a wealth of information. Team exhibits include all-time rosters, year-by-year records and statistics, uniform number history, and a whole lot more.

Exquisitely designed and well organized, PittsburghHockey. net is packed with tons of priceless photos, including some archival shots you won't find anywhere else. It also features detailed articles and stories about the origins of hockey in Pittsburgh, dating back to the late 19th century.

Trivia buffs will fall in love with this site. For instance, did you know that the Western Pennsylvania Hockey League was widely regarded as the first, full-blown professional league? Ever heard of the immortal collegiate star, Hobey Baker? He played his last hockey game in Pittsburgh.

Among the more colorful features are the Uniform History sections that can be found under each team's exhibit page. Photos of virtually every jersey style are prominently on display, along with myriad interesting facts and tidbits. For example, the Pirates—Pittsburgh's original NHL club—switched from black and gold (borrowed from the city crest) to orange and black for the 1929–30 season. When the franchise moved to Philadelphia, the renamed Quakers kept the new color scheme. It was later adopted by—you guessed it—the Flyers.

Likewise, the section on early Penguins history is most enjoyable. "The Very Beginning," which can be found under the header "Franchise and More," makes for an especially interesting read. It features a fascinating and detailed account of the birth of the team, expertly blended with some wonderful quotes and recollections by the club's first owner, Pennsylvania senator Jack McGregor. The article includes a link to "The History of the Pittsburgh Penguins

Logo," another entertaining and informative piece, as well as a list of the players picked in the 1967 Expansion Draft.

Perhaps the finest compliment to PittsburghHockey.net is paid by Penguins fan Regina D'Amico.

"The site is simply tremendous!" she wrote. "My father was an usher at the Civic Arena for many years and loves the Penguins. He doesn't own a computer and knows little about the Internet, but every time he comes over to see his grandchildren he asks us to 'bring up that Pittsburgh hockey thing on the computer.' What a neat discovery."

79 The Pittsburgh Kid

The eldest son of former Penguins player and head scout Greg Malone, Ryan Malone played two years of high school hockey in suburban Upper St. Clair and dreamed of one day skating for his hometown team.

"I thought that, by my junior year, I was as good as anyone in the area, but it wasn't easy getting recognition," Malone told Dejan Kovacevic of the *Pittsburgh Post-Gazette*. "The summer after that school year, I tried out for Team Pittsburgh, which plays annually at the national Chicago Showcase, and I was cut. I was pretty angry about it at the time, but maybe it helped me. That summer, I just wanted to show everybody they made a mistake."

In 1997 the tall, rangy center decided to play for fabled Shattuck-St. Mary's Boarding School in Fairbault, Minnesota. He moved on to the Omaha Lancers of the fast United States Hockey League during his senior year of high school, where he drew the attention of NHL scouts—including his dad. That summer, the elder Malone selected his son in the 1999 Entry Draft.

"I didn't know who would take me, but I just wanted someone to do it," Ryan recalled. "When it was the Penguins in the fourth round, it was a dream come true."

Following in his father's footsteps, Malone cracked the Penguins' opening day lineup in 2003–04, becoming the first Pittsburgh-born player ever to skate for the club. Although the "X Generation" Pens were woeful, Ryan enjoyed a fine rookie campaign. He scored a team-leading 22 goals to earn a spot on the NHL's All-Rookie Team.

After playing in Europe during the lockout season, the big forward returned to the Pens in 2005–06. Playing left wing and center, the 6'4", 224-pounder equaled his first-year output of 22 goals. His game, however, was plagued by inconsistency. On some nights he was the best player on the ice. On other nights he was barely noticeable.

The trend continued in 2006–07, when Malone dipped to 16 goals. He often ran afoul of Penguins coach Michel Therrien, who benched the big winger in a crucial game during the 2007 Stanley Cup playoffs.

Taking Therrien's criticism to heart, a different Ryan Malone emerged in 2007–08. Displaying a new level of focus and intensity, he drove to the net with authority and dropped the mitts when necessary to defend a teammate. Duly impressed by Bugsy's trans-formation, Therrien named him as an alternate captain.

Malone credited former Pen John LeClair for helping him with his game.

"John made a living by keeping the game simple and using his physical assets," Malone said.

Penguins general manager Ray Shero had his own take on No. 12's surprising metamorphosis.

"Maybe it's maturity," Shero said, "maybe it's the fact he got married [to his college sweetheart Abby], maybe it's because it's his contract year, but it's been like a perfect storm for Ryan."

Suddenly one of the league's premier power forwards, Malone established new career highs with 27 goals and 51 points. He continued his gritty, determined play during the team's march to the Stanley Cup Finals. Already playing with a broken nose, he absorbed a Hal Gill slap shot to the face during the early stages of Game 5.

"When you stand in front of the net, you have to be willing to pay a price," Malone said.

In an extraordinary display of courage, he packed his nose with cotton balls and returned to skate a regular shift during the Pens' marathon triple-overtime victory.

Following his postseason heroics, Malone became an unrestricted free agent. In a different era, the Penguins no doubt would have made a strong bid to keep the budding star. Due to salary cap restrictions, however, Shero was unable to extend a competitive offer. On June 28, 2008, he traded negotiating rights to the big winger to Tampa Bay for a third-round draft choice.

80 Herbie

At age 62, Herb Brooks had settled quite comfortably into his post-coaching career. The United States hockey legend was serving as a scout for the Pittsburgh Penguins, which afforded him the opportunity to spend more time at home with his family.

However, in December of 1999 he received a phone call from Penguins general manager Craig Patrick. The team was badly

Coaching legend Herb Brooks was behind the bench for 57 games in 1999–2000. He passed away in August of 2003.

Miracle

In the summer of 1979 Herb Brooks was named general manager and head coach of Team USA for the 1980 Winter Olympics. Determined to defeat the powerhouse Soviet team that had dominated international hockey, he devised a hybrid system that combined aspects of the Soviet's highly effective weaving style with the NHL's more traditional game.

Still, most experts thought the callow Americans would be fortunate to earn a medal. After all, Brooks' club was comprised of college players, while the Soviets and Czechs boasted essentially pro teams.

"Unless the ice melts," wrote *The New York Times* columnist Dave Anderson, "or unless the United States team or another team performs a miracle, as did the American squad in 1960, the Russians are expected to easily win the Olympic gold medal for the sixth time in the last seven tournaments."

Inspired by Brooks-isms such as "the legs feed the wolf" and "hard work beats talent when talent doesn't work hard," the United States scrambled to a last-minute tie with Sweden, followed by a 7–3 upset over heavily favored Czechoslovakia. Employing their coach's swirling, creative style they downed Norway, Romania, and West Germany to set up an epic medal-round clash with the Soviets.

In the locker room prior to the game, Brooks gave one of his most stirring speeches.

"You were born to be a player," he said. "You were meant to be here. This is your night."

Skating before a packed house of 8,500 fans at the Field House in Lake Placid, New York, the young Americans did the unthinkable. In perhaps the greatest upset in the history of sports, they stunned the powerhouse Soviets 4–3. As the final seconds ticked off the clock, play-by-play announcer Al Michaels capped the countdown with his famous call, "Do you believe in miracles? YES!"

The improbable victory had a strong Pittsburgh flavor. Buzz Schneider, the Penguins' sixth-round choice in the 1974 Amateur Draft, scored Team USA's first goal. Center Mark "Magic" Johnson, another Pens draft pick and the son of future Pittsburgh coach Bob Johnson, notched a pair of game-tying goals, including a stirring tally in the final second of the first period. The team's assistant coach, Craig Patrick, would go on to build two Stanley Cup winners in the Steel City.

The triumph over the Soviets and the subsequent gold-medal victory over Finland earned Brooks everlasting acclaim as one of the sport's most brilliant teachers, innovators, and motivators. He, too, joined the Penguins, serving as a scout and later as the team's coach during 1999–00 season.

underperforming under incumbent coach Kevin Constantine and needed a spark. Patrick asked his old friend and mentor to take over the coaching duties. Brooks agreed.

"We agree on a lot of philosophies, and I believe he is a better fit for what we have on the ice," Patrick said. "I believe he can get the best out of what we have."

Under Constantine, the Penguins played a rigid, defensive system that served to stymie some of the team's star players like Jaromir Jagr and Alexei Kovalev. Brooks preferred a swirling, creative style that blended the best attributes of the North American and European games.

"The idea is to give the game to the players," Brooks said. "Not to suffocate them. Not to treat them like a bunch of robots and say, 'You do this and you do this.' We want to try and provide an environment that brings out their talents."

Brooks opened the door for players who had mysteriously fallen from grace with Constantine. He recalled feisty Tyler Wright from Wilkes-Barre and gave him a prominent role. Matthew Barnaby, who likewise was relegated to the shadows, joined Wright and Aleksey Morozov on what proved to be a very effective third line.

The Penguins flourished under the crafty old coach, going 10–3–1 in his first 14 games. An incident in Colorado on January 13, 2000, cemented his popularity with the players. In the late stages of a 4–3 loss to the Avalanche, Barnaby was knocked unconscious courtesy of a borderline hit by Alexei Gusarov. When Avs play-by-play announcer John Kelly suggested the Penguins' agitator was faking it, Brooks went ballistic.

"Did you make that call on Barnaby?" Brooks shouted. "You say he has a tendency to embellish? What the hell kind of call was that?"

The tirade earned him a two-game suspension—and the undying admiration and respect of his team.

"It's just ridiculous," Barnaby said of Brooks' suspension. "He gets suspended indefinitely for standing up for one of his players."

With the team firmly united behind their coach, the Penguins finished in third place in the Atlantic Division. In the Stanley Cup playoffs that spring, they stunned the heavily favored Capitals before bowing to the powerful Flyers in six games.

Despite the presence of coach-in-waiting Ivan Hlinka, Patrick would have undoubtedly welcomed Brooks back for another season. However, the mastermind of the Miracle on Ice Olympic hockey team elected to return to his role as scout.

In 2002 he came out of retirement one last time to lead the United States team to a silver medal at the Winter Olympics in Salt Lake City. Always in demand, he was courted by New York Rangers general manager Glen Sather. Brooks decided to remain with the Penguins, who named him as their director of player development.

Sadly, Herb's life came to a tragic and untimely end on August 11, 2003, when he was killed in a car accident near Forest Lake, Minnesota. He was posthumously inducted into the Hockey Hall of Fame in 2006.

Although his time at the Penguins' helm was brief, Brooks made a lasting impression on his players.

"It was awesome," Ron Tugnutt recalled in an interview with the *Pittsburgh Post-Gazette*. "My oldest son, he goes, 'You played for Herb Brooks, Dad?' because he watched [the film *Miracle*] over and over again. He was a special man. He was totally different than everyone else. I really enjoyed playing for him."

81 Gardsy

When Paul Malone Gardner arrived in Pittsburgh in November of 1980 via a big trade with Toronto, he already was an established goal scorer. The son of former NHL All-Star Cal Gardner, he tallied 30 goals in each of his first three NHL seasons, including 30 in just 46 games in 1977–78.

Paul made his living in the trenches. Although neither especially big nor fast, the 6'0", 195-pounder planted himself in the slot in a style reminiscent of Boston's Phil Esposito and scored on rebounds and deflections. Although he absorbed tons of abuse, the tactic paid off handsomely.

"Garbage goals or whatever, I'll take 'em any way I can get 'em," he said.

While Gardner undeniably possessed a nose for the net, he also carried a rap for less-than-inspired defensive play. When the Maple Leafs broke training camp in 1980, Gardner was shocked to learn that he'd been demoted to Springfield of the American Hockey League.

Fortunately, he soon was granted a reprieve. With top centers Mark Johnson, Orest Kindrachuk, and Gregg Sheppard shelved due to injuries, the Penguins were in desperate need of a scoring punch. General manager Baz Bastien acquired Gardner's services for fringe players Kim Davis and Paul Marshall.

The mustachioed center proved to be a godsend. Less than a month after his arrival Gardsy exploded for four goals in 30 minutes, including three power-play tallies, during a contest with the Flyers.

"It was like my 10th game with the team, and it was a big thing in helping me fit in and feel comfortable," Gardner said. "They had gotten me to help on the power play, and to score goals, and I proved in a hurry I could do just that."

Gardner enjoyed an outstanding first season with the club, tallying 34 goals and 74 points in only 62 games. Thanks in large part to his willingness to pay a price in front of the net, he became a fixture on the Pens' deadly power play, striking for 18 goals with the man advantage.

The 24-year-old center continued his hot hand in 1981–82. Gardner was rolling along at better than a point-per-game clip when the Pens visited Winnipeg on January 13, 1982. Late in the second period of a chippy game, he skirmished with Jets agitator Doug Smail.

As players from both sides milled around, Winnipeg goon Jimmy Mann hopped over the boards and made a beeline for Gardner. Catching the Pens' scoring leader unaware, Mann unleashed a brutal sucker punch that knocked Gardner's jaw off its hinges. The emergency room doctors were astonished by the damage, comparing it to an injury one might sustain in a car accident.

The mugging robbed Gardner of a chance to score 50 goals. Although it was one of the most vicious attacks ever to take place on an NHL rink, Mann received a relatively mild 10-game suspension.

"It just didn't seem fair that I missed 21 games because I was hurt, and [Mann] got a 10-game suspension," Gardner recalled.

Paul returned to the lineup wearing a cage mask to protect his jaw. Incredibly, he tied young gun Mike Bullard for the club scoring lead with 36 goals. Even more remarkably, Gardner led the league with 21 power-play goals.

Following a solid 28-goal season in 1982–83 misfortune struck again. During the Penguins' 1983 training camp Gardner fell from a ladder while installing storm windows at his home and suffered two broken heels. When he struggled to regain his form, the Penguins unceremoniously shipped him to Baltimore of the AHL.

"They wanted to revamp the team and build for the future, so they got rid of many veterans," he said. "I had scored 201 goals, and it hurt to get sent down like that."

Still, he nearly returned to the Steel City when new Penguins coach Bob Berry contacted him the following season.

"He called me to see if I wanted to come back to Pittsburgh, but I had already signed with Washington," Gardner recalled. "I've often wondered what it would've been like to have played with Mario [Lemieux]."

82 The Heartbreak Kids

Following an up-and-down regular season, the Penguins squared off against the powerhouse New York Islanders in the opening round of the 1982 playoffs. The Islanders' dynasty was in full bloom. They had won back-to-back Stanley Cups. Worse yet, the pesky Pens had drawn their ire during a rugged regular season finale. The Islanders were out for blood.

Predictably, the defending Cup champions thrashed the Penguins by a combined score of 15–3 in Games 1 and 2. Bruised and battered, the Steel City sextet limped back to Pittsburgh, where they hoped to regroup on home ice. Instead, they received a tongue-lashing from owner Edward DeBartolo Sr.

"No one is more upset and disappointed with the play of the Pittsburgh Penguins than me," he said. "I am not attending Saturday night's playoff game and I empathize with you fans who have decided not to come to the Civic Arena tomorrow night."

Stung by DeBartolo's harsh words, the undermanned Penguins pulled together. They staved off elimination with a thrilling 2–1 victory, thanks to Rick Kehoe's game winner in overtime. In Game 4 they stunned the Islanders 5–2 to set up a deciding fifth game in Uniondale.

The momentum had shifted. Now it was the mighty Islanders who were back on their heels. Skating before a sold-out crowd at the Nassau County Coliseum, the teams battled through a scoreless first period. Although the Islanders had the better scoring chances, Michel Dion was a veritable fortress in goal.

"All year he's been outstanding," Pens coach Eddie Johnston said. "Tonight he was phenomenal."

When New York finally scored midway through the second period, the partisan crowd breathed a collective sigh of relief. But rugged rookie Kevin McClelland ignited a Penguins rally just 43 seconds later when he tipped in a Greg Hotham blast from the point.

The Islanders were stunned by the sudden turn of events. Before they could regroup, Mike Bullard and Randy Carlyle struck for a pair of beautiful goals to stake Pittsburgh to a 3–1 lead. Only 20 minutes stood between the Penguins and arguably the greatest playoff upset of all time.

Watching their dreams of a third straight Stanley Cup evaporate before their eyes, the Islanders unleashed a furious offensive assault at Dion. Playing the game of his life, the spirited goalie held firm until 14:33, when Mike McEwen struck for a power-play goal.

Then, with two minutes remaining, ex-Penguin farmhand Gord Lane dumped the puck into the corner and Carlyle skated over to retrieve it. The puck skipped by the young defenseman to John Tonelli, who rifled it past Dion. Although shocked, the Penguins held the swarming Islanders at bay and forced the game into overtime.

The Pens grimly dug in for one last stand. Bullard almost scored the game winner early in overtime, but his shot rang off

Michel My Belle

During the summer of 1981 the Penguins were seeking a goaltender to replace Greg Millen. They gambled on Michel Dion, a former WHA phenom who had faltered badly the previous season. Before they signed Dion they sent him to an eye doctor, who told him he needed contact lenses.

"The doctor said I had no depth perception," he said. "Last year I noticed more screen shots and blue-line shots were going in. I just didn't realize it was because I needed contacts."

His vision problems corrected thanks to the new lenses, Dion enjoyed a brilliant start to his Penguins career. He quickly became a darling of the Civic Arena faithful with his spectacular, acrobatic style. Organist Vince Lascheid broke into a rendition of The Beatles' "Michelle My Belle" whenever Dion made one of his electrifying saves.

By midseason the Penguins were battling the New York Islanders for Patrick Division supremacy. One of the big reasons was the extraordinary play of Dion, who earned a spot on the Wales Conference All-Star Team. He appeared in 62 games and tied a club record with 25 wins, while posting a respectable 3.79 goals-against average.

That spring the Penguins met the Islanders in the opening round of the playoffs. After being strafed for 15 goals in Games 1 and 2, Dion held New York to just three goals in the next two contests as his team rallied to tie the series. Twenty minutes away from a stunning upset in Game 5, the Penguins couldn't keep the determined Islanders at bay. John Tonelli struck for the series winner in overtime to overcome a heroic 42-save effort by Dion.

As the dejected goalie knelt in front of his net, Islanders netminder Billy Smith—who usually avoided any fraternization with opposing players—skated the length of the ice to console his adversary.

"They should stop everything and give him the Conn Smythe right now," Smith said. "I've watched him this whole series and I've never seen anything like him. He's incredible."

a goalpost. At the six-minute mark the ever-present Tonelli beat Dion again to bring the final curtain down on the Penguins' Cinderella story.

"I was feeling really high because I thought we had it in our back pockets," Johnston said. "We were two goals ahead with six minutes to go, then they got a questionable penalty and a lucky bounce. A great club capitalizes on those breaks and, let's face it, they're a great hockey club."

Although understandably downtrodden, the Penguins consoled themselves with the knowledge that they had battled a much stronger opponent to the bitter end.

"A lot of people counted us out, including our owner," Carlyle declared. "But we showed people we weren't about to be kicked when we were down...that we're a proud hockey club."

The victorious Islanders had nothing but praise for their plucky adversaries, especially Dion.

"What can you say about Dion?" asked New York coach Al Arbour. "The kid was just fantastic."

83 Baz

It seemed written in the stars that Aldege "Baz" Bastien would one day serve as the Penguins' general manager. Three decades earlier he'd been a promising young goalie for the Pittsburgh Hornets until he was struck in the right eye by a puck during training camp. The damage was so severe the eye had to be removed.

Unfazed by the abrupt end to his playing career, the plucky Bastien assumed the Hornets' coaching reins that very same year. The following season the 31-year-old was named general manager.

In 1953 he returned to the team's bench, guiding the Wasps to a fourth-place finish.

Still one of the boys at heart, Baz wasn't above hobnobbing with his players. During card games he was known to pluck out his glass eye and set it on the table, a move that never failed to elicit the appropriate groans and moans.

When the Hornets resumed operations in 1961 after five years in cold storage, Bastien was a key member of the organization. He was appointed general manager for the second time, a role he would fill until the team ceased operations in 1967. In a storybook ending, Bastien coached the Hornets to a Calder Cup in their final year of existence.

The next year Baz began a long apprenticeship in the NHL, serving as assistant general manager to Sid Abel in Detroit. When Abel took over the expansion Kansas City Scouts in 1974, Bastien once again served as his aide. During the Scouts' first season, he convinced his boss to trade for Denis Herron, the Penguins' promising goalie. Herron quickly emerged as a star for a bad team.

In 1976, Bastien's odyssey came full circle when he returned to Pittsburgh as Wren Blair's handpicked successor. The move was well-received among Steel City fans, who felt he had been unjustly passed over by the club a decade earlier.

"You can't imagine how happy I am to come back to the city where I played my hockey," he said. "I always loved Pittsburgh. And I go back to the days when if you wore a white shirt, at noon you had to change it."

Although thrilled to be back in Pittsburgh, he faced a daunting task. Following a respectable three-year run in the mid-1970s, the aging Penguins were beginning to fade. The team had virtually no farm system. Worse yet, the club's marginal finances did not afford Bastien the luxury of building through the draft.

Adept at plugging short-term gaps from his years as a minor league executive, the cigar-chomping Bastien used the only

A Higher Calling

Penguins general manager Baz Bastien was quite pleased when he acquired defenseman Tom Edur from Colorado on December 2, 1977, and with good reason. By all accounts, the former third-round pick of the Boston Bruins was regarded as a rising star.

Following three solid seasons in the World Hockey Association, Edur tallied 32 points for Colorado in 1976–77 while pacing a terrible Rockies team with a remarkable plus-14. Possessing good mobility and excellent offensive skills, the 23-year-old defender enjoyed similar success with the Penguins. In just 58 games in the Steel City he piled up 43 points while manning the right point on the power play.

However, Edur was a young man of deep convictions. A devout Jehovah's Witness, he believed there was a higher calling on his life. Prior to the 1978 training camp he decided to retire.

"I quit hockey," he explained in an interview with *MacLean's* magazine, "but not because I don't love the game. I do. My dream had been to become a National Hockey League player. But serving Jehovah, the Most High God, is not just a one-day-a-week affair. It is a way of life."

The Penguins tried their best to coax the promising young defender out of retirement. They offered him a new contract that included a hefty raise and gave him permission to sit out Sunday games. But Edur would not be swayed. The team grudgingly accepted his decision.

"We got compensation from God," quipped Penguins marketing director David Rubinstein. "Two miracles."

collateral at his disposal. He traded draft choices—lots of them—to acquire players from other teams. Over the course of his six-plus seasons as general manager, he dealt four first-round picks, as well as second- and third-round choices.

In one of his more infamous trades he sent a first-round pick to Montreal for Rod Schutt. According to Penguins folklore, Bastien thought he'd acquired *Steve Shutt*, a brilliant left wing who once scored 60 goals for the Canadiens.

Still, the moves worked for a time. Fueled largely by Bastien-acquired talent, the Pens finished a solid second in the Norris Division in 1978–79. The club's strong showing earned the veteran GM Executive of the Year honors. However, the improvement was largely a case of smoke and mirrors.

"The problem was, every year you went into training camp and there was never a young star to hang your hat on," announcer Paul Steigerwald recalled. "We always traded our draft picks."

Following three fair-to-middling seasons the practice of robbing Peter to pay Paul finally caught up to Bastien and the Penguins. Bereft of young talent, the team spiraled to a last-place finish in 1982–83.

Sadly, Baz would not live to preside over a revival. While driving home from a hockey writers' dinner held in his honor, he died from injuries sustained in an automobile accident on March 15, 1983.

84 The Boys of Winter

If ever a team was destined for failure, it was the 1983–84 Pittsburgh Penguins. Only a season removed from a rousing near-miss against the powerhouse Islanders in the 1982 playoffs, the Pens had fallen on hard times with a pronounced thud. Longtime general manager Baz Bastien tragically died in a car accident the previous spring. In one of his final moves he unwittingly traded the first overall choice in the 1983 Entry Draft to Minnesota, a pick that could've netted the team Peterborough scoring sensation Steve Yzerman.

The club's new GM, Eddie Johnston, surveyed the rubble with an unflinching eye. He was determined to break with the club's tradition of trading away draft choices for veterans.

"Other franchises were getting top young players like Bobby Smith and Sylvain Turgeon, and I remember Mike Lange saying, 'Why can't we get one of those guys?'" Paul Steigerwald recalled.

Building through the draft was a luxury that the Penguins seemed ill-equipped to afford. Although owner Edward J. DeBartolo Sr. had deep pockets, he had grown weary of all the losing.

Fortunately, there was a flickering light at the end of the tunnel. A franchise player would be available in the upcoming draft, one universally hailed as the finest prospect to come out of junior hockey since the Great One, Wayne Gretzky. His name was Mario Lemieux.

With his eyes fixed firmly on the prize, Johnston began to rebuild in an unusual fashion. He released Paul Baxter, arguably the club's second-best defenseman, and dealt productive Greg Malone to Hartford for a draft pick.

Newcomers Ted Bulley, Rocky Saganiuk, and Greg Tebbutt were added at bargain-basement prices. Mitch Lamoureux, a 57-goal scorer at Baltimore, and defenseman Phil Bourque were promoted from the minors. Nineteen-year-old Bob Errey, selected with the first-round pick acquired from Minnesota, also made the squad.

The Penguins wisely switched their marketing theme from "We Have a Hockey Team," to the more appropriate "The Boys of Winter." Indeed, there would be many nights during the upcoming season when the Pens appeared to be a collection of boys attempting to compete in a man's game.

With a lineup that consisted mainly of aging veterans, minor league retreads, and inexperienced youngsters, the team flopped out of the starting blocks. Attendance plummeted along with the club's on-ice fortunes. Rumors circulated that the team would move to Hamilton, Ontario, or Saskatoon, Saskatchewan, following the season.

While the sad-sack Pens stumbled along, Lemieux was shattering junior hockey scoring records. Knowing full well the only way

The Bullet

The 1983–84 Penguins were terrible. Easily one the worst non-expansion teams of all time, "The Boys of Winter" essentially were a minor league club competing in the National Hockey League.

Predictably, no one did much to distinguish themselves. However, one player who shone through the wreckage was All-Star center Mike Bullard. Displaying a nose for the net and pit-bull determination, the Bullet struck for a remarkable 51 goals and 92 points.

His performance was all the more amazing when compared to his teammates. Bullard outdistanced the team's second-leading goal getter (Ron Flockhart) by 24 goals, and outpaced the second-best point scorer (Doug Shedden) by 35 points.

A virtual one-man show, the gritty Ottawa native led the Pens in nearly every major offensive category, including goals, assists, points, even-strength goals, power-play goals, and shots. His extraordinary efforts earned him team MVP honors, along with the Booster Club Award.

the franchise would survive was to land the Laval wonder, Johnston redoubled his efforts to ensure the Penguins would finish dead last.

In a shrewd trade that stirred quite a bit of controversy, he dealt former Norris Trophy winner Randy Carlyle to Winnipeg for a first-round pick and future considerations. Under the guise of evaluating talent, Johnston called up Vincent Tremblay and watched as the overmatched goalie allowed a staggering 24 goals in four games.

"EJ sent down Roberto Romano, who was not great, but good," Steigerwald explained. "Vincent Tremblay wasn't very good."

Predictably, the Pens finished the season in a death spiral. Posting a dismal record of 16–58–6—the worst in the league for the second straight season—they were unquestionably among the most hapless teams of all time.

Two months later Johnston strode to the podium at the Montreal Forum and proudly announced in halting French that the Penguins had selected "numer soixante-six" of the Laval Voison with the first choice in the Entry Draft. The team had its savior.

"I thought EJ did a great job of 'positioning' the team that year," said vice president of advertising Tom Rooney. "Because, otherwise, the place was empty, and the team was getting hammered."

85 Scorin' Warren

The rags to riches (to rags again) tale of Warren Young is truly one of the most remarkable stories in the history of the National Hockey League.

By all accounts a late bloomer, Young played one season of Junior B hockey before attending Michigan Tech. Following a solid if unspectacular collegiate career with the Huskies, the former California Golden Seals draft pick was assigned to Baltimore of the Eastern Hockey League. The rough-and-tumble EHL was no picnic.

"Coming out of college, I wanted to be known only as a skillful hockey player," Young said. "But if you're a big guy and you won't fight and take the body, they'll take advantage of you."

Young soon emerged as a sturdy, no-nonsense player. He scored 53 goals with the Clippers to earn a promotion to Oklahoma City, Minnesota's top farm club. Although he appeared in a handful of games for the North Stars over the next several seasons, he was never given a real opportunity to establish himself.

"All those years and I kept wondering, *Can I do it? Can I play in the NHL?*" he said.

Desperate for anything resembling big-league talent, Penguins general manager Eddie Johnston signed Young to a free-agent deal during the summer of 1983. When the big winger was called up by the Pens for a late-season cameo in a meaningless game against the Rangers, he made the most of the opportunity.

"Their defenseman, Steve Richmond, was running a lot of our guys, and Warren stood up to him," Johnston recalled. "Fought him. Beat him pretty good. A lot of guys would've said, 'Why should I stick my nose in when I know I'm going back down tomorrow?' Warren got involved."

Young had made an impression. When training camp broke in the fall of 1984, he was on the Penguins roster. Not only had he made the team, but he found himself skating alongside prized rookie Mario Lemieux.

The pair quickly developed a wonderful chemistry. Young was a step slow, but he read the play very well. Standing 6'3" and weighing 195 pounds, he was a fearless and capable fighter, which afforded him and his gifted linemate extra time and space to make plays.

"The criticism of Warren was always that he had to work on his skating," said his minor league coach Gene Ubriaco. "But he's got great hands, can handle the puck well, he's tough, and he can score."

Aided by Lemieux's picture-perfect setups, the 29-year-old rookie found the net with stunning regularity. He scored 40 goals and led the league with a 30.8 shooting percentage, a remarkable achievement for a player who was previously regarded as a career minor leaguer. Young's outstanding play earned him a spot on the NHL's All-Rookie Team and folk hero status in Pittsburgh.

With his contract up for renewal, Scorin' Warren was surprised when Eddie Johnston encouraged him to field offers from other clubs. Although he preferred to remain a Penguin, Detroit made Young an offer he couldn't refuse—$1 million over four years.

"I really didn't want to leave," Young said. "The situation was forced on me."

He did his best to live up to the big contract. However, the Red Wings were a terrible team, even worse than the Penguins. With little help, Young's output dipped to 22 goals and 46 points. Respectable totals for sure, but not enough to justify the money he was making.

Seeking to unload his fat contract, the Red Wings sold Young back to the Penguins on the eve of the 1986–87 season. He was thrilled to return to Pittsburgh, but this was one fairy tale that would not have a happy ending. In his second go-around with the club, Warren struggled to rediscover his scoring touch. He finished the season with eight goals in 50 games, hardly the stuff of legend.

Following a brief seven-game stint with the Pens in 1987–88, Young was shipped to the Muskegon Lumberjacks, where he finished his career. Although Scorin' Warren endured an inglorious end, his sudden rise to stardom remains one of the true feel-good stories in the team's long and colorful history.

86 Read *Penguin Profiles: Pittsburgh's Boys of Winter*

For Penguins fans who thirst for in-depth stories about the team's early stars and history, *Penguin Profiles: Pittsburgh's Boys of Winter* is an absolute must read. Beautifully crafted by Jim O'Brien, one of Pittsburgh's preeminent sportswriters, *Penguin Profiles* was published in 1994 during the club's first golden age.

A former columnist and reporter for *The Pittsburgh Press* who was born and raised in the Glenwood section of the city, Mr. O'Brien possesses a deep and abiding love for Pittsburgh sports. The seventh book in his "Pittsburgh Proud" series, *Penguin Profiles* is a veritable gold mine of information about the team's rich and colorful past. It features biographies on more than 30 of the team's most prominent players, coaches, and executives, from Hall of Famers such as Mario Lemieux, Ron Francis, and Larry Murphy to All-Stars like Syl Apps, Dave Burrows, and Jean Pronovost.

Nestled comfortably within its 448 pages like a pair of old slippers is an "Other Voices" section, which includes highlights, stories, and recollections from Ron Cook, Guy Junker, Stan Savran, and other notable sportswriters and personalities. The book also details the early history of Pittsburgh hockey as seen through the eyes of venerable old-timers such as Jimmy Jordan, Roy McHugh, and Jackie Powell, who served as a goal judge for the Hornets and Penguins.

"This book is about beginnings," wrote Mr. O'Brien. "It's about some of the players and people who have been associated with the Penguins through the years. It's about where they came from, how they got started, the families that fashioned them, how they got hooked on hockey. Sportswriters and sports broadcasters who have been close to the club share their stories, their beginnings, as well.

"It's a scrapbook, a family album of sorts, for Penguins fans, stories to savor, to smile about, perhaps to shed a tear about. It's not meant to be a history of the Penguins, but rather profiles, anecdotes, tall tales, highlights, and lowlights, featuring a classic collection of photographs, to help us all better appreciate Pittsburgh and its Penguins."

Describing Mr. O'Brien's unique style, Jim Kriek wrote, "O'Brien is not really in one breath an historian, not really a storyteller, or narrator, or biographer in a single essence of each by itself. Rather, he is a combination of all those attributes."

A masterful writer, Mr. O'Brien does a marvelous job of letting his subject tell the story. One can picture him sitting back in an easy chair, asking thought-provoking questions and scribbling notes on a yellow legal pad, while his subject opens up. You see the glow in Joe Mullen's eyes as he shares what it was like to play roller hockey as a kid on the rough-hewn streets of Hells Kitchen. You feel the ache in Red Kelly's heart as he talks about visiting Michel Briere in a Montreal hospital. You sense the joy in Eddie Johnston's voice as he describes learning the secrets of the basketball pick play from Tommy Heinsohn in a Boston bar. It gives the book a wonderful intimacy and rhythm, and makes it a remarkably easy read.

Penguin Profiles can be purchased online at amazon.com.

87 Rats

Heading into the 1996 Eastern Conference Finals, the Penguins were understandably upbeat. Their opponent—the upstart Florida Panthers—was hardly an imposing team. Constructed mainly of retreads and castoffs from other clubs, the Panthers had clawed their way to a playoff berth in their third year of existence. Although they played a gritty, close-checking style, they appeared to be no match for the black and gold.

The series opened on May 18, 1996, before a sold-out crowd at the Civic Arena. Despite Florida's reputation for stingy defensive play, the high-octane Penguins had a surprising number of good scoring chances. Mario Lemieux nearly struck for the opening goal a minute into the contest, but goalie John Vanbiesbrouck made a big save. Galvanized by the big stop, the Panthers proceeded to pound five pucks past Ken Wregget to coast to an easy victory.

Dismayed by his team's poor showing, Pens coach Eddie Johnston gave Tom Barrasso the starting nod in Game 2. The move worked like a charm. Backed by Barrasso's 30-save performance and timely scoring from Lemieux, Jaromir Jagr, and Sergei Zubov, the Pens won 3–2 to even the series.

However, Games 3 and 4 would be contested in the unfriendly confines of the Miami Arena. Florida fans had developed a unique ritual of tossing plastic rats onto the ice when the Panthers scored, a craze that started when Scott Mellanby famously one-timed a real rat to its death in the locker room before the season opener.

"You have to sneak the rats into the building," said Panthers fan Dan Platt. "You can't just walk into an arena carrying a rat, you know. They check you. Security. They make men take off their hats. They open women's pocketbooks. If you get caught, you have to check the rats at Guest Relations. That's *if* you get caught."

To counteract the effects of the vermin-flinging crowd the Penguins donned their third uniform, affectionately known as the "third bird." The team was undefeated in 11 games when wearing the lucky uniforms.

Unfortunately, the jersey's magical powers were no match for the rats. After grabbing a 2–1 lead on goals by Bryan Smolinski and Petr Nedved, the Pens morphed into disinterested spectators. The hustling Panthers pelted Barrasso with 61 shots to turn a nailbiter into a 5–2 rout.

Although stunned by Florida's tenacity, the Penguins refused to fold. With blue-liners Zubov and J.J. Daigneault pacing the attack, the Pens captured Games 4 and 5 to snatch the series lead.

The comeback was nearly complete. A lone victory separated the Penguins from a return to the Stanley Cup Finals. Once again, however, the venue shifted to the Miami Arena. Almost on cue, each Florida goal was accompanied by a fusillade of rubber rodents, forcing the beleaguered Barrasso to seek refuge in his goal cage. The Panthers won 4–3 to force a seventh and deciding game.

Relieved to return to the relative safety of the Civic Arena, the Penguins hoped to break Florida's stranglehold in Game 7. But the Panthers continued to employ the neutral-zone trap to perfection.

Banana Suit

Over the course of his 16-year NHL career, Sergei Zubov established himself as one of the finest two-way defenders of his era. A smooth, effortless skater, the three-time All-Star was an exceptional puck handler who excelled at quarterbacking the power play.

Seeking a puck-moving defenseman to replace the departed Larry Murphy, Penguins GM Craig Patrick acquired the mobile Russian from the Rangers on August 31, 1995, in a big four-player swap.

Upon learning of the trade, Zubov no doubt choked on his pelmeni. During his stay in the Big Apple he enjoyed the comforts of home in Brighton Beach, one of the largest Russian-speaking communities in the United States. The Steel City offered no such amenities. For the 25-year-old Moscovite, it was like being sent to a Siberian gulag in the dead of winter.

Nor was Zubov afforded a hero's welcome. When he arrived at a Penguins function decked out in a yellow suit, a teammate couldn't resist poking fun. "Hey, check out Zubie's banana suit." Sergei was not amused.

Still, the quicksilver defenseman enjoyed a strong season with the Penguins. He tallied 66 points in 64 games while pacing the club's blue-liners with a plus-28. However, he failed to mesh—on ice or otherwise—with reigning superstar Mario Lemieux.

Zubov's ordeal ended the following summer. In a trade heartily endorsed by Lemieux, Patrick shipped the skilled defender to Dallas for Kevin Hatcher. Although Hatcher would give the Pens three solid seasons, he was far outshone by Zubov, who emerged as a world-class player.

Their diligence was rewarded when Mike Hough scooped up a pass from Robert Svehla and beat Barrasso on a two-on-one break.

Midway through the second period the momentum began to shift when Barrasso made a sensational save to thwart a breakaway attempt by Bill Lindsay. As the Penguins' attack gathered steam, Nedved blew the game-tying goal by Vanbiesbrouck.

The revival was fleeting. With 14 minutes remaining on the scoreboard clock Tom Fitzgerald gained the Pittsburgh blue line and cut loose an ordinary slap shot before chasing off for a line change. The puck glanced off the stick of defenseman Neil Wilkinson and fluttered under Barrasso's blocker pad. Moments later the Panthers tacked on an insurance goal to dash the Pens' Stanley Cup hopes.

The Rat Pack had prevailed.

Gronk

When Jordan Staal arrived at the Penguins' training camp in the fall of 2006, no one truly expected him to make the team. Although he'd been taken second overall in the Entry Draft that summer, the 18-year-old center had only two seasons of junior hockey under his belt.

As the team began exhibition play, Staal made a strong impression. Remarkably well schooled and responsible for a youngster, the Thunder Bay, Ontario, native surprised everyone by earning a spot in the opening day lineup.

Coach Michel Therrien used Staal primarily in a defensive role through the early going. Acting on a hunch, Therrien moved Jordan to left wing with stunning results. Staal finished his rookie season with 29 goals, a remarkable achievement given that he was playing an unfamiliar position.

He also gained a colorful new nickname—Gronk.

"Colby Armstrong gave it to me and it has stuck with me," Staal said. "I think it's pretty funny."

"He's huge, he's like a big monster," Armstrong explained. "We used to call a kid I played with in junior [hockey] 'Gronk' because he was a huge guy like Staal; so that's why I started calling him Gronk."

Jordan Staal has become an anchor of the new-age Penguins and helped the team win its third Stanley Cup in 2009.

Staal set a slew of NHL records during his magical first season. He was the youngest player in league history to score a hat trick; the youngest to score on a penalty shot; and the youngest to score two shorthanded goals in one game. His league-leading seven shorthanded goals were the most ever by a rookie. He was the third-youngest player—behind only Ted Lindsay and teammate Sidney Crosby—to score 20 goals.

Jordan had set the bar high, perhaps too high. Suffering a case of the sophomore jinx, his production tumbled to 12 goals and 16 assists in 2007–08.

Entering the 2008–09 campaign, Therrien once again tried Staal at left wing with fellow wonder boy Evgeni Malkin. This time, however, the combination didn't work. Jordan was returned to his natural position of center. He clicked with feisty wingers Matt Cooke and Tyler Kennedy. Buoyed by the presence of his new linemates, Staal closed with a rush to tally 22 goals and 27 assists, excellent totals for a third-line center.

He came of age during the playoffs that spring. The Pens had dropped two of the first three games of their Stanley Cup Finals rematch with Detroit and trailed 2–1 in the second period of Game 4. Worse yet, Brooks Orpik was serving a minor penalty.

With his team on the ropes, Staal stepped forward. Gathering in a lead pass from Max Talbot, the big center bulled his way past Brian Rafalski and wristed the puck into the net. The play was arguably the turning point of the series.

"Jordan's goal was huge," Crosby said. "They had a little bit of momentum at that point. They had two power plays right in a row and it was three minutes into the power plays before he scored. That was a huge momentum shift. We bounced back right away after that."

After helping the Penguins capture the Stanley Cup, Staal took his game to new heights in 2009–10. Now regarded as one of the finest two-way players in the league, the durable center tallied

49 points while running his iron-man streak to 302 games. The 21-year-old was nominated for the Frank J. Selke Trophy for his superb defensive work.

The 2010–11 season would prove to be the most difficult of Staal's budding career. After sitting out a dozen games while recovering from surgery to repair a tendon in his big toe, Jordan suffered a broken hand during a team practice on November 1. He would not suit up until the Winter Classic on New Year's Day.

Staal's timely return helped take the sting out of losing Crosby to a concussion. When Malkin went down with a season-ending knee injury, Jordan assumed the role of No. 1 center. He proved up to the challenge, notching 11 goals and 30 points in 42 games while leading the banged-up Penguins to a fifth consecutive playoff berth.

"He carries a lot of minutes, plays a lot of situations, and does it unbelievably well," teammate Pascal Dupuis said. "He's a big piece of the puzzle."

89 Friday Night Fights

On Friday night, February 11, 2011, the Penguins and the New York Islanders engaged in a brawl-filled contest, the likes of which hadn't been seen in the NHL for decades.

The seeds for the epic battle were sown nine days earlier, when the Pens shut out the Islanders 3–0 at the CONSOL Energy Center. Max Talbot sent New York forward Blake Comeau to the locker room with a concussion, courtesy of a clean but jarring hit. When the Islanders retaliated in the final minute of play, Pens goalie Brent Johnson decked his counterpart Rick DiPietro with a crushing left, breaking his cheekbone.

Deadly Force

During the 1981–82 season Penguins defensemen Paul Baxter and Pat Price were regarded by opposing teams as latter-day versions of the famous outlaws Frank and Jesse James.

Arguably the NHL's most despised player, Baxter piled up a league-leading 409 minutes in the slammer—the highest single-season total in club history—including 21 fighting majors. Price was no Caspar Milquetoast, either. The bellicose 6'2", 200-pounder served 322 minutes in the sin bin while dropping the mitts 19 times.

No opponent was spared the duo's wrath, not even the two-time Stanley Cup champion New York Islanders. During the late stages of a wild 7–2 Penguins victory in the season finale, Baxter bloodied the nose of big Dave Langevin with a flurry of lefts.

The rough treatment continued as the two teams squared off in the Patrick Division Semifinals. Staying true to form, Baxter and Price combined for 42 penalty minutes during the hard-fought five-game set. Baxter was a particular thorn to the defending champs, pounding the Islanders' forwards with hard body checks throughout the series.

Afterward it was revealed that the pugnacious pair had been the target of not one, but two death threats. The first threat was received at the Civic Arena switchboard on April 12, 1982. The second was phoned in the following day, two hours before the fifth and deciding game. Both incidents were immediately reported to the NHL Security Office, which contacted Detective Joseph Clark of the Nassau County Police. A 22-person detail was promptly dispatched to the Nassau County Coliseum.

"They did a great job of protecting our players without letting them know of the threats," said Penguins general manager Baz Bastien. "Fortunately, nothing happened."

"We were wondering who those guys were hanging around us all day," Price said. "Do you believe that? Welcome to New York."

Itching for revenge, New York called up battler Micheal Haley from their Bridgeport farm club. Burly enforcer Trevor Gillies—who had scored eight goals during his 12-year pro career—also dressed for the game.

The tone was set during a rugged first period. Midway through the frame the hyper-aggressive Haley pounded Craig Adams to the ice with a barrage of heavy rights. Minutes later Gillies and Penguins heavyweight Eric Godard slugged it out. The bouts were mere preliminaries to the main events that would follow.

After running up a commanding 6–0 lead, the Islanders clearly were out for blood. The powder keg exploded five minutes into the second period. New York's Matt Martin spied Talbot carrying the puck through center ice and chased him down. Sneaking up behind the Penguins' forward, he shed his gloves and unleashed a right-handed sucker punch. At the last possible second Mad Max saw the punch coming and dropped to the ice. As Martin prepared to pummel the prone Talbot, Pens defenseman Deryk Engelland rushed to his teammate's aid.

With the officials preoccupied with the pileup at center ice, two more fights broke out. Pens tough guy Mike Rupp took on Travis Hamonic, while Pascal Dupuis and Isles winger Josh Bailey engaged in a lively scrap. Seeking to stem the violence, embattled referees David Banfield and Dan O'Halloran banished each of the combatants—with the exception of Talbot.

The hostilities ceased, but only briefly. At 4:47 of the third period, Gillies spotted Eric Tangradi digging for a loose puck along the boards in the Islanders' zone. Gathering a full head of steam, the 227-pounder stormed at the Penguins' rookie with a 10-yard charge and walloped him with an elbow. As Tangradi crumbled to the ice, the Islanders' bully set upon his victim with bad intentions. Fortunately, Adams jumped in and tackled Gillies before he could inflict further damage.

"I don't know what they were so frustrated about," said Pens defenseman Brooks Orpik. "[Brent Johnson] got into a fight with their goalie, who was very willing, and you've got guys like Trevor Gillies who are out to hurt people."

Once again, all hell broke loose. Haley squared off with Talbot and made short work of his outgunned foe. Having disposed of the plucky Pens forward, he went looking for more action. In a scene straight from the movie *Slap Shot*, he spotted Johnson at the far end of the rink and skated the length of the ice to challenge the big goalie.

"He just came down," said Johnson, who admitted to being surprised. "I don't know. It's all a blur right now. One of those things in hockey that just kind of happens."

As the Islanders' tough guy dashed toward Johnson, Godard hopped over the boards. Knowing full well he faced a 10-game suspension for leaving the bench, the rugged winger intercepted Haley and pounded him with a volley of rights.

"I'm aware of the rules and stuff like that, but at that moment, you're not thinking about what the [repercussions] are," Godard said. "I'm going to try to defend my teammates."

The adversaries barely had enough players to finish the game. Thanks to 21 misconducts doled out by Banfield and O'Halloran, the Pens had six players left on their bench, while the Islanders had nine. All told, the teams combined for a whopping 346 penalty minutes, including a club-record 163 issued to the Penguins.

"We knew coming in here it would be a chippy game," Johnson said. "Things just got carried away."

90 Trots

During an outstanding 15-year run with the New York Islanders, Bryan Trottier established himself as one the finest two-way centers in the history of the game. In addition to winning four Stanley Cups, he'd captured virtually every major award the game had to offer, including the Art Ross, Hart, Conn Smythe, and Calder Trophies.

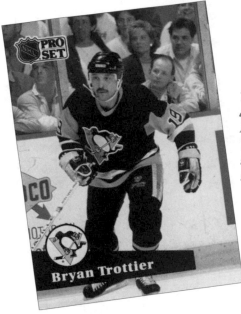

Thought to be past his prime after 15 years with the New York Islanders, Bryan Trottier joined the Penguins in 1990 and provided invaluable veteran savvy.

At 34 years of age, however, there was no denying Trottier had slowed a step. His once lofty production had tailed off dramatically during his final two years on Long Island. Convinced the seven-time All-Star was nearing the end of the line, the Islanders bought out his contract following the 1989–90 season.

"I was pretty scared," Trottier said. "The two people I thought the most of in my hockey career, Bill Torrey and Al Arbour, didn't want me anymore. They were telling me I was through. I kept telling myself I had something left, but I looked upon these two men as being so wise. I respected them so much. But things weren't working, and they made a change."

Fortunately, Trottier soon received a phone call from Penguins general manager Craig Patrick.

"He said simply, 'Why do you want to keep on playing?' Trottier recalled in Jim O'Brien's book, *Penguin Profiles*. "And I said, 'I want to win.' And Craig said, 'If you're committed to winning, we'll do it.'"

Patrick wasn't expecting big numbers from Trottier. He was seeking a veteran leader for his young team, someone to be the voice of experience on the ice and in the locker room. It was a role the Val Marie, Saskatchewan, native was perfectly suited to fill.

Thanks to his savvy, work ethic, and attention to detail, Trottier became an effective checking center for the Penguins. Skating with fellow lunch-pail gang members Phil Bourque, Bob Errey, and Troy Loney, Trots played 52 games for the Pens in 1990–91 and scored 28 points. In the playoffs, he served as a stabilizing influence during the team's march to the Stanley Cup.

His leadership was never more evident than during the difficult 1991–92 season. Following the tragic death of the team's beloved coach, Bob Johnson, the Penguins looked to their veterans for support. Trottier was there to provide it, along with his characteristically sturdy defensive play.

In honor of his outstanding on-ice achievements, Trots was named to the Wales Conference All-Star Team as a special Commissioner's selection. Old No. 19 didn't disappoint, notching a goal early in the third period.

Remarkably, Trottier could still provide offense when called upon. When back problems sidelined Mario Lemieux for six games in February, interim coach Scotty Bowman slotted the veteran center on the top line between Mark Recchi and Kevin Stevens. He promptly went on a tear, piling up 11 points in five games. Fueled in part by Trottier's drive and desire, the Pens went on to capture their second Stanley Cup that spring.

After watching his venerable teammate take Lord Stanley's chalice for several slides on a rain-slicked tarpaulin during the team's victory celebration, Rick Tocchet grinned and said, "He's like the little boy in all of us. He's got six [Stanley Cup] rings and he acts like this is the first."

Suffering from chronic back problems of his own, Bryan retired over the off-season to take a front office position with the Islanders.

However, he quickly grew bored. When the Penguins offered to bring him back as a player/assistant coach in the summer of 1993, he jumped at the chance.

Displaying his typical fun-loving attitude and zest for the game, Trottier played 41 games for the Penguins in 1993–94 before hanging up his skates for good. Three years later he was inducted into the Hockey Hall of Fame.

91 Make a Road Trip to Philadelphia to Watch a Pens-Flyers Game

High on the bucket list for any true Pittsburgh fan is making a road trip to Philadelphia to watch the Penguins take on their in-state brethren, the Flyers.

Separated by only 300 miles of rolling hills and grasslands, the cities are worlds apart in terms of culture. Accordingly, few rivalries have sparked such unbridled hatred and venom. For Pens supporters, it's a clear-cut case of good versus evil. Syl Apps versus Bobby Clarke; Sidney Crosby versus Mike Richards; Gary Roberts versus Ben Eager.

Bad blood began to flow as far back as the second game of the 1969–70 season, when Pens policeman Bryan "Bugsy" Watson fought Flyers tough guy Earl Heiskala in the main event, while Wally Boyer engaged Philly enforcer Reg Fleming on the undercard.

The simmering rivalry intensified in 1972–73 with the emergence of the Broad Street Bullies. Armed with bruisers such as Dave "the Hammer" Schultz, Bob "Hound" Kelly, Don "Big Bird" Saleski, and Andre "Moose" Dupont, the Flyers made mincemeat out of the peace-loving Pens. In direct response to Philly's terror

Who Is That Guy?

For those of us who've never played the game (and for some of us who have), it's hard to fathom just how good professional hockey players are.

Take the case of former Penguins heavyweight Jay Caufield. A quick glance at the record book tells you all you need to know about the rugged 6'4", 237-pounder. Over the course of his five-plus National Hockey League seasons, "Jaybird" played in 208 games and notched five goals, eight assists, and 13 points while racking up 759 minutes in the slammer. Plain and simple, Caufield made it to the NHL because of his willingness to use his fists.

Or so it would seem. My younger brother, Dan Buker, played hockey in local industrial leagues for several years. A lot of former high school and college players skated in those leagues, as well as the occasional former pro. So the quality of competition was pretty high.

I asked Dan who was the best he'd ever played against.

"Jay Caufield," he answered without hesitation. "You wouldn't believe how good a skater and puck handler he is. He was by far the best player on the ice."

tactics, the Penguins acquired heavyweights Steve Durbano, Bob "Battleship" Kelly, and Bob Paradise the next season to keep the peace.

Not surprisingly, the antagonists waged some epic battles through the years. On March 8, 1975, the host Pens bombed the defending Stanley Cup champions 8–2. Six years later the teams combined for 225 penalty minutes during a wild slugfest at the Spectrum. In the spring of 1984 the Flyers folded, spindled, and mutilated the locals by a count of 13–4. Mario Lemieux tallied five goals and eight points to pace a 10–7 rout of Philly during the 1989 playoffs. And, of course, there is "the Streak," when the Pens went a thoroughly dismal 0–39–3 in Philadelphia over a 15-year period.

Be forewarned: traveling to the City of Brotherly Shove to catch a Pens-Flyers game isn't for the faint of heart. After all,

Philadelphia fans once famously booed Santa Claus at an Eagles game and pelted him with snowballs.

Longtime Penguins fan Kelli Zappas attended a game at the Wells Fargo (then Wachovia) Center during the 2006–07 season. She gave a rather chilling account of her experience.

"My initial reaction when I was invited to go was, 'Don't do it,'" Kelli wrote. "But it really is something everybody should do once.

"All the horror stories you hear about how downright vicious Flyers fans can be are all true," she continued. "It truly is a hostile place. The fans are loud, obnoxious, and hateful. They will say or do anything to try to intimidate you, despite the fact that they really have only one thing to fall back on: calling 'Cindy' Crosby a crybaby.

"The Penguins won the game and my friends and I walked toward the car, ignoring the taunting. The Flyers fans didn't know what to do. They tried attacking the Steelers for a minute (they had missed the playoffs and the Eagles had made it that season). But none of us were die-hard football fans, so we refused to take the bait. They stood there with blank looks in their eyes and then renewed their verbal attacks on Crosby.

"I was offered a ticket during one of the Cup runs for a game in Philly and flat-out refused to go. I had no desire to experience the heightened hostility of the playoff atmosphere. After later hearing about the unprovoked threats of physical violence toward my friends and how stuff was thrown at them, I was glad I opted not to go. There are rivalries and then there is just plain outright ridiculous, juvenile behavior."

On second thought, perhaps making the trek to Philadelphia isn't such a good idea after all.

92 The Luck of Riley

As the Penguins' first general manager, Jack Riley takes umbrage whenever he hears someone knock his old Penguins teams.

"I get a little tired of people saying this team was nothing before the Cup," he told Tom McMillan in *The Penguins: Cellar to Summit*. "Sure, there were some horrible teams in Pittsburgh. But we had some good teams, too. And some exceptional hockey players. [Syl] Apps, [Jean] Pronovost, [Lowell] MacDonald, Bryan Hextall, Ron Schock, Kenny Schinkel."

An experienced and knowledgeable hockey man, Riley had served as president of the American Hockey League before taking the Penguins' job in 1966.

"It was a thrill to put a team together from scratch," he said. "Starting a hockey team is an interesting challenge. You know you're going to get leftovers. There was no Amateur Draft as such for the first two years after expansion. That was part of the deal. The new teams couldn't take any players from the NHL-sponsored junior teams."

Undaunted, Riley and his staff worked wonders at the 1967 Expansion Draft. The Penguins' first lineup featured two future Hall of Famers—Andy Bathgate and Leo Boivin—and solid pros such as Schinkel, Earl Ingarfield, and Ab McDonald.

"We were the first expansion team to beat one of the old clubs," Riley proudly recalled. "We beat the Chicago Black Hawks here on a Saturday night."

Good things were expected of that inaugural team. However, the organization was totally devoid of a farm system due to shaky ownership and tight finances, an all-too familiar refrain that would be repeated many times over during the coming years.

Role Call

The Penguins' great Stanley Cup teams of the early 1990s boasted no fewer than six Hall of Famers. However, Stanley Cups aren't won on talent alone. Role players, too, fill a vital role. The Penguins were blessed to have three of the best in Bob Errey, Troy Loney, and Phil Bourque.

Selected with the 15th overall pick in the 1983 Entry Draft, the speedy Errey struck for 53 goals during his final season of junior hockey. He made the talent-starved Penguins as a 19-year-old rookie in 1983–84, but struggled to produce. After being sent to the minors for seasoning, Errey worked hard to transform himself into a gritty, all-around player who was capable of filling a checking role.

Following an 18-goal season at Baltimore in 1983–84, Loney gradually worked his way into the Pens' lineup. Although Big Red lacked the foot speed to be a consistent scoring threat, he was defensively reliable and strong in the corners. Not averse to dropping the gloves, the husky 6'3", 209-pounder became a protector on an emerging young team.

Bourque was the last to earn regular duty. After winning the Governor's Trophy as the International Hockey League's top defenseman in 1987–88, he was converted to left wing by Penguins coach Gene Ubriaco to take advantage of his natural speed and aggressiveness. Skilled enough to play on the top two lines yet gritty enough to fill a defensive role, Bourque developed into a versatile and valuable performer.

During the 1988–89 season the trio established themselves as the heart and soul of the Pens' lunch-pail gang. In a savvy move, Ubriaco placed Errey on a line with big-time scorers Lemieux and Rob Brown. Serving as the unit's defensive conscience he notched a career-high 26 goals. Loney potted 10 goals while evolving into a solid grinder and penalty killer. Sporting his trademark mullet and beard, Bourque scored 17 goals and helped spark the team to its first playoff berth in seven years.

Their collective value was never more evident than during the cauldron of the Stanley Cup playoffs. During the Penguins' first Cup run in 1991, Bourque filled an important two-way role, chasing down loose pucks and mucking in the corners while scoring six big goals. The following spring he notched a pair of game-tying goals during a first-round matchup with the Capitals. His power-play goal in Game

1 of the Finals sparked a Pens rally and helped pave the way to a second Stanley Cup.

Loney enjoyed his moment in the sun during Game 5 of the 1991 Finals. With the Penguins nursing a one-goal lead late in a tight game, he rambled to the net and muscled the puck past Minnesota goalie Brian Hayward to seal a victory. A year later he scored a crucial game-tying goal in Game 4 of the Patrick Division Finals.

Perhaps no one contributed more mightily to the second Cup win than Errey. The Penguins trailed Washington 3–1 during their opening-round series. With his team facing almost certain elimination, Pens coach Scotty Bowman handed the plucky winger the daunting task of shadowing feisty Dino Ciccarelli. In Game 5 Errey held the Capitals' winger without a shot on goal while scoring two huge goals of his own. With Ciccarelli completely neutralized, the Penguins rallied to beat the Caps in seven games.

Phil Bourque, Troy Loney, and Bob Errey were key contributors to the Penguins teams of the early 1990s.

"The toughest part of the early years was dealing with the owners," Riley recalled. "They weren't bad guys; they just didn't have much hockey know-how or enough money."

Using every means at his disposal, Riley worked hard to cobble together a decent club. He traded for future mainstays Pronovost, Duane Rupp, and Bryan Watson and added the likes of Glen Sather and Dean Prentice through the Intra-League Draft. When Riley finally got an opportunity to draft a legitimate player, he plucked Michel Briere from the ranks of the Quebec League.

His tenure was interrupted following the team's rousing playoff run in 1970. Owner Donald Parsons appointed Red Kelly to the dual role of coach and general manager. Kelly insisted that his boss be retained, so Riley was promoted to club president.

With the club still struggling to meet expectations, Riley reassumed the GM duties on January 29, 1972. By the following season the energetic Irishman had assembled a talented nucleus, including rising young stars Apps, Dave Burrows, and Greg Polis. However, Riley was unable to lead the club over the hump to contender status. In January of 1974 he was replaced by his longtime assistant, Jack Button.

Riley remained with the Penguins as a scout through the 1974–75 season. After leaving the organization, he stayed active in hockey. From 1975 through January of 1977 he served as commissioner of the Southern Hockey League, overseeing teams such as the colorful Macon Whoopees. In 1979 he began a four-year stint as commissioner of the International Hockey League. At the end of his term, Riley continued to work as a consultant for the IHL and the East Coast Hockey League. He also served as a goal judge at the Civic Arena, but retired in 1993–94 so he could enjoy the games.

In December of 2009 he received a special token of appreciation for his years of service: the Penguins awarded him a Stanley Cup ring.

"I was kind of surprised when I saw the ring, even though I knew I was getting it," Riley said. "Tom McMillan gave it to me in a jewelry box. I tried it on, and it was perfect. I thanked Ray Shero personally. I told him to thank Mario [Lemieux] and Ron [Burkle]. I thought it was really nice of them to think of me."

93 Pass the Gatorade

After spending nearly a decade on a short list of Stanley Cup contenders, the Penguins entered the 2000 postseason in the unfamiliar role of underdogs. The club had nosedived early under demanding coach Kevin Constantine before rebounding to earn a playoff spot under USA hockey legend Herb Brooks.

Despite their less-than-inspired record, the Pens had jelled into a quick, resourceful team. Scoring champion Jaromir Jagr paced an underrated attack that featured the likes of Alexei Kovalev, Robert Lang, and Martin Straka. At the trade deadline Craig Patrick imported dependable defenders Bob Boughner and Janne Laukkanen, along with goalie Ron Tugnutt. They proved to be just the right tonic.

In the opening round of the playoffs the Pens dispatched the heavily favored Capitals with shocking ease. Even more remarkably, they swept the first two games of their Eastern Conference Semifinal series with the powerful Flyers—in Philadelphia, no less. Although the Flyers bounced back to win Game 3 in Pittsburgh, it did little to undermine the Pens' burgeoning confidence.

The Penguins got the jump on Philly in Game 4, as Kovalev struck at 2:22 of the opening frame. It was all the offense either side could muster for the next 40 minutes. The unheralded Tugnutt, who was proving to be a marvel, stopped the Flyers dead in their tracks. When not as active as his counterpart, Philadelphia's Brian Boucher made key saves when called upon.

A slashing penalty to Straka early in third period opened the door. Four seconds into the power play, John LeClair rambled to the net and snapped the puck past Tugnutt. Once again the defenses stiffened, forcing the game to overtime.

With the goaltenders serving up goose eggs, the teams churned through a first overtime. A second overtime came and went. Then a third and a fourth. When his stars ran out of gas, Herb Brooks turned to his fourth line of Rob Brown, Pat Falloon, and Ian Moran. While the energetic trio produced a number of good scoring chances, they couldn't beat Boucher.

As the game rolled into a *fifth* overtime with no end in sight, the players teetered on the brink of exhaustion...and delirium.

"You can't even describe how it felt," Pens defenseman Darius Kasparaitis said. "You don't even think what you're doing... When you're tired, it's tough to think. You make mistakes. Things happen."

Something, indeed, happened at 12:01 of the fifth overtime. Big Keith Primeau swooped down the right side of the Penguins' zone and made a sharp skate stop to elude the onrushing Kasparaitis. Then he pulled the puck back to his forehand and beat Tugnutt with a missile that clanged off the crossbar and into the net.

"We gave our best," Kasparaitis said. "We competed so hard. This is hockey; somebody has to lose. Unfortunately, it was our team."

The plucky Tugnutt was hardly at fault. Over the course of 152 minutes he'd stopped an astounding 70 of 72 shots to earn the No. 1 star in a losing cause.

"He was great," Brooks said.

Despite the deflating loss, the Penguins remained surprisingly upbeat.

"We feel good about ourselves," Tugnutt said afterward. "The series is still up for grabs."

"Our psyche is fine," said Matthew Barnaby, who drank six Gatorades and ate nine slices of pizza to maintain his energy during the marathon loss. "I mean, I think I could speak for all of us and say, 'Let's get back at it tomorrow.'"

Then he grinned and added, "Maybe I'll resist saying that since I'm so tired. But I will say, 'Let's go at it again Sunday.' We'll see what happens then."

Unfortunately for the Pens, the Flyers capitalized on their momentum and won Games 5 and 6 to end Pittsburgh's season.

94 Brownie

Rob Brown was born to score goals. It came as naturally to him as breathing. And he scored lots of them, a whopping 616 over the course of a junior, minor league, and NHL career that spanned 20 years.

Brown first drew the attention of the scouts while skating for the Kamloops Blazers under future NHL coach Ken Hitchcock. Although neither big nor fast, the youngster possessed magical hands and terrific instincts. At the callow age of 17, he piled up 173 points. In 1986–87 he upped that total to an astronomical 212 points to win the Canadian Major Junior Player of the Year Award.

Seeking to add punch to his emerging young team, Penguins general manager Eddie Johnston selected Brown with his fourth pick in the 1986 Entry Draft. Following his final season at Kamloops, the offensive whiz earned a spot with the Penguins in 1987–88. A natural center, Brown was converted to right wing

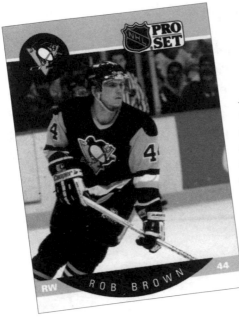

A natural high-scoring winger, Rob Brown transformed himself into a reliable defensive player during his second tour of duty with the Penguins.

and slotted next to another former junior scoring champion, Mario Lemieux.

"I played with Mario in my first game and he put me in on a breakaway," he said. "I was like, 'I could get used to this.'"

The two players instantly clicked. Thanks to his keen sense of anticipation, Brown was able to read and react to Lemieux and vice versa. In 1988–89 Mario rolled up a career-high 199 points, while Brownie exploded for 49 goals and 115 points.

Respect came grudgingly despite his huge numbers. Many opponents believed Brown was riding Mario's coattails.

"I'd like to take Lemieux out of the lineup and see how good Brown and the other guys are," said Minnesota coach Pierre Page after the colorful winger tallied six points during a 9–2 rout of the North Stars.

The charge seemed to gain some validity in 1989–90. With Lemieux missing a large chunk of time due to a back injury, Brown's output dipped to 33 goals and 80 points. Following a slow start in 1990–91, Penguins GM Craig Patrick dealt him to the Whalers for swift-skating Scott Young.

Brown played well in Hartford. Joined by former Pens teammates John Cullen and Zarley Zalapski, he scored 34 goals and 73 points in 86 games with the Whalers. However, on January 24, 1992, he was traded again, this time to the Blackhawks for defenseman Steve Konroyd. He skated against the Penguins in the Stanley Cup Finals, but was cut loose following a dismal 1992–93 campaign.

After washing out in the Windy City, Brown entered the next phase of his career. For the next four seasons he held the distinction of being the most dominant player in the minor leagues.

The Great Escape

Lively and fun-loving, Rob Brown was always popular with his teammates. However, the same could not be said for the opposition. In a 1990 poll the trash-talking winger was voted the least-liked player in the league by his colleagues.

In particular, Philadelphia's hot-tempered goalie, Ron Hextall, was a mortal enemy. When asked to comment on the high-scoring Penguin, Hextall fairly spat out his words, referring to Brown as a "goal-suck."

During the 1989 playoffs the duo was involved in one of the most famous incidents in Penguins history. After scoring a goal during a 10–7 rout of the Flyers, Brown launched into his colorful windmill celebration.

Brownie's antics were too much for Hextall to bear. Shaking his big goaltender's blade, the frazzled Flyer chased after the plucky winger, who skated away as though his life depended on it.

"Back then I used to celebrate after every goal," Brown recalled. "It was 9–2 and if I was about to celebrate, Hextall was going to be sure he got his piece of me. I was in the corner and Dan Quinn was coming in to give me a high five and I could just see Hextall behind him. I just remember skating up the boards with my head turned back, hoping someone would grab the crazy goalie."

Starring for Kalamazoo, Phoenix, and the Chicago Wolves, he amassed an incredible 522 points during that span to capture three International Hockey League scoring titles.

It appeared the productive winger was destined to finish out his career as the best player outside of the NHL. However, opportunity came knocking when Craig Patrick invited him to the Penguins' training camp in 1997. Determined to seize what might be his last chance to make it back to the big show, Brown hired a trainer and whipped himself into top shape.

Showing a ton of heart and desire, Brown earned a spot with the Pens, albeit in a brand-new role. Remarkably, he was cast in a *defensive* role on the checking line. Even more remarkably, he excelled, providing the team with solid two-way play.

Brown has fond memories of his second stint with the Penguins.

"The biggest thing for me was when I made a comeback years later and made it back here in Pittsburgh," he recalled. "The reaction from the fans I got then was amazing. I think I was even more appreciative then of how lucky I was to play in a city like this and to be treated as well as I was."

95 Visit the Site of the Schenley Park Casino

The Oakland neighborhood is home to Pittsburgh's most prominent cultural and academic institutions, as well as some of its most impressive structures. Situated within close proximity are the Carnegie Library and Museum, Heinz Chapel, Soldiers and Sailors Memorial Hall, and the University of Pittsburgh's Cathedral of Learning. Famed sporting venues such as Forbes Field, Duquesne Gardens, and Pitt Stadium once graced the landscape. However, few realize the area once was home to the city's first indoor skating facility—the Schenley Park Casino.

Located at the entrance to Schenley Park, the Casino was a magnificent structure. Completed in the spring of 1895 at a cost of $400,000, it was constructed of limestone and brick. The roofline featured a series of wooden corbels and copper cornices. Above the large, arched entryway rested a grand patio, an ideal viewing space for parade reviews and political rallies. At night, the Casino glittered like a crown jewel, thanks to more than 1,500 incandescent, arc, and white calcium lights.

The artificial ice surface truly was a marvel. Measuring 225 feet by 70 feet, it rested on a main floor that sat below the viewing area in an elliptical bowl. Constructed of a concrete and marble chip aggregate, the floor was specially designed to hold water. A series of looping chiller pipes that carried ammonia gas from a nearby ice-making room served to freeze the concrete floor and the one-inch-thick ice surface above.

"The body of ice has a remarkable smoothness and the excellence of its surroundings is unsurpassed anywhere in the world," boasted an article in the *Pittsburgh Press*.

Pittsburghers agreed. During the grand opening on May 29, 1895, they flocked to the Casino to try out the city's newest attraction. More than 2,800 tickets were sold for the afternoon skating session, which lasted from 1:00 PM to 4:30 PM.

"The skating rink was the scene of great gliding," noted the *Pittsburgh Commercial Gazette*. "Between 500 and 600 lovers of the sport continually circled the arena. Many ambitious skaters tasted the humiliation of doing some of their fancy feats in getting up off the ice instead of cutting figures on the ice, to the great amusement of the spectators."

The Casino was open to the public on weekdays. For an admission fee of five cents, patrons could rent a pair of steel skate blades and cruise around the ice during public skating sessions. On the

Lalime the Dream

Although the Pens have employed a handful of top-flight netminders, including Les Binkley, Tom Barrasso, and Marc-Andre Fleury, the Steel City has never been renowned as a hotbed for puck stoppers.

However, the team can boast of at least one record-setter between the pipes. During an extraordinary six-week run in 1996–97, a skinny rookie named Patrick Lalime took the NHL by storm.

Lalime started the 1996–97 campaign with the Cleveland Lumberjacks, but was summoned to Pittsburgh when Barrasso went down with a shoulder injury. On December 6 he made his first career start against Washington. Although he was pulled after 40 minutes of solid work (16 saves on 17 shots), Lalime earned his first NHL victory. Over the next few weeks the 22-year-old rookie split the goaltending chores with the more experienced Ken Wregget. He registered his first career shutout on December 13 with a 4–0 whitewash of San Jose.

Misfortune appeared to strike the Pens again on December 26 when Wregget was injured during a tie with Montreal. Although Lalime had yet to lose a game, the Pens weren't sure if he was ready for full-time duty. The unassuming youngster quickly caught lightning in a bottle. Employing the butterfly style popularized by his idol, Patrick Roy, Lalime started the next 10 games and won nine of them. The only blemish on his sterling record was a 3–3 tie with Ottawa. On January 15, 1997, he stopped 31 shots in a 3–0 victory over Hartford to establish a new league goaltending record with a 15-game unbeaten streak to start his career. Three days later he upped his string to 16 games, turning aside 49 shots to pace a 4–2 win over Calgary. His record run was finally halted on January 23, when Colorado eclipsed the Pens in overtime.

Lalime posted a 14–0–2 record during the streak, along with a microscopic 1.69 goals-against average and an extraordinary .947 save percentage. Remarkably, Lalime's brilliance failed to earn him the support of the Penguins' brass.

"When Patrick got back there, we started to tighten up defensively," coach Eddie Johnston explained.

Embroiled in a contract dispute with general manager Craig Patrick, Lalime was unceremoniously shipped back to the International Hockey

League the following season. Patrick traded Lalime's rights to Anaheim on March 24, 1998, for journeyman Sean Pronger. He didn't appear in another NHL game until he joined Ottawa in 1999–00.

Given a new lease on life in the Canadian capital, Lalime re-emerged as a solid big-league goalie. He registered a sparkling 2.32 goals-against average over the course of five seasons with the Senators while earning All-Star honors in 2002–03. During the 2002 Stanley Cup playoffs he tied a 57-year-old league record by recording three consecutive shutouts. His postseason goals-against average of 1.77 (in 41 games) is the third best of all time.

weekends, the ice surface was reserved for hockey exhibitions and private parties.

As the Casino's fame spread, it attracted the attention of hockey players throughout the United States and Canada. Hockey clubs from across North America would soon travel to the Steel City to challenge the Pittsburgh Keystones, which was comprised of players from Carnegie Tech and Western University (later the University of Pittsburgh).

Convinced the city would fall in love with speed, grace, and athleticism of the sport, building manager James Conant began to organize hockey exhibitions on Friday evenings following the public skating session. Thanks to its large balcony the Casino provided a bird's-eye view of the ice surface 20 feet below. In December of 1895, the *Pittsburgh Press* mentioned a "friendly hockey match" that drew some 10,000 spectators. While the attendance figure seems heavily inflated, the sport had clearly taken hold in the Steel City.

Sadly, the Casino would not survive to play a part in hockey's growing popularity. Early in the morning of December 17, 1896, a pipe carrying the ammonia gas began to leak. Although no one can be certain, it's believed that the gas mixed with grease to set off an explosion. By the time firefighters arrived on the scene, the blaze was already out of control. A second, deadlier explosion of the main ammonia storage tank razed the rear of the building. Heat from the conflagration grew so intense it melted the glass at the nearby Phipps Conservancy.

Overwhelmed by a cauldron of flames, flying debris, dense smoke, and deadly ammonia fumes, the firefighters were forced to withdraw. Within an hour the Casino had burned to the ground.

96 Black Wednesday

March 20, 1996, is a date that will live in infamy among Penguins fans. On that fateful Wednesday Craig Patrick dropped a bomb (or laid an egg) that would become legendary in hockey circles.

The brilliant general manager—who'd made a living out of fleecing his front office brethren—engineered what is widely regarded as the worst hockey trade of all time. Seeking to add size and toughness to his club, he sent promising winger Markus Naslund to Vancouver for Alek Stojanov.

It may be hard to believe in hindsight, but there was some justification for the trade. As undeniably talented as Naslund was, there were questions about his character. Coach Eddie Johnston, who had a keen eye for young talent, had soured on the 22-year-old Swede.

Stojanov did possess some pedigree. Selected with the seventh overall pick in the 1991 Entry Draft, the husky 6'4", 220-pounder enjoyed a breakout season during his final year of junior hockey, notching 36 goals and 71 points in only 50 games. A darn tough fighter to boot, Stojanov had made headlines by pummeling future

Penguins GM Craig Patrick dealt promising winger Marcus Naslund to Vancouver in 1996 for Alek Stojanov, perhaps the worst trade in franchise history.

Flyers star Eric Lindros. Blessed with surprisingly soft hands and good offensive instincts for a tough guy, scouts felt he would develop into a decent if not prolific power forward.

When asked to evaluate the deal, Patrick readily admitted that the Penguins hadn't given Naslund enough ice time.

"I wouldn't say that Markus didn't succeed," he offered. "He's a gifted goal scorer. We couldn't—or didn't—allow him the playing time to accomplish what others have."

Regarding his new acquisition, Patrick was upbeat. "He's going to get better as time goes on. He scored well in junior, both playmaking and scoring goals," Patrick said. Then he added, rather prophetically, "One thing he'll need to improve to play on the top two lines is his skating."

Determined to prove his worth, Stojanov made a favorable first impression. During his Pens debut he engaged Buffalo's rugged Bob Boughner in a spirited slugging match. The following night he scored his first NHL goal to help Pittsburgh to an 8–2 rout of the Rangers.

Unfortunately, it proved to be Alek's high-water mark. Due in part to his pronounced lack of speed and complications from earlier reconstructive shoulder surgery, he tallied only one more goal for the Penguins.

Reduced to the role of a fourth-line mucker, Stojanov contributed the only way he could—with his fists. In 1996–97 he served as the team's chief enforcer and pounded out victories in five of his seven fights. However, his chances at even a modestly successful NHL career were snuffed out in December when he was injured in a car accident.

The following season Stojanov returned to the minor leagues. Over the next five years the burly winger plied his trade for teams such as the Syracuse Crunch and the New Mexico Scorpions before hanging up his skates in 2002. Baring no trace of bitterness over what could've been, the good-natured giant became a firefighter in Hamilton, Ontario.

"How many guys get a chance to play in the NHL with Mario Lemieux?" he told Christine Simpson in a rare interview.

Naslund quickly dispelled any concerns about his heart in the Pacific Northwest. Serving as the Canucks' team captain he blossomed into a perennial All-Star. Beginning in 2000–01, he topped the 40-goal mark in three straight seasons while earning First Team NHL All-Star honors and the Lester B. Pearson (Ted Lindsay) Award. Following 11 standout years in Vancouver, he departed as a free agent during the summer of 2008 as the team's all-time leading scorer.

97 Singing the Blues

Although the Penguins finished a distant third in the Norris Division in 1980–81, there was reason to believe the team might do some damage in the playoffs. Following a dreadful first half, the Pens played better than .500 hockey over the final 37 games. Thanks to fiery coach Eddie Johnston, the club boasted one of the top power-play units in the league, striking for 92 man-advantage goals. Newcomers Paul Gardner, Paul Baxter, and Pat Price added some badly needed scoring and aggression to the mix.

The Pens' opening-round playoff opponents were the St. Louis Blues, their old rivals from the early 1970s. Under the guidance of former star Red Berenson, the resurgent Blues had rolled up 107 points to capture the Smythe Division crown. A powerful offensive club, St. Louis boasted five 30-goal scorers, including Wayne Babych, Bernie Federko, and Jorgen Pettersson.

Remarkably, the Penguins proved to be an even match for their high-flying foe. After dropping the series opener 4–2, they took two of the next three contests. All-Star defenseman Randy Carlyle was enjoying a sensational series, as was third-year goalie Greg Millen.

The fifth and deciding game was played before a standing-room-only crowd of 18,150 at the Checkerdome. The Penguins drew first blood, as Gardner deflected a Rick Kehoe slap shot past Mike Liut. Typifying the back-and-forth nature of the series, the Blues knotted the score on second-period goals by Brian Sutter and Federko, sandwiched around a tally by George Ferguson.

St. Louis grabbed the lead early in the final period on a goal by Rick Lapointe. But once more the pesky Pens battled back. At 10:36 Greg Malone gathered in a pass from Rod Schutt and beat

Liut to tie the game at 3–3. Following nine minutes of thrilling end-to-end action, the game went to overtime.

The Blues opened the extra stanza firing on all cylinders. Greg Millen was up to the task, making a series of highlight-reel saves.

"I don't think I've ever seen any goaltender play as well as Millen played in my five years in the NHL," Carlyle said later.

Inspired by their little goalie, the Penguins suddenly sprang to life. They fired the last seven shots of the period at Liut, who likewise was in top form. At the 15-minute mark the Blues' netminder stopped Gardner's jam attempt from the slot to snuff out the Pens' best scoring chance.

Five minutes into the second overtime Blues winger Mike Zuke scooped up the puck and flew into the Penguins' end. Mark Johnson quickly pinned Zuke against the boards. However, he couldn't prevent a bounce pass that hopped past Carlyle and onto the stick of Mike Crombeen, who was camped in the slot. Crombeen whipped the game winner into the upper-left corner of the net.

Afterward, the vanquished Penguins struggled to come to terms with their emotions.

"It's almost a shock to your system to play so well and fall short," Baxter said. "You just can't comprehend what happened. It's almost agonizing to fall so short, though not for a lack of effort. I've never seen a group of guys give so much of themselves as we did tonight. A game like this builds character. Guys grow from these kind of games."

While understandably heartbroken, Eddie Johnston had nothing but praise for his troops.

"I was just very, very proud of them," he said. "I have never seen a series like that—never mind a game like that. When you get into overtime it's just a guts thing. You push yourself. You do it with determination and intestinal fortitude. Both teams had that tonight, although I really felt in my heart we should have won."

98 Slats

Noting that the rugged St. Louis Blues had made it to the Stanley Cup Finals two years in a row in the late 1960s, Penguins general manager Jack Riley was determined to make his mild-mannered team more difficult to play against. In January of 1969 he'd acquired tough guys Tracy Pratt, George Swarbrick, and Bryan Watson from Oakland with favorable results. Continuing the trend, he snatched peppery winger Glen Sather from Boston in the 1969 Intra-League Draft.

A native of High River, Alberta, Sather had helped the Edmonton Oil Kings win the Memorial Cup in 1962–63. Following a three-year minor league apprenticeship, he earned a spot with the Bruins in 1967. While not a big scorer, Slats developed into an effective energy player who worked his tail off every shift. More importantly, he knew how to win.

Penguins fans immediately took a shine to the blond-haired winger. They loved his hell-for-leather style. Colorful and abrasive, he constantly agitated opponents in an effort to gain an edge.

Thanks to the presence of Sather and his fellow toughies, the 1969–70 Pens were infinitely more entertaining. The results, however, were no different. The team was floundering well below the .500 mark until St. Louis arrived in town on January 31, 1970, for a key West Division matchup.

Armed with bruisers such as Noel Picard and the Plager brothers, Barclay and Bob, the division-leading Blues were no strangers to the penalty box. The stage was set for a battle royale, one that would mark an early turning point in Penguins franchise history.

The fuse was lit early in the second period when Barclay Plager jousted with Watson. Later in the frame, the St. Louis

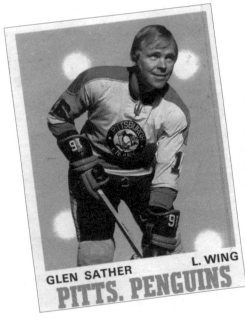

Long before he guided the Edmonton Oilers to five Stanley Cups, Glen Sather skated for six NHL teams, including the Pittsburgh Penguins.

defender spotted his antagonist again and made a beeline for him. Before Plager could reach his intended target, he was intercepted by Sather.

In an instant, the combatants shed their sticks and gloves and started swinging. As the battle intensified, players from both teams joined the fray. The powder keg quickly exploded into a bench-clearing brawl. At the eye of the storm, Sather engaged Plager in two separate fights. When order was finally restored the St. Louis bad boy was nursing a broken nose.

Although Slats received a double-major and a misconduct for his pugilistic efforts, the fight had the desired effect. The fired-up Penguins dominated the Blues in the third period and rallied to earn a 2–1 victory.

Afterward, St. Louis coach Scotty Bowman was livid.

"[Sather] couldn't lick his lips," Bowman fumed. "He's all mouth. What a little [expletive]."

The Penguins had a decidedly different reaction. Buoyed by Sather's team-first actions, the club promptly went on a 9–5 run over the next 14 games to secure its first-ever playoff berth. Sather capped off a solid first season with the Pens, tallying 12 goals and 26 points to go with 114 minutes in the sin bin.

Now one of the most treasured members of the team, Slats enjoyed similar success in 1970–71. When Watson went down with a broken ankle, he stepped forward to become the team's chief protector, dropping the mitts seven times. On December 19, he scored the fourth hat trick in club history to pace the Pens to a 9–1 rout of Detroit.

It appeared Sather would enjoy a long and eventful stay in Pittsburgh. But the New York Rangers, desperate for muscle, made the Penguins an offer they couldn't refuse. On January 26, 1971, Sather was sent to the Big Apple for promising youngsters Syl Apps and Sheldon Kannegiesser.

Crestfallen, the Steel City faithful hung a bed-sheet banner at the Civic Arena asking, "Why Slats?" Apps quickly provided the answer, scoring a breathtaking breakaway goal against Jacques Plante in his Penguins debut.

99 Visit the Site of the Winter Garden

When one takes a leisurely stroll along the tree-lined walkways of Pittsburgh's scenic Point State Park, it's hard to imagine that this was once the site of the Winter Garden—the city's third great ice palace. Indeed, nothing remains of the once-proud structure that served as a mecca for Steel City hockey.

In the early part of the 20th century, hockey enjoyed a period of unprecedented popularity and growth in Pittsburgh. As the sport flourished, it became a challenge for the proliferation of amateur, college, and professional teams to secure ice time at the Duquesne Gardens, the city's preeminent indoor skating facility.

A solution would soon present itself. Noting the ever-increasing demand for ice, the Western Pennsylvania Exposition Society decided to convert the Main Hall of the Pittsburgh Exposition, which was located near the Point, into an indoor skating rink. An impressive structure, the Main Hall had been rebuilt following a fire that had devastated the Exposition in 1901. Constructed of steel, stone, and brick, it was built to withstand even the worst conditions. A city guidebook boasted "nothing short of an earthquake would cause it to even shake."

Following the Exposition of 1915, 125,000 feet of chiller pipe and a concrete floor were installed in the building. Using the latest technology of the day, a brine solution was pumped through the pipes from a refrigeration plant located in nearby Machinery Hall. The system maintained the floor temperature at a chilly minus-30 degrees and produced a dry, hard ice surface.

Completed in 1916, the new indoor rink was named the Winter Garden. Several teams from the former Western Pennsylvania Hockey League, including Pittsburgh Duquesne and Pittsburgh Lyceum, began playing their home games at the new facility. The Winter Garden also played host to one of the city's earliest women's hockey leagues.

The Winter Garden enjoyed its shining moment on March 24, 1917. The immortal Hobey Baker came to town with an all-star team from Philadelphia to play an exhibition match. The former Princeton star scored a hat trick, including the game winner in the third overtime, to best the local sextet.

It was the final game Baker would ever play. Enlisting in the U.S. Army as a pilot, he soon departed for France. After being awarded the Croix de Guerre for his service in World War I, he was killed just a few short weeks after the armistice when his newly repaired Spad crashed during a test flight. Orders to return home were found tucked inside his jacket.

The Winter Garden would meet an untimely end as well. Although truly a wonderful facility, it had its drawbacks. The ice sheet measured a massive 300 feet by 140 feet, compared to today's NHL standard of 200 feet by 85 feet. Playing on such a large expanse of ice was a test of even the hardiest player's spirit and endurance. A polio epidemic had forced the Exposition to close its doors in 1916, which left the Winter Garden as the lone attraction still open to the public. Located in an increasingly rough and seedy area of town, the Exposition became an undesirable place to visit.

After just four short years the Winter Garden ceased operations following the 1920 season. A sale of the Exposition properties was reported in the *Pittsburgh Post-Gazette* on April 9, 1920, but the transaction was never completed. With a white elephant on its hands, the city of Pittsburgh agreed to lease the property for an annual fee of $30,000. Soon it would serve as the city's auto pound.

In the mid-1930s a movement to revive the Expo site failed, and the city ended its lease agreement. One by one the monolithic old buildings were torn down. Machinery Hall was dismantled in 1942 to provide scrap metal for the war effort.

The Main Hall, which housed the Winter Garden, was the last building to be cleared, meeting with the wrecker's ball in 1951. Although it was an inglorious end for the once-magnificent hockey arena, it paved the way for the city's First Renaissance.

100 The Muskegon Line

Following a dramatic rally to overcome Washington in the opening round of the 1992 playoffs, the Penguins suddenly found themselves in hot water. Forty-goal men Mario Lemieux and Joe Mullen were injured during Game 2 of a bitterly fought Patrick Division Finals series against the Rangers. To make matters worse, rugged winger Rick Tocchet was out with a separated shoulder. The rash of injuries threatened to derail the Penguins' march to a second Stanley Cup.

With his stars dropping like flies, general manager Craig Patrick dipped into the farm system. He recalled minor league linemates Jock Callander and Mike Needham from the Muskegon Lumberjacks and pressed them into service for Game 3.

The newcomers were not without pedigree. A former International Hockey League scoring champ, the 31-year-old Callander had skated on a line with Lemieux during the 1987–88 season and performed well. Although a lack of speed prevented him from earning steady work at the NHL level, he was a skilled, heady player who could adapt to a checking role.

A sixth-round pick in the 1989 Entry Draft, Needham displayed genuine promise. In 1991–92 the 22-year-old right wing notched 41 goals for Muskegon.

It didn't take long for the former Lumberjacks to make an impact. With the Penguins down 2–1 in the series and trailing early in Game 4, Needham stepped forward with a terrific individual effort. Twenty-four seconds after Tony Amonte struck to give the Rangers a 2–0 lead, he snapped off a quick shot on Mike Richter. The New York goalie made the initial save, but Needham scooped up the rebound and fired the puck home.

The goal proved to be the turning point. Buoyed by the rookie's sensational play, the undermanned Penguins rallied to stun the Rangers 5–4 and even the series.

Unfortunately, the injury bug bit again. Sparkplug Bob Errey, the Pens' crackerjack checker and penalty killer, went down with a separated shoulder. Once again Craig Patrick turned to the Lumberjacks for help, summoning veteran left wing Dave Michayluk.

Like Callander, the 30-year-old Michayluk was a former IHL scoring champ who lacked the speed to make it in the NHL. However, he was a capable, resourceful player who gave 100 percent each and every shift.

"Dave Michalyuk is a very hard worker and he comes to play every game," said his minor league coach Rick Ley. "He's a complete player."

Noting that Callander, Michayluk, and Needham were linemates at Muskegon, Penguins coach Scotty Bowman decided to play them as a unit. Given the trio's lack of NHL experience, it was a bit of gamble. However, it proved to be a savvy move. Dubbed "the Muskegon Line" by the local press, the erstwhile Lumberjacks provided invaluable depth as the underdog Pens ousted the Rangers in six hard-fought games.

"It was a total team victory in that series," winger Phil Bourque recalled. "We were without our big gun, but we had other weapons."

The Muskegon Line enjoyed a collective moment in the sun during Game 1 of the Wales Conference Finals. After being victimized for a goal midway through the opening period by Boston's Ted Donato, Bowman showed his faith in the unit by keeping them on the ice for the ensuing face-off.

He was rewarded on the next rush. Michayluk forced a turnover deep in the Bruins' zone and threaded a seeing eye pass to Callander, who popped the equalizer past Andy Moog.

Following the series opener the Pens' wounded warriors gradually returned to the lineup, signaling the end of the Muskegon

Line. Needham gave way to Lemieux in Game 2. Michayluk was bumped aside by Errey, but not before scoring the series capper in Game 4. Callander suited up for every game during the Pens' exhilarating sweep of Chicago in the Finals. As a reward for their gritty, unselfish play, each had his name engraved on the Stanley Cup.

The Cup Runneth Under

Stanley Cup lore is filled with zany stories of colorful antics and over-the-top victory celebrations. Perhaps no team had more fun with the Cup—or gave it rougher treatment—than the 1991 Penguins.

After spending a tranquil first night in Pittsburgh on Tom Barrasso's front lawn, the Cup made its way to Mario Lemieux's house for a pool party the following day.

Clad only in his underwear, Phil Bourque decided to take hockey's holy grail for a swim. Depending upon the account of the story, Bourque either jumped into the pool with Lord Stanley's silverware in tow or flung it into the pool from an artificial waterfall.

The Cup promptly sank like a stone. Due to suction, it became firmly anchored to the bottom of Mario's 10-foot-deep pool. It took the efforts of three Penguins to free the Cup from its roost and haul it back to the surface.

"I think [the Cup] had a good time," Bourque said.

The incident was so infamous that it spawned a book about Stanley Cup misadventures.

Acknowledgments

Although writing a book is often a solitary endeavor, such a project would not be possible without the kindness and support of family, friends, and loved ones.

I wish to acknowledge Rich Arthurs, Tom Blanciak, Melanie Blaser, Valerie Chouinard, Roger Costello, Danielle Danzuso, Ric Drake, Evan Freshwater, Travis Gracey, Ken Griffin, Parker Johnston, Sandy Joseph, Kathryn Kluk, Stasi Longo, Bob Mazuer, Mike Morton, Dennis Murphy, Bill Ogden, Kevin Solecki, Linda and John Tinnemeyer, and Dave and John Wright for their inspiration and encouragement.

I'd also like to thank hockey journalist Joe Pelletier, *LCS Hockey* hosts Michael Dell and Jerry (a.k.a. Larry) Fairish, and Phil Krundle, as well as my fellow bloggers at PenguinPoop.com for their generosity and steadfast support.

It goes without saying that I owe an enormous debt of gratitude to Tom Bast at Triumph Books. Tom provided me with a truly wonderful opportunity to write this book. My editor, Adam Motin, has been an invaluable resource, friend, and ally throughout the creative process. Likewise, the design team and promotional staff at Triumph deserve a shout out for their tireless efforts on my behalf.

A special note of thanks goes to Mario Lemieux and the Pittsburgh Penguins for providing so many thrilling memories down through the years, and to all of the hockey fans who made my first book, *Total Penguins*, a success.

Last but not least, I wish to thank my Lord and Savior Jesus Christ. His blessings, goodness, and mercy know no bounds.

Sources

Books

Diamond, Dan, ed. *Total Hockey.* Andrews McMeel Publishing, 1998.

Dryden, Ken. *The Game.* John Wiley and Sons, Ltd., 1983.

Fischler, Stan. *Bad Boys: Legends of Hockey's Toughest, Meanest, Most Feared Players!* McGraw-Hill Ryerson, 1991.

Fischler, Stan, and Fischler, Shirley. *Who's Who in Hockey.* Andrews McMeel Publishing, 2003.

McMillan, Tom. *Pittsburgh Penguins: Cellar to Summit.* Ironist Press, 1995.

O'Brien, Jim. *Penguin Profiles: Pittsburgh's Boys of Winter.* James P. O'Brien Publishing, 1994.

Schultz, Dave, with Stan Fischler. *The Hammer: Confessions of a Hockey Enforcer.* Summit Books, 1981.

Starkey, Joe. *Tales from the Pittsburgh Penguins.* Sports Publishing, LLC, 2006.

Magazines

Hockey Player Magazine
MacLean's
Pittsburgh Magazine
Sports Illustrated
The Hockey News

Newspapers

Hamilton Spectator
Pittsburgh Press
Pittsburgh Post-Gazette
Pittsburgh Sun-Telegraph
Pittsburgh Tribune-Review
The Gazette Times

The Globe and Mail
The New York Times
The Toronto Sun

Videos

A Portrait of Courage: The Story of the 1992–93 Pittsburgh Penguins. The Pittsburgh Penguins with Ross Sports Productions, 1993.

Against the Odds: The Story of the 1991–92 Pittsburgh Penguins. KDKA Sports with Ross Sports Productions, 1992.

One from the Heart: The Story of the 1990–91 Pittsburgh Penguins. KBL with Ross Sports Productions, 1991.

Stanley Cup: 2009 Champions. Warner Home Video with the NHL, 2009.

Websites

dropyourgloves.com

greatesthockeylegends.com

hhof.com

hockeydb.com

hockeydraftcentral.com

hockey-reference.com

hockeystoughguys.blogspot.com

legendsofhockey.net

letsgopens.com

nemesisfl.tripod.com

penguinpoop.com

penguinslegends.blogspot.com

penguins.nhl.com

pittsburghhockey.net

mashf.com

sports.yahoo.com

thehockeyblog.com

thereginapatsalumni.com